Frommer's
Crete
day BY day™

by Jos Simon

A John Wiley and Sons, Ltd, Publication

Contents

15 Favourite Moments 1

1 Strategies for Seeing Crete 7

2 The Best Full-Day Tours 11
The Best in Three Days 12
The Best in One Week 16
The Best in Two Weeks 20

3 The Best Special-Interest Tours 25
Minoan Crete 26
Venetian Crete 32
Ottoman Crete 36
Crete in World War II 42
Crete & The Arts 48
Oddball Crete 52
Family Crete 58

4 The Best Urban Tours 65
The Best of Chaniá 66
Where to Stay 71
Where to Dine 73
The Best of Réthymnon 74
Where to Stay 79
Where to Dine 80
The Best of Iráklion 82
Where to Stay 88
Where to Dine 89
The Best of Ágios Nikólaos 90
Where to Stay 95
Where to Dine 96

5 The Great Outdoors 99
Best Beaches 100
Best On Land 104
Best At Sea 112

6 The Best Regional Tours 115
Chaniá Region 116
Where to Stay 124
Where to Dine 125
Réthymnon Region 126
Where to Stay 134
Where to Dine 135
Iráklion Region 136
Where to Stay 143
Where to Dine 144
Lasíthi Region 146
Where to Stay 154
Where to Dine 155

The Savvy Traveller 157
Before You Go 158
Getting There 162
Getting Around 162
Fast Facts 163
Crete: A Brief History 168
Useful Words & Phrases 172

Index 175

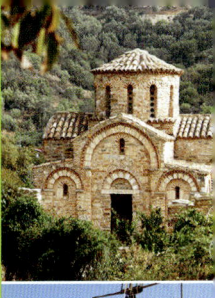

Copyright © 2010 John Wiley & Sons Ltd, The Atrium, Southern Gate, Chichester, West Sussex PO19 8SQ, England

Telephone (+44) 1243 779777

Email (for orders and customer service enquiries): cs-books@wiley.co.uk.
Visit our Home Page on www.wiley.com

All Rights Reserved. No part of this publication may be reproduced, stored in a retrieval system or transmitted in any form or by any means, electronic, mechanical, photocopying, recording, scanning or otherwise, except under the terms of the Copyright, Designs and Patents Act 1988 or under the terms of a licence issued by the Copyright Licensing Agency Ltd, Saffron House, 6-10 Kirby Street, London EC1N 8TS, UK, without the permission in writing of the Publisher. Requests to the Publisher should be addressed to the Permissions Department, John Wiley & Sons Ltd, The Atrium, Southern Gate, Chichester, West Sussex PO19 8SQ, England, or emailed to permreq@wiley.co.uk, or faxed to (+44) 1243 770620.

Designations used by companies to distinguish their products are often claimed as trademarks. All brand names and product names used in this book are trade names, service marks, trademarks or registered trademarks of their respective owners. The Publisher is not associated with any product or vendor mentioned in this book.

This publication is designed to provide accurate and authoritative information in regard to the subject matter covered. It is sold on the understanding that the Publisher is not engaged in rendering professional services. If professional advice or other expert assistance is required, the services of a competent professional should be sought.

UK Publisher: Sally Smith
Executive Project Editor: Daniel Mersey
Commissioning Editor: Mark Henshall
Development Editor: Mary Anne Evans
Project Editor: Hannah Clement
Photo Research: Jill Emeny
Cartography: John Tulip

Wiley also publishes its books in a variety of electronic formats. Some content that appears in print may not be available in electronic books.

British Library Cataloguing in Publication Data

A catalogue record for this book is available from the British Library

ISBN: 978-0-470-71708-0

Typeset by Wiley Indianapolis Composition Services

Printed and bound in China by RR Donnelley

5 4 3 2 1

A Note from the Editorial Director

Organizing your time. That's what this guide is all about.

Other guides give you long lists of things to see and do and then expect you to fit the pieces together. The Day by Day guides are different. These guides tell you the best of everything, and then they show you how to see it *in the smartest, most time-efficient way.* Our authors have designed detailed itineraries organized by time, neighborhood, or special interest. And each tour comes with a bulleted map that takes you from stop to stop.

Hoping to wade through crystal clear waters or enjoy Crete's rolling vineyards and olive groves? Planning to eat mezzedes in traditional tavernas or devour fresh fish under the shady trees? How about getting to grips with Europe's first civilisation—the Minoans, absorbing the atmosphere in its monasteries. Whatever your interest or schedule, the Day by Days give you the smartest routes to follow. Not only do we take you to the top attractions, hotels, and restaurants, but we also help you access those special moments that locals get to experience—those "finds" that turn tourists into travelers.

The Day by Days are also your top choice if you're looking for one complete guide for all your travel needs. The best hotels and restaurants for every budget, the greatest shopping values, the wildest nightlife—it's all here.

Why should you trust our judgment? Because our authors personally visit each place they write about. They're an independent lot who say what they think and would never include places they wouldn't recommend to their best friends. They're also open to suggestions from readers. If you'd like to contact them, please send your comments our way at feedback@frommers.com, and we'll pass them on.

Enjoy your Day by Day guide—the most helpful travel companion you can buy. And have the trip of a lifetime.

Warm regards,

Kelly Regan

Kelly Regan, Editorial Director
Frommer's Travel Guides

About the Author

Born and raised in Pwllheli on the Llŷn Peninsula, **Jos Simon** ventured into the world beyond Snowdonia as an LSE student in mid-60s swinging London. Having married a Greek, he embarked on a teaching career in various parts of the UK, his life enriched by Greek in-laws, Greek food and Greek holidays. Early retirement brought new challenges as a freelance travel writer, specialising (of course) in stories about Greece. As a result of continued Hellenic touring, with children, then alone, then with grandchildren, writing about Greece for UK magazines, and researching this book, he has come to feel like an honorary Greek.

Acknowledgments

Many thanks to the following for all their help in the writing of this book:

- at John Wiley and Sons, to all the usual suspects: Mark Henshall, Fiona Quinn, Jill Emeny, Scott Totman et al.
- to Mary Anne Evans, for encouragement and really sympathetic development editing.
- to a host of tourism professionals for sharing their expertise and providing practical input—Emma Wilde of Small Luxury Hotels of the World, Anna Kadianakis of Elounda Gulf Villas, Janet Stimson of Crete Escapes, Marlen Taffarello of Aldemar Hotels, Linda Diamandis of Sunvil, Frankie Miles, author of *Crete on the Road,* Nick McKenna of Sunisle Holidays, and particularly, via Vanessa Barbara Smethurst, whose selfless sharing of her local knowledge took my breath away.
- to Peter Lynch for help with the turtles.
- to Ray Bennett, of the Turnpike, for providing a hassle-free place to work, and advice on Crete's limited golfing opportunities.
- to my wife and family, who let me go to Crete on my own, and made allowances whilst I was writing the book.

Dedication

For Mike Dafnis, my source of all wisdom on Greece for over forty years.

An Additional Note

Please be advised that travel information is subject to change at any time — and this is especially true of prices. We therefore suggest that you write or call ahead for confirmation when making your travel plans. The authors, editors, and publisher cannot be held responsible for the experiences of readers while traveling. Your safety is important to us, however, so we encourage you to stay alert and be aware of your surroundings.

Star Ratings, Icons & Abbreviations

Every hotel, restaurant, and attraction listing in this guide has been ranked for quality, value, service, amenities, and special features using a **star-rating system.** Hotels, restaurants, attractions, shopping, and nightlife are rated on a scale of zero stars (recommended) to three stars (exceptional). In addition to the star-rating system, we also use a **kids icon** to point out the best bets for families. Within each tour, we recommend cafes, bars or restaurants where you can take a break. Each of these stops appears in a shaded box marked with a coffee cup–shaped bullet.

The following **abbreviations** are used for credit cards:

AE American Express	DISC Discover	V Visa
DC Diners Club	MC MasterCard	

Travel Resources at Frommers.com

Now that you have this guidebook to help you plan a great trip, visit our website at www.frommers.com for additional travel information on more than 4,000 destinations. We update features regularly to give you instant access to the most current trip-planning information available. At Frommers.com, you'll find scoops on the best airfares, lodging rates, and car rental bargains. You can even book your travel online through our reliable travel booking partners. Other popular features include:

A Note on Prices

In the "Take a Break" and "Best Bets" sections of this book, we have used a system of dollar signs to show a range of costs for 1 night in a hotel (the price of a double-occupancy room) or the cost of an entree (main course) at a restaurant. Use the following table to decipher the dollar signs:

Cost	Hotels	Restaurants
$	under $100	under $10
$$	$100–$200	$10–$20
$$$	$200–$300	$20–$30
$$$$	$300–$400	$30–$40
$$$$$	over $400	over $40

An Invitation to the Reader

In researching this book, we discovered many wonderful places—hotels, restaurants, shops, and more. We're sure you'll find others. Please tell us about them, so we can share the information with your fellow travelers in upcoming editions. If you were disappointed with a recommendation, we'd love to know that, too. Please write to:

Frommer's Crete Day by Day, 1st Edition
Wiley Publishing, Inc. • 111 River St. • Hoboken, NJ 07030-577

15 Favourite **Moments**

15 Favourite Moments

1. Loutró
2. Naval Museum, Chaniá
3. Elafonísi
4. Argiroúpolis
5. Arkádi Monastery
6. Bali
7. Crete's premier wine region
8. Mátala
9. Nikos Kazantzákis' Grandparents House, Mirtiá
10. Hersónisos
11. Archaeological Museum, Iráklion
12. Spinalónga
13. Lasíthi Plateau
14. Crete's South-West Coast
15. Mochós tavernas

Previous page: Elounda Harbor.

15 Favourite Moments

Crete is an island of extremes—the biggest Greek island, the farthest south, the hottest, with the longest summers, with people who are the hardest, proudest, most unforgiving of the Greeks, yet with a reputation for hospitality, love of family, and loyalty to friends. Crete is divided by three two-thousand-metre-plus mountain ranges into four prefectures or regions. The north coast has all the major towns and holiday areas, joined together by the single National Road, whilst the south boasts pretty villages and some of the best coastal scenery in Europe. Everywhere there are excellent beaches, and a highly developed tourist infrastructure. So enjoy the hotels and restaurants, the tourist attractions, and water sports, but also get away from it all into the mountains, visit the relics of its long and august history, seek out its village life, its music, dance, art and craft, its first-rate walking and cycling, its wildlife. Here are my fifteen favourite moments from many weeks and months touring the island.

❶ **Being dropped off by the coastal ferry** in the pretty fishing village of Loutró—walking down the ramp and enjoying the peace and tranquillity left behind after the ferry continues its journey along the coast. *See p 120.*

❷ **Touring the Naval Museum in Chaniá,** full of information about the Venetians—their harbours and ships, lighthouses and boatyards—and about the ferocious Battle of Crete and the German occupation of the island, whilst catching glimpses of this beautiful city from the museum's windows. *See p 67.*

❸ **Wading through crystal clear waters** from a baking sandy beach to the islet of Elafonisi, on Crete's west coast. *See p 101.*

❹ **Devouring fresh fish** under the trees in the hill village of Argiróupolis, surrounded by the roar of rushing water amid eddies of cool, clean mountain air. *See p 128.*

❺ **Absorbing the uplifting yet sombre atmosphere** in the Arkádi Monastery, scene of one of the greatest events of the struggle against Ottoman domination. Here, hundreds of Cretan men, women, and children preferred to blow

The coastal ferry nearing the fishing village of Loutró.

Family Life In Crete

Central to social life in Crete is family. Children in Crete are cherished. Kids are smiled at and indulged, parents are complimented on their offspring. If you're asked how many children (or grandchildren) you have, and what they're like, answer in full—you can be confident that the questioner really wants to know. And do the polite thing—ask back. The indulgent attitude of most Greeks to children is also extended to pregnant women. Seats will immediately be given up on buses, and chairs provided in shops. If a pregnant woman catches a whiff of cooking as she passes a restaurant, and fancies a taste, it is considered a matter of honour by the cook or restaurateur to ensure that she immediately has her fancy satisfied—free of charge. This is because there's an old wives' tale that, if a pregnant woman wants something particular to eat and doesn't get it, her baby will have a birthmark relating to that food. I wonder if unscrupulous pregnant women ever use this tradition to eat out for nothing! Finally, the elderly are widely respected—there is little of the ageist contempt for the old that prevails in many societies.

themselves and their enemies to smithereens rather than surrender. *See p 128*.

6 Dropping down to Bali, one of Crete's loveliest seaside towns, from the National Road, and delighting in its picturesque perfection, its numerous beautifully sited tavérnas, and its busy water-borne traffic. *See p 102*.

7 Driving through the rolling vineyards and olive groves of Crete's premier wine-producing region south of Iráklion, and

Absorbing the uplifting yet sombre atmosphere at the Arkádi Monastery.

15 Favourite Moments

Bali, one of Crete's most attractive seaside towns.

stopping off to sample the wine and buy a few bottles. *See p 139*.

⑧ **Exploring the caves of Mátala**, once early Christian burial tombs, later a hippy, happy hunting ground of the 1960s, visited by numerous rock, pop, and folk music celebrities. *See p 103*.

⑨ **Finding out about Crete's greatest writer**, Nikos Kazantzákis, in the museum that has been established in his grandparents' house in Mirtía and in Iráklion's National Museum, then paying respects at his tomb high upon the city's ramparts. *See p 50*.

⑩ **Enjoying the vast array of family fun activities** available in and around Hersónisos—water parks, aquaria, karting, bungee-jumping, golf (both real and crazy), and lots more. *See p 62*.

⑪ **Getting to grips with Europe's first civilization**—the Minoans—in the Archaeological Museum in Iráklion, following up with a visit to the world-famous Minoan palace at Knossós, then drinking in the atmosphere in some more of Crete's Minoan sites. *See p 83*.

⑫ **Chugging out across a sparkling sea** to investigate the formidable Venetian fortifications of the island of Spinalónga, which was designed to protect the port of Eloúnda, but which became a refuge for Turks seeking sanctuary after independence, and then, until 1957, Europe's last leper colony. *See p 149*.

⑬ **Pottering around the Lasithi Plateau**, spread out like a patchwork quilt high in the mountains of

Take a tour around the Minoan Palace at Knossós.

Entrance to the Diktean Cave in Lasíthi Plateau.

eastern Crete, visiting stunning caves and admiring home-produced textiles. *See p 153*.

⑭ Thrilling to some of Europe's most majestic coastal scenery along Crete's south-west coast, stopping on the way to enjoy attractive beaches and homely villages. *See Chapter 5, p 99*.

⑮ Eating mezzedes and drinking raki in one of the traditional tavernas in the main square at Mochós, hoping that the locals will start dancing or, even better, that a wedding celebration will pass by and draw you in. *See p 55*.

1 **Strategies** for Seeing Crete

Strategies for Seeing Crete

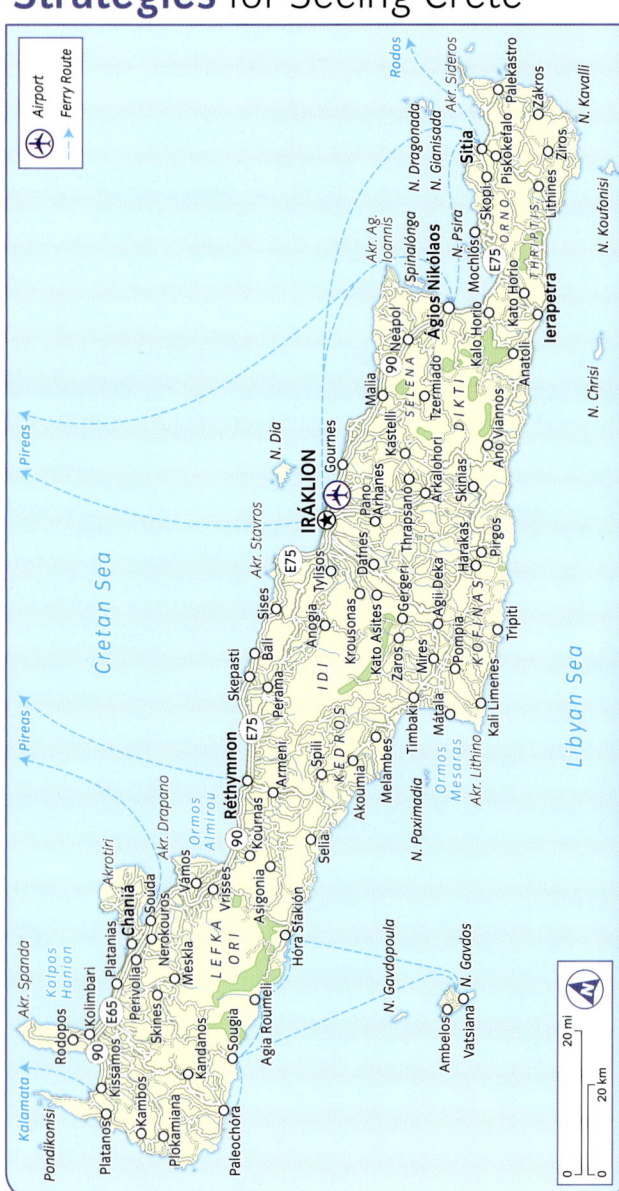

Previous page: Painted boat, Chaniá.

Crete is a long, thin island—260km long and varying from around 80km to 20km in width. It therefore requires a number of strategies to ensure that you make the best of your visit.

Strategies for Seeing Crete

Rule #1: Hire a car
To get the best out of your visit, you really need the freedom to explore that a car will give you. If you're tempted to rent motorcycles or quad bikes, think carefully. They're cheap and convenient, but dangerous—ask any local A&E staff. Cars are safer.

Rule #2: Whilst driving around Crete, allow plenty of time
Roads are often so winding that, on any but the National Road, you'll be lucky to average 30mph.

Rule #3: Check opening times
Cretans can be cavalier about published times. I visited one restaurant at a time when, according to its published hours, it should have been open, only to be told that the owner 'had things to do', so decided to close. Even attractions such as museums where the hours are literally 'inscribed in stone' (or brass) have a tendency simply to stick a bit of paper over them, bearing totally different hours. Big tourist attractions like the water parks also play it by ear—whatever the official closing date, when visitor numbers have slowed to a trickle in October, they simply make a pragmatic decision that it's not worth opening, and shut up shop for the winter.

Rule #4: Remember that many things close for the siesta after lunch
Do what the Cretans do, divide your day into three—plan activities for the morning and evening, and rest up in the afternoon.

Rule #5: Despite what you may hear to the contrary, there's no need to stick slavishly to the main roads
The quality of even quite minor roads in Crete is excellent. If a route that you want to take is marked down as a dirt road, check with locals—you'll often find that they've been recently resurfaced (the roads, that is, not the locals). Distances in this book are approximate as there are often several ways to get from A to B.

Rule #6: Look out for tourist road trains
They're a cheap and easy way of getting an overview of a region. Most holiday areas and large towns have them. They can be very bumpy, though—you could end up with loose fillings!

Rule #7: Coastal ferries are inexpensive and efficient
They're usually quicker than doing the same route by car (even where that's possible. Some villages are accessible only from the sea). Be sure you're waiting on the jetty at the required time—crews

Coastal ferries are inexpensive and efficient.

Look out for tourist road trains.

have got unloading and loading down to a fine art, and it's unbelievable how quickly they can turn around.

Rule #8: If using taxis for longer journeys, agree a price before embarking
And don't be afraid to haggle.

Rule #9: Petrol stations are plentiful, even in rural areas
But most don't take credit cards, so have lots of cash ready. Even those that advertise that they do take credit cards will seemingly go to any length to avoid doing so—saying that the machine is broken, or the phone lines are down, or flatly denying that they accept them, even when you can see the sticker! ●

Agritourism—A Different Way To See Crete

Rural areas in Crete are dying. Young people leave in search of work and entertainment. Old people die. In the worst-hit areas, cottages lie empty, walls crumble, and fields return to nature. In response, and with the full backing of successive governments, a movement has developed called 'agritourism' (or 'agrotourism'). Characterful old buildings are sympathetically renovated and turned into villas or small hotels, and working farms are encouraged to provide accommodation for holidaymakers. As urban Greek or foreign holidaymakers flood in to fill the void left by departing youngsters (or oldsters), new customers are provided for local restaurants and shops, traditional crafts are given a boost, and faltering festivals take on a new lease of life. Agritourism offers a refreshingly different kind of experience—the chance to enjoy a peaceful holiday (and even to help with the animals on a farm, or with the olive harvest) whilst supporting Greek community life. Have a look at the entry on Vamos in Chapter 6 (p 123).

Not for everybody, perhaps, but win-win, all the way!

2 The Best **Full-Day Tours**

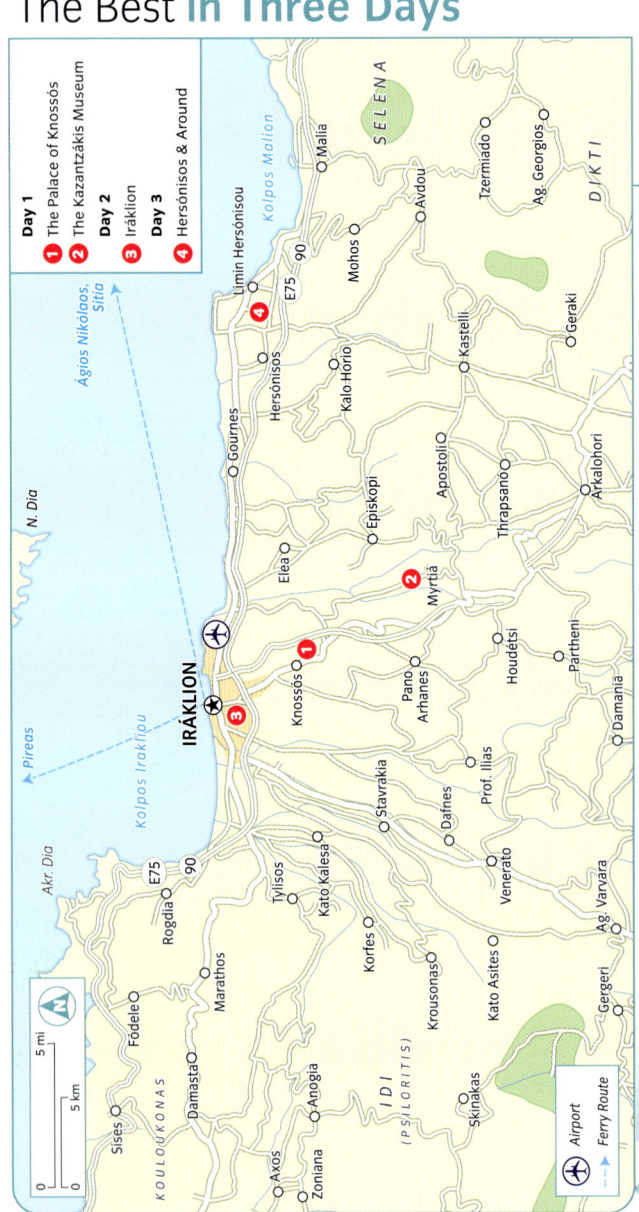

The Best in Three Days

Because of its size, there's no way that you could try to see most of what Crete has to offer in three days. Therefore I've gone for itineraries that include the two things on the island that are of undeniable world importance—the Palace of Knossós and the associated Archaeological Museum in Iráklion—whilst at the same time offering tasters of other parts of the Cretan experience. Each day's trip starts and ends in Iráklion.

Day 1 (Round trip 28km)

Get onto the National Road south of the capital, and follow signs to Knossós. As you approach the entrance to the site, (about 6kms from the city centre), there are several car parks. Use the one which also has spaces for coaches, or even park right outside the gates if there's room. 8km.

1 ★★★ **kids** **The Palace of Knossós.** In what is really a suburb of the capital, the Minoan Palace of Knossós is fascinating not only for the picture it provides of life in a wonderfully sophisticated palace-city of three and a half thousand years ago, but also for the amazing *Indiana Jones*-like story of its discovery by Englishman Arthur Evans. An easy bus or taxi ride from the centre of Iráklion, the palace spreads over a hilltop with views of the surrounding countryside. It is well-served by information boards and by professional guides who can be hired at the entrance. ⏱ *3 hr. See p 27,* **2**, *p 137,* **1**.

Continue south from Knossós, past an aqueduct. Then turn left, following signs to Mirtia and the Kazantzákis Museum. About 10km.

2 ★★★ **The Kazantzákis Museum.** After driving through the vineyards and olive groves to the south of Knossós you arrive at Mirtia and the museum devoted to Nikos Kazantzákis (1883–1957). The town is pretty and peaceful, with an attractive square dotted with modern sculptures—well worth a visit in its own right. The museum is in a large house that once belonged to the writer's grandparents. It's stuffed with memorabilia—the books, the plays, the theatre models, the busts and photographs, but also a teapot, tobacco pipes and such. ⏱ *1 hr. See p 13,* **2**.

Return to Iráklion by the same route.

The Minoan palace of Knossós.

The Best Full-Day Tours

Kazantzákis's grandfather's house, now a museum.

Day 2

3 ★ **Iráklion.** Despite getting a panning in most guidebooks, and despite the noise, heat, dust, and traffic in the modern parts, Crete's capital city is, in fact, well worth a visit, with its excellent **Archaeological, Historical, and Battle of Crete museums**, its Venetian walls, fortress, relics, and port, and its pedestrianized old city. Stroll around **Platia Nikoforou Foka** and **Platia Venizelou**, admire the **Morosini Fountain** and the **Loggia**, have a look at Ágios **Tito's church** (his head's still there, in a reliquary), or take a rest in **El Greco Park**. ⏱ *1 day. Iráklion tourist office, 1 Xanthoudidou.* ☎ *28102 28225. For more on Iráklion, see p 83 in Chapter 4.*

Day 3 (Round trip 60km)

Follow signs for Ágios Nikólaos east on the National Road or on the old coast road—either will do. After about 28km look out for signs to Hersónisos.

4 ★ **kids Hersónisos & Around.** Hersónisos and its surrounds contain the single greatest concentration of holiday attractions for families on the island. Hersónisos itself is surprisingly user-friendly, with a small harbour offering boat trips, a pleasant beach, a tourist road train, a captivating hands-on little aquarium, an outdoor museum of Cretan life (**Lychnostatis**), and the excellent **Star Beach** complex with a wide range of water sports and facilities. Outside Hersónisos, all in less than half-an-hour's drive, there are, to the east, the remains of the **Minoan Palace of Mália**, to the south a succession of attractive villages in the hills above the town and to the west, two large water parks, Crete's only 18- hole golf course, and the first-rate **Cretaquarium**. ⏱ *1 day. For more information on Hersónisos see p 59 in Chapter 3.*

Take a break by the Morosini Fountain in Iráklion.

Check out the boat trips on offer in Hersónisos harbour.

Daedalus & King Minos

Crete's central myth involves a great inventor, Daedalus, servant of King Minos. On his accession, Minos had asked his uncle, the god Poseidon, to send him a bull to sacrifice. But the bull was so magnificent that Minos decided not to sacrifice him, but to put him in amongst the royal herd of cows. Big mistake. A vengeful Poseidon caused Minos's wife Pasiphae to fall in love with the bull. She asked Daedalus to help her consummate her passion, so he invented a hollow cow into which she crawled—you get the idea! Pasiphae gave birth to the Minotaur—half man, half bull. The monster started trashing the island, so Daedalus designed a labyrinth in which it was imprisoned. Minos fed it Athenian youths and maidens, paid as tribute. In due course, Theseus, the son of the King of Athens, demanded that he be included to see if he could vanquish the Minotaur.

On his arrival, Minos's daughter Ariadne fell in love with him, and offered to help. She approached Daedalus, who gave her a ball of thread for Theseus to unravel as he made his way through the labyrinth. It worked—he killed the Minotaur and, following the thread, led his compatriots to safety. Minos was so furious with Daedalus that he imprisoned him, together with his son Icarus, in the labyrinth. Not a smart move—Daedalus had designed it, so knew how to get out. Daedalus built wings from wax and feathers, and escaped from Crete, warning Icarus not to fly too close to the sun. Icarus ignored his father's instructions, the wax melted, the wings fell apart, and Icarus fell to his death.

Daedalus flew on to Sicily, where Minos tracked him down. So Daedalus scalded him to death as he lay in his bath. A clever bloke, Daedalus, but not to be messed with.

The Best in One Week

Day 1
1. Iráklion

Day 2
2. The Palace of Knossós
3. The Wine Roads
4. The Kazantzákis Museum

Day 3
5. Górtys
6. Festós
7. Agía Triáda
8. Mátala

Day 4
9. Ágia Galíni
10. Hóra Sfakíon

Day 5
11. Loutró

Day 6
12. Réthymnon

Day 7
13. Samariá Gorge Walk
14. Chaniá

The Best in One Week

Rather than cherry-picking attractions from the whole island, I feel that in a week, it is best to see central Crete plus one end of the island. The east is lovely, but I feel that the west boasts the prettier towns, the nicer beaches, the grander scenery, and the more interesting history. On days 1, 2, and 3 tours start from Iráklion, days 4 and 5 from Réthymnon, and days 6 and 7 from Chaniá.

Day 1

① ★ Iráklion. Spend your first full day in the capital. In Iráklion you can experience the easy-going street life around **Platia Venizelou**, but also the vibrant (and noisy!) life of modern Crete at **Platia Eleftherias**, with its constant swirl of cars and mopeds, or along the road past the harbour. Dip into Minoan history at the **Archaeological Museum**, Cretan life and art at the **Historical Museum**, or World War II in the **Battle of Crete Museum**. Walk the city walls and tour Iráklion's Venetian relics, or examine some of Greece's most famous icons in the **Museum of Religious Arts**. Or wander around Iráklion's shops or the cafés and restaurants in Dedalou. *For more on Iráklion see p 83 in Chapter 4.*

Bust of Sir Arthur Evans in Knossós.

Day 2 (Round trip 28km to 80km, depending on which vineyards you visit)

For directions to Knossós, see above, p 13, ①. 6km.

② ★★★ kids The Palace of Knossós. The great palace was discovered in the early 20th century by Sir Arthur Evans, a British archaeologist who identified it (on what some consider tenuous grounds) as the palace of the legendary King Minos (see Daedalus box, p 15). He reconstructed parts in ways which many archaeologists think irresponsible, but it can't be denied that the site stirs the imagination and inspires awe. It also led to a great scramble by archaeologists from all over the world to discover and identify other palaces, towns, and burial sites from Europe's first great civilization. *See p 13, ①. 3 hr.*

③ The Wine Roads. The area south of Knossós is Crete's greatest wine region, so after the Minoan site explore the vineyards and wineries. *The Winemakers' Network of Iráklion Prefecture* has produced some informative guides and itineraries of 22 participating vineyards. Most provide introductory videos, guided tours, tastings, and of course the opportunity to buy wine. *1 hr upwards. See p 139, ⑦.*

④ ★★★ The Kazantzákis Museum. Right in the heart of the wine region, the Kazantzákis Museum in Mirtía will tell you all you need to know (and more!) about Crete's greatest writer. *1 hr. See p 13, ②.*

Day 3 (Round trip 140km)

South-west of Iráklion, turn off the National Road towards Agia Varvara (signposted 'Mires'). Pass Siva to Agia Varvara and down onto the Messara Plain. Drive

Ancient ruins at Górtys.

through Agii Deka ('Ten Saints') towards Mires. Górtys is just outside the village. 44 km.

5 ★★ **Górtys.** Ancient Górtys saw its heyday in Dorian and Roman times. Its fame rests on three connections. In mythology, it's the place where Zeus made love to Europa after abducting her from the mainland; it has a wall inscribed with the law code of the Dorians; and it's where Christianity, in the person of St Titus, entered Crete. ⏱ *1 hr. See p 140,* **8**.

After Mires, take a left turn off the main road to Festós. About 16 km.

The lighthouse in the port of Réthymnon.

6 ★★ **Festós.** One of Crete's great Minoan palace sites, Festós has extensive views across this part of the island. Apart from the site itself, Festós is also famous as the place where the exquisite *Phaistos Disc* was found—made of clay, it has a spiral of hieroglyphics on it which have still not been interpreted. ⏱ *30 min. See p 140,* **10**.

Turn right out of the car park, then follow signposts to Agia Triáda. 3km.

7 ★★ **Agía Triáda.** A hillside archaeological site with similar views to Festós, Agía Triáda is odd—nobody is really sure what it is. The best guess so far is that it was a summer palace for royalty from Festós. ⏱ *30 min. See p 141,* **11**.

Return to the fork just before Festós and turn right. The road descends for 10 km to the Messara Plain and Mátala.

8 ★★ **kids Mátala.** After all the dry tramping around archaeological sites, Mátala comes like water to one dying of thirst. On a graceful cove hemmed in by two headlands, Mátala has a sandy beach, cafés and tavernas, plus caves (celebrated by, amongst others, Joni Mitchell) on the right-hand headland. ⏱ *3 hr. See p 103,* ⑫.

Return to Iráklion the way you came.

Day 4 (Round trip 240km. This tour takes you through some of Crete's most beautiful scenery)
From Réthymnon take the main road due south through Spíli to the coast at Ágia Galíni. 60km.

⑨ ★ **Ágia Galíni.** Here you can chill out, take a boat ride along the coast to **Palm Beach** or the **Paximadia islands**, or go dolphin-watching. ⏱ *1–2 hr.*

Continue towards Réthymnon for about 10 km then turn left towards Sellia. Follow the coast road west past Frangokástello to Hóra Sfakíon.

⑩ ★★ **Hóra Sfakíon.** This was the port from which the defeated Allied army was lifted off during World War II—look out for the monuments. ⏱ *30 min. See p 120,* ⑭.

⑪ ★★★ kids **Loutró.** Take the ferry to congenially laid-back and insanely photogenic Loutró to eat, drink, and/or go for a swim. ⏱ *2 hr to half a day, depending on ferry timetable. See p 60,* ⑥.

From Hóra Sfakíon, drive north through the Askífou Plateau, turn east onto the National Road at Vrísses and return to Réthymnon. About 68km.

Day 5
⑫ ★★★ **Réthymnon.** Spend your fifth day exploring Réthymnon, with its narrow lanes, overhanging balconies, tiny Venetian port, and impressively massive castle. *For more information on Réthymnon, see p 75 in Chapter 4.*

Day 6
⑬ ★★★ **Samariá Gorge Walk.** Crete is renowned for its fine walking. So, if you're relatively fit and you want to make a full day of it, head for the Samariá Gorge's 16-km descent to the sea (see p 105, ①). But it's gruelling, hot, and crowded. An easier option is the Ímbros Gorge. *See p 106,* ②.

Day 7
⑭ ★★★ kids **Chaniá.** I've saved my favourite Cretan town for last—Chaniá. Enjoy the Venetian harbour, the boatyards and lighthouse, the attention-grabbing Naval Museum, and much else. *For more information on Chaniá see p 67 in Chapter 4.*

The Venetian harbour of Chaniá.

The Best in Two Weeks

Day 8
① Hersónisos

Day 9
② The Lasíthi Plateau

Day 10
③ The western edge of the Gulf of Mirabéllo

Day 11
④ Ágios Nikólaos

Day 12
⑤ Gourniá
⑥ Móchlos
⑦ Sitía

Day 13
⑧ Moní Tóplou
⑨ Vái
⑩ The Zákros Gorge & the Palace of Zákros

Day 14
⑪ Inland Crete

A **fortnight's stay gives you the chance to get a firm** handle on Crete—though you won't be able to boast an intimate knowledge of the whole of the island, you will certainly get a comprehensive overview, and the chance to 'bookmark' parts you particularly like for more detailed exploration. START: **Hersónisos**.

The Best in Two Weeks

Day 8 (Round trip 80km)
Drive 24km east along the National Road to Hersónisos, then explore the region—the town, the Palace at Mália, Acquapulp Water Park, Crete Golf Club and Cretaquarium.

① ★ kids Hersónisos. Whilst not to everyone's taste, Hersónisos and its hinterland offer the most varied range of attractions and probably the largest concentration of hotels and restaurants on the island. A favourite with the sun, sea, and sand package holiday companies, Hersónisos is the place to go for family friendliness, Mália for bars and nightlife. *For more information on Hersónisos see p 62 in Chapter 3.*

Day 9 (Round trip 115km)
Drive north on the National Road to Neápoli, then follow signs for Lasithi Plateau.

② ★★★ The Lasithi Plateau. High up in the Dikti Mountains, the Lasithi Plateau was, for a long time, one of the island's remotest and most distinctively individual regions. Cut off by the surrounding ring of peaks, the people lived for centuries by farming its rich soil, raising livestock, and spinning and weaving textiles. From the latter 20th century onwards, tourism has become increasingly important, though more through coach parties visiting for the day than from longer-stay holidaymakers. The villages are spaced at intervals around the edge of the plateau, making it an attractive day-long circular route. There are shops selling locally produced textiles, several museums, a couple of caves (one, it is claimed, the birthplace of Zeus), and many cafés, tavernas, and small hotels. The much-photographed windmills of the plateau look nothing when their sails are furled but when the sails are spread, the plateau looks like a field of flowers. *For a tour of the Lasithi Plateau, see p 152 in Chapter 6.*

Day 10 (Round trip 76km)
Drive north on the National Road towards Iráklion. After 26km follow signs to the right for Sisi.

③ The western edge of the Gulf of Mirabéllo. Probably the most attractive area in Lasíthi Province is the region from Mália to Ágios Nikólaos. Here you can experience the seaside village of Sisi, surrounded by rocks and palm trees (5km from the National Road), the impressive Milatos Cave (a further 6km), the upland monastery of Moní Aréti (24km from the cave), sweeping views across the Gulf of Mirabéllo

A Lasithi windmill.

The Best Full-Day Tours

Take a relaxing stroll around Ágios Nikólaos.

from the escarpment above Eloúnda, and Eloúnda itself—one of Crete's prettiest and most upmarket small towns (16km from the monastery). It has a good range of shops, varied restaurants, an agreeable municipal beach in the centre, and the Roman remains at Oloús, just south of the town. And from Eloúnda's tiny harbour you can catch a boat out to the odd island of Spinalónga. *For a tour of the Lasíthi Plateau see p 152 in Chapter 6.*

Day 11

❹ ★★ **Ágios Nikólaos.** Once heading for the worst excesses of mass tourism, Ágios Nikólaos has, in the 21st century, gone upmarket, appealing to an older, more family-orientated demographic. Though still dominated by tourism, it's beautifully situated on hills above its famously bottomless lake, it's cheerfully unassuming, and it has a mix of bars and restaurants, beaches and day cruises—good for a day's low-stress strolling, window-shopping, and grazing. A 10-minute drive out of the town brings you to one of Crete's premier craft villages—**Kritsá**—and the impressive ruins of **Lató**, a Roman city. *For a tour of Ágios Nikólaos see p 91 in Chapter 4.*

Day 12 (Round trip 78km)
Head south along the National Road towards Sitia. In about 20km, turn right along a dirt road to the ruins of Minoan Gourniá, just off the main road.

❺ ★★ **Gourniá.** Driving around the Gulf of Mirabéllo, you leave Crete's tourist hotspots for a more authentic Crete. There's still plenty of holiday infrastructure, but without the same high-season congestion. Gourniá is one of Crete's most satisfying and easily understood Minoan city sites, yet you might find

One of many lace and embroidery shops in the craft village of Kritsá.

Visit the Minoan ruins on the tiny island off the harbour of Móchlos.

yourself alone as you clamber around its paths and ruined walls. ⏲ *30 min. See p 22,* ❺.

Continue along the main Sitia road, through Kavousi, Lastros, and Sfaka. After the Panorama Tavern (terrific views!), turn left down a switchback road through huge quarries to Móchlos. 23km.

❻ ★ **Móchlos.** The village of Móchlos is just the place for a coffee-break, lunch, or afternoon swim. It is also worth visiting for the Minoan ruins on the tiny island just off the harbour—ask at any of the tavernas on the waterside about getting out to it by boat. *See p 23,* ❻.

Continue east after Móchlos, back to the main coast road, and drive the pleasantly bendy road to Sitía, about 35km. In the town follow signs for the port—after the last roundabout, just before the sea, the (free) main car park is on the right.

❼ ★ **Sitía.** Once the object of attempts by the Venetians to develop it as a regional capital ('La Sitis'—hence Lasithi), Sitía is once again in the sights of the developers. But despite rumours of an expansion of the local airport into an international destination, the town currently remains a quiet, charming Cretan port, lined by locals with fishing rods and overlooked by a fort, numerous tavernas, and a few hotels mostly frequented by Cretans. There's an extensive sandy beach south of the port, and a considerable archaeological museum covering important finds from eastern Crete—don't be put off by the rather grim, garage-like exterior. ⏲ *half a day. See p 23,* ❼.

Stay the night in Sitía.

Day 13 (Round trip 174km)
Leave Sitia, following signs to Palaiokastro, Vái, and Zákros. After about 12km, turn left off the main road, across 3km of bleak terrain to Moni Tóplou.

❽ ★ **Moní Tóplou.** Beyond Sitia you are entering Crete's 'far east', a land of small villages, serpentine roads, and empty hills, but with several places well worth visiting, starting with the handsome monastery of Moní Tóplou. Enjoy its tranquillity, read up on its bloodthirsty history, and have a drink and a snack in its very Cretan café. ⏲ *30 min. See p 23,* ❽.

The Best Full-Day Tours

Continue across 9km of bleak terrain to Vái.

9 ★ kids **Vái.** The beach at Vái is the star of a thousand photoshoots. With its dazzling sand and its swaying palm trees, you could be on a desert island. Except for the crowds! ⏱ *1 hr. See p 24,* **9**.

From Vái, head south 30km through Zákros to Káto Zákros. Just before the village, look out for a sign on the left 'Footpath Zákros Gorge—Cheese Dairy—Zákros Springs'. Park the car and take the path.

10 ★★★ **The Zákros Gorge & the Palace of Zákros.** South from Vái a footpath takes you down the Zákros Gorge to Káto Zákros on the coast. Flower-decked in spring, glorious at any time, the ravine is also called *The Valley of the Dead,* for the caves which were used as burial places by the Minoans. At the bottom of the gorge, just outside the village, is the Palace of Zákros, the most recently excavated of Crete's Minoan sites. The village itself—Káto Zákros—is a tranquil place to stop for refreshment, sunbathe on the pebble beach, or have a swim.

Return to the car on foot, or by bus or taxi. 1 hr for the return walk, 1 hr for the palace. See p 152 in Chapter 6.

To get back to Ágios Nikólaos, return to Zákros, then turn left 3km north of the town, up a series of hairpin bends, towards Karidi. From there, a 15km drive across good mountain roads brings you to the main Sitia–Ierapetra road. Turn left to Ierapetra, then follow signs for Ágios Nikólaos. About 116km.

Day 14

11 **Inland Crete.** There could be few more agreeable ways of spending your final day on Crete than exploring the quiet rural roads and hill villages of inland Crete as you head back to the airport and home. Depending on how much time you've got, lose yourself in the mountains, stop to feed roadside donkeys, or park up and enter tiny whitewashed hamlets to try to communicate with villagers who will almost certainly speak little or no English. Take a look at the map, trace a route from Káto Zákros at random, and follow it. And remember—however isolated you feel up in the mountains, you're rarely more than half an hour's drive from one of the excellent main roads. Once on them, you can get to Iráklion airport within a couple of hours, wherever you are! ●

An old windmill infront of Moni Tóplou.

3 The Best Special-Interest Tours

Minoan Crete

The Best Special-Interest Tours

1. Archaeological Museum
2. The Palace of Knossós
3. Knossós Palace Snack Bar
4. The Palace of Festós
5. Agía Triáda
6. The Palace of Mália
7. Tavérna Kalyba
8. Archaeological Museum, Sitía
9. The Palace at Zákros
10. Káto Zákros Bay
11. Gourniá
12. Mochlos
13. Tavérna Sofia

Previous page: Port of Iráklion, with Venetian fortress in the background.

Minoan Crete

Crete's very own, and Europe's first, civilization, the **Minoan golden age**, precedes that of classical Greece by a thousand years. And yet the Minoans emerged from the mists of Homeric myth little more than a hundred years ago. The first two sites below are essential visits for understanding Minoan Crete—the remaining ones depend on where you're staying. And keep two key dates in mind—repeated discoveries all over the island have established that there was massive destruction at the end of the First Palace Period in around 1700 BC (probably by earthquake), and the final destruction at the end of the New Palace Period (possibly by tidal waves, followed by invasion) around 1450 BC. START: **Iráklion. Trip length 142km.**

① ★★★ Archaeological Museum. The essential first stop on any tour of Minoan Crete has to be the Archaeological Museum in Iráklion. What started as a rather ramshackle collection of antiquities in 1883 was properly housed in its own building just before World War I, and re-housed in an earthquake-proof building just before World War II. A massive renovation and rebuilding programme was begun at the start of the 21st century which, at the time of writing, still hadn't been completed. No fixed date has been published for the re-opening—until then, the highlights of the Minoan collection are on show in temporary accommodation—the artefacts spectacular, the presentation uninspiring. Once fully open, the museum will undoubtedly be a world superstar ⏲ *30 min. See p 83,* ①.

Get onto the National Road south of the capital, and follow signs to Knossós. As you approach the entrance to the site, (about 6km from the city centre) there are several car parks. Use the one which also has spaces for coaches, or even park right outside the gates if there's room. 8km.

② ★★★ kids The Palace of Knossós. The other Minoan must-visit is the Palace of Knossós, about 5km south of the capital. Entrance to the site is past the bust of archaeologist Sir Arthur Evans, who, though he didn't discover it (that honour goes to Cretan Minos Kalokairinos), bought the site and excavated it from 1900 onwards. Dating from the New Palace Period, it was more an administrative and religious centre than a palace, and contains all the features that have come to be recognised as typical of the Minoan civilization—the inclusion of light-wells within the structure, sophisticated water and drainage systems, and broad flights of steps. Knossós had over a thousand

The Minoan palace at Knossós.

The archeological site of Festós.

rooms. The first ones you come to were for storage, then, clustered around a central court, there are a number of staircases, a throne room, royal apartments, a theatre, workshops, and several separate houses. Always remember, though, that many of Evans's interpretations and reconstructions have been questioned—even his identification and naming of the civilization as 'Minoan' has been disputed. *See p 137,* ❶.

The excavation site at Agia Triáda.

❸ **Knossós Palace Snack Bar.** Stop for a cold drink in the snack bar, one of a cluster of buildings near the entrance. For more substantial refreshment, try one of the unnamed tavérnas that line the road opposite the entrance. *No phone. $.*

Return to the National Road into Iráklion. To the south-west, turn off the National Road towards Agia Varvara and the south (signposted 'Mires'). After Siva a new road runs as far as Agia Varvara, a rural town notable mainly for its 'navel of Crete'—a huge conical rock topped by a chapel. Beyond it, the road winds down onto the Messara Plain. Drive through Agii Deka ('Ten Saints') and Mires, then look out for signposts to Festós on the left. 68km.

❹ ★★ **The Palace of Festós.** Festós is interesting both for its similarities with Knossós—typically Minoan grand stairway, storage rooms, workshops, royal apartments and so on, built around a central court—and for its differences (in particular, the considerable surviving remains from the first, pre-1700 BC palace). The initial excavation was by Italian Federico

Halbherr (1857–1930) at around the same time that Evans was excavating Knossós, and he did a more austere job, largely eschewing reconstruction. This is both good and bad news—modern archaeologists approve far more of Halbherr's methodology, but for the non-specialist, Evans's reconstructions and interpretations at Knossós stir the imagination far more effectively. However, some interesting artefacts were discovered at Festós—in particular, the exquisite and mysterious *Phaistos Disc*—between 3500 and 4000 years old, 15cm in diameter, made of fired clay, and with a spiral of hieroglyphic symbols on both sides that you feel should have been easy to interpret, yet never have been.

Turn right out of the car park, then follow signposts along the road after right fork, signposted Agia Triáda. 3km.

❺ ★★ **Agía Triáda.** Agía Triáda was also excavated by Halbherr, whose bust decorates the ticket office. The complicated ruins are difficult to interpret and don't seem to fit in with anything known about Minoan Crete. Indeed, nobody has managed to work out exactly what the site represents—a summer palace, perhaps, or the house of a great prince. It hasn't even got a name—it is called Agía Triáda (Holy Trinity) after a nearby church (not the one on site). And the mystery doesn't end there—the layout is different to anything else in Crete, and looks far more like a small town with an attached palace. Despite all this, it has yielded some of the best known Minoan artefacts ever found—the Boxer Vase, Harvest Vase, and Chieftain Cup, and a wonderful sarcophagus, all now held by the **Archaeological Museum** in Iráklion (see p 83, ❶.) *See p 141,* ⓫.

Return to Iráklion 63km.

If you don't have time to take in Festós/Agia Triáda, then Mália, 20 minutes drive east along the National Road, is a lot closer to Iráklion. Round trip Iráklion to Mália and back 76km.

❻ ★ **The Palace of Mália.** Details, models, and maps at the entrance give a good idea of the palace in its heyday. Furthermore it was never reoccupied after the 1450 BC destruction, and so is much more clear-cut in its layout. The excavation is a work in progress, so there's a lot of new stuff to see—beyond and around the palace a whole Minoan town is beginning to emerge. Under protective roofs, there are walkways and information boards which will be extended as finds are made.

❼ **Tavérna Kalyba.** Three hundred metres beyond the palace is a clean, sandy beach. End your day with a swim to wash away the day's dust, then have something to eat and some cold drinks at the Tavérna Kalyba on the beach. *No phone. $.*

Work in progress at the Palace of Mália.

Minoan Crete

The Best Special-Interest Tours

Eastern Crete

If you are staying in Crete's far east, it is possible to get an insight into Minoan culture without travelling out of the region. Start this tour in Sitia. Trip length 174km.

❽ ★ Archaeological Museum, Sitía. Like its Iráklion counterpart, Sitía's Archaeological Museum is a good starting point for the local Minoan sites. Many of the treasures discovered at the Palace of Zákros and the attached town give a unique insight into ordinary life in Minoan Crete, partly because, as in Roman Pompeii, its destruction appears to have come so suddenly that the inhabitants had no time to gather up their possessions before fleeing, and partly because it was an important staging post for trade with Egypt. Look out for a large millstone and several clay pots outside the museum, and, in the main room, practical objects such as a bronze saw, a wine press, a clay grill, and cooking utensils. There's also a case full of clay tablets bearing Linear A inscriptions baked by the very fire that destroyed the palace. Linear A, found on many Minoan artefacts, has, unlike the later Linear B, not yet been deciphered. *See p 150,* ⓬.

Take the road from Sitia across to the east coast. 36km.

❾ ★ The Palace at Zákros. The excavation of the palace (and town) of Zákros was initially done by British archaeologist David Hogarth during the great burst of activity in the early 20th century. However, the site was abandoned, and the main excavation was done by Greek archaeologist Nikolaos Platon, starting in 1961 and continuing to the present. This makes it one of the few to use the most up-to-date methods. Though smaller than the other great Minoan palaces, it was nevertheless important—one of four Minoan administrative centres, and a celebrated port on the route to Egypt. *See p 152,* ⓱.

❿ Káto Zákros Bay. Eat at Nikos Platanakis's Káto Zákros Bay tavérna in the village—most of the food is locally sourced, and the position at the start of the village, on the beach, couldn't be better. ☎ *28430 26887. $.*

Stepping around the excavations at the Palace of Zákros.

Gourniá was excavated by the intrepid female archaeologist Harriot Boyd.

Go back across the mountains to the Sitía–Ierapetra road, and from Ierapetra cross the island back to the National Road. Gourniá is on the road to Ágios Nikólaos, on the left. 87km.

11 ★★ Gourniá. A small, easily understood site on a hill-top, Gourniá was one of the few in the early 20th-century, macho world of archaeological exploration to be excavated by a woman—the admirably intrepid American archaeologist Harriet Boyd (later Boyd-Hawes). A mass of narrow lanes and small houses, many occupied by craftsmen, it is worth a climb up to the hill-top, and a larger residence—probably the governor's. *See p 149,* **8**.

Return along the National Road towards Sitía, and take the loop down to the sea and Móchlos. 23km.

12 ★ Móchlos. Móchlos is an unassuming little fishing village which has a small island just offshore with substantial Minoan remains. Indeed, it was probably attached to the mainland in Minoan times, forming a hilly promontory that protected the harbour. Tombs on the western end of the islet were excavated from 1908, and the main settlement on the side facing the village is a joint US–Greek venture from the late 1980s (see www.uncg.edu/~jssoles/Mochlos/first.html). Get to the island by asking at one of the waterside tavérnas—strong swimmers could even get across under their own steam. The excavations are explained by information boards, and in the summer there may well be archaeology students around helping with the dig. *See p 149,* **9**.

13 Tavérna Sofía. Take a quick dip off the rocks next to the harbour, refreshment at the tavérna, and then head off home. ☎ *28430 94554. $.*

Return to the National Road, and Sitía. 28km.

Venetian Crete

The Best **Special-Interest** Tours

1. The Harbour at Chaniá
2. The Fortezza at Réthymnon
3. Iráklion
4. Spinalónga

Airport
Ferry Route

Venetian Crete

The Venetian conquest and occupation of Crete lasted from 1204 to 1669. To the Venetians, Crete was just another part of their mercantile empire, and the beauty of Venice's installations—their harbours, lighthouses, boat repair sheds, mariners' mansions, and Venetian houses (many now restaurants)—can sometimes blind us to the ferocity of their occupation. The Venetian influences are most evident in Chaniá, Réthymnon, and Iráklion and several fortified islands. This tour starts in Chaniá and goes eastwards. If you don't have time to do the complete tour, spread it across several days. If you only have a day, a visit to Iráklion plus Spinalónga is a good introduction to Venetian Crete. START: **Chaniá. Trip length 192km.**

1 The Harbour at Chaniá. The harbour gives the most complete idea of how the Venetians handled the needs of their great merchant fleet. Protected by a kilometre-long sea wall, the harbour entrance has a lighthouse on one side and a powerful fortress on the other. On the inner harbour, a series of arches indicates the 'Arsenali', the covered boat sheds built to protect ships whilst they were being repaired and maintained. A group of seven stands just beyond the offices of the port police, and there are a further two at the eastern end of the harbour. Inside the fortress, the excellent Naval Museum (see p 67, **3**) has a series of models and plans showing what Chaniá looked like in Venetian times, and exactly how the Arsenali were used. ⏱ *2 hr. For detailed information on Chaniá, see p 67 in Chapter 4.*

Take the National Road east from Chaniá. 61km.

2 ★★ kids **The Fortezza at Réthymnon.** The fortress, erected between 1573 and 1580 according to designs by Sforza Pallavicini, was a direct result of pirate attacks on the town—by Barbarossa in 1538, and Uluch Ali in 1562 and 1571. Like the Koules in Iráklion (see below), the fortress is easy to understand—a series of powerful bastions joined together by a massive curtain wall, accessed through a tunnel. ⏱ *2 hr. For detailed information on Réthymnon, see p 75 in Chapter 4.*

The Arsenali by the inner harbour of Chaniá.

One of the powerful bastions on Réthymnon fortress.

Continue east along the National Road to Iráklion. 61km.

③ ★ Iráklion. The town's fortress, the Koules **kids**, was built between 1523 and 1540 by Michele Sanmicheli in response to the ever-westward spread of the Ottoman Empire and is similar to Réthymnon's Fortezza. If the yardstick by which we judge the success of the Venetian fortresses is how effective they were in action, Koules wins hands down. In the Turkish invasion of 1645, whilst the Fortezza at Réthymnon held out against the Turks for a day, Koules resisted the Turkish siege until 1669! Iráklion's Venetian town walls are the most complete in Crete. They curve around from the Ágios Andreas bastion on the seafront west of the city, via numerous other bastions, to the Sabbionera bastion above the ferry dock east of the Venetian harbour, and enclose the whole of the old part of the city. There's a path along the walls—park next to the Ágios Andreas bastion, or near the tomb of Nikos Kazantzákis. As you walk, notice the design of the walls—a series of interlocking bastions ensure that each part of the wall is overlooked by at least one other part. Iráklion has the best group of Venetian buildings within its walls. From Platía Venizelou in the old town's centre you see the Morosini Fountain, the Loggia, and San Marco basilica. ⏱ *2 hr. For detailed information on Iráklion, see p 83 in Chapter 4.*

Head east on the National Road towards Ágios Nikólaos. Before the town, at the first set of traffic lights, turn left and follow the coast road for 10km to Eloúnda and Spinalónga. 70km.

Crete & the Venetian Empire

Crete became part of the Venetian Empire in 1204, when the 4th Crusade forgot its mission statement to free the Holy Land from Moslem domination and instead sacked Byzantine (Christian) Constantinople. Crete was separated from the Byzantine Empire and handed over to Venice. To the island's new rulers, Crete was just another part of their mercantile empire, a source of food and raw materials, a staging post to provide safe harbours, and the means to repair and maintain their ships. They spent the first 250 years imposing strict feudalism and ferociously putting down insurrections, the middle hundred years going through a cultural revival sparked by the sack of Constantinople, and a final century desperately building and reinforcing fortresses, shipyards, city walls, and island redoubts against both the westward spread of the Ottoman Empire and increasing attacks by pirates.

Venetian Massacre

It is sometimes forgotten that the Venetian occupation led to as many massacres and as much brutality as the Ottoman one. Most infamous of these incidents was the early 16th-century Kandanoleon Massacre, south of Chaniá. Following much friction between the Cretans and their Venetian rulers, peace was apparently restored through an arranged marriage between the son of a Cretan overlord, Gadhanole, and the daughter of a Venetian nobleman, Molini. On the day of the wedding feast, when 450 Cretan men, women, and children were off their guard, asleep, and in many cases the worse for drink, a Venetian force was summoned. After hanging Gadhanole, his son and several others, they took the rest of the guests away in chains and hanged them at the gates of Chaniá, and in towns and villages across north-western Crete. (There isn't much hard evidence that the massacre ever took place, though don't say this to a Cretan.)

❹ ★★ kids Spinalónga. Finally, to appreciate the military achievements of the Venetians, visit the fortified island of Spinalónga, in the Gulf of Mirabéllo. Built in the late 1570s by military engineer Genese Bressani, the fortifications served a dual purpose—to protect the salt pans that the Venetians had built in Eloúnda (see p 148, ❹) from pirates, and to defend the port of Eloúnda from the Turks. It was certainly successful—the Turks couldn't take it after their 1649 occupation of Crete, and had to wait until it was ceded by treaty in 1715. Similarly, Turks used the island as a refuge from Cretan reprisals towards the end of the 19th century during the series of uprisings that led to independence. ⏲ *2 hr. See p 149,* ❼.

Iráklion's fortress and port.

Ottoman Crete

The Best Special-Interest Tours

1. The Mosque of the Janissaries
2. Other Turkish relics in Chaniá
3. The Venizélos Graves
4. Anópoli
5. Frangokástello
6. Réthymnon
7. Arkádi Monastery
8. Melidóni Cave
9. Iráklion
10. Milatos Cave

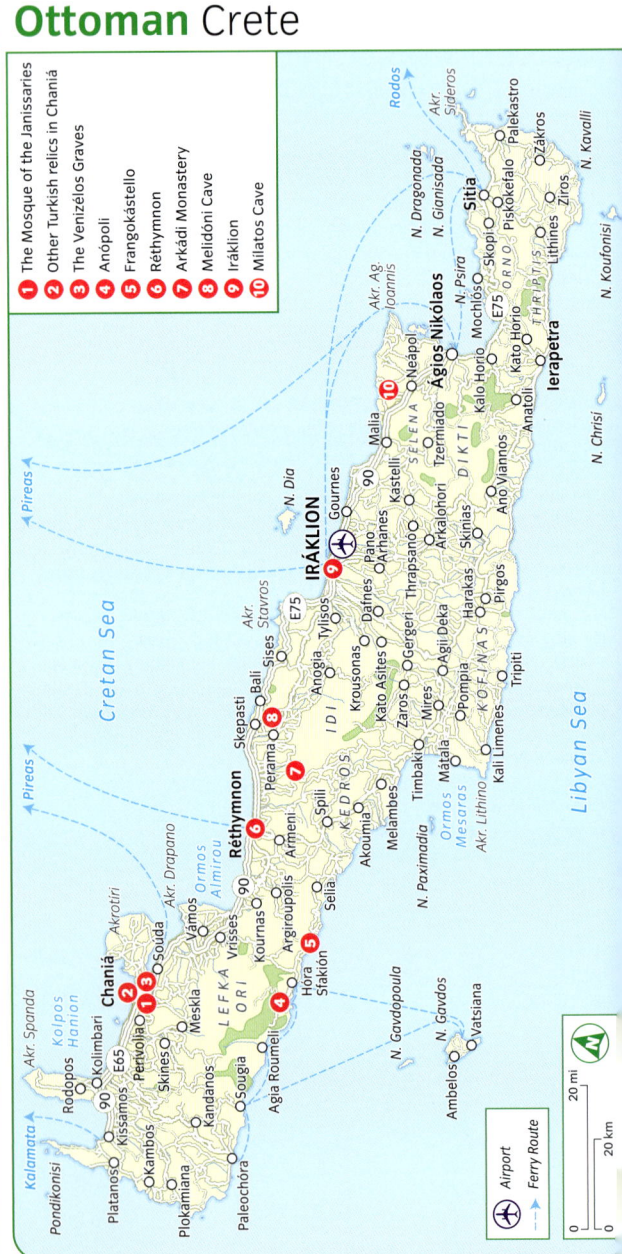

Ottoman Crete

Relics of the Ottoman occupation of Crete are, as one would expect, few and far between, and are not much celebrated. With one exception. Sites of Turkish atrocities are usually fulsomely commemorated—stories of Turkish cruelty played an important part in stiffening Cretans' determination to throw off the Ottoman yoke, and the places where they occurred have become popular day-visit destinations much relished by the Cretans themselves. Even if it were possible, a tour of all these sites might become depressing. So take your pick of the tour sights according to which part of the island you are in. But if you can, include both Chaniá and Réthymnon.

START: **Chaniá**.

Tour 1 begins and ends in Chaniá. Round trip 196km.

❶ The Mosque of the Janissaries. On the harbour front, the mosque is Chaniá's principal Ottoman relic. Also Crete's oldest Ottoman structure, it was built from scratch, rather than, as was more usual, adapting existing Christian churches, and was intended as thanks to Allah for the successful capture of the city during the 1645 invasion. This did the Turkish commander little good—on returning home he was executed for losing 40,000 men during the siege.

Because of its idiosyncratic design—a large dome, four strange flying buttresses, and a ring of subsidiary domes—and its position on the beautiful Venetian harbour, the mosque is Chaniá's signature building. There's not much to see inside, though the mirhab—a niche which marked the direction of Mecca—is still there. ⏱ *15 min. See p 69,* ❽.

❷ Other Turkish Relics in Chaniá. Elsewhere in Chaniá, two minarets survive—one on Platía 1821, the other on Daliani. The Public Gardens, south-east of the Old

Mosque of the Janissaries on Chaniá's harbour front.

Town, were laid out by a 19th-century pasha, and now contain a small zoo of local animals and a stage for open-air performances. Houses with the characteristic ornate Turkish wooden balconies crowd together in Splantzia, up against the Old Town's eastern wall. Finally, the fortress on the western side of the entrance to the harbour, though built by the Venetians, was used by the Turks, and is the spot where the Greek flag was first raised when Crete was united with mainland Greece in 1913. ⏱ *30 min. For detailed information on Chaniá, see p 67 in Chapter 4.*

From Chaniá, follow signs east towards the airport. As you climb the hill out of the town, look out for signs for the Venizélos Graves off to the left. 6km.

❸ ★ The Venizélos Graves. On a hillside above Chaniá are the graves of Eleftherios Venizélos and his son Sophocles, both of whom served at various times as Prime Minister of Greece. The site was chosen to commemorate one of the most famous episodes in Eleftherios Venizélos's life. In 1897 yet another Cretan rebellion against Turkish rule started, supported by the independent state of Greece. However, despite widespread sympathy from people all over Europe, the great powers not only refused to help the rebels, but actually sent a combined fleet to forestall a Greek invasion and stop the rebellion. When a Greek flag was raised on the hillside above Chaniá, a naval bombardment destroyed the pole, only for the flag to be seized and held aloft by hand. A statue in the grounds surrounding the graves commemorates the event. Crete finally gained its independence in 1898. ⏱ *1 hr. See p 121,* ⓱.

Drive to Hóra Sfakion (see directions on p 120 in Chapter 6). Continue up 12km of hairpin bends to Anópoli. 84km.

❹ Anópoli. The statue of Ioannis Vlachos, better known as Daskaloyannis ('John the Teacher'), one of Crete's great heroes, stands in the main square. In 1770, encouraged by the promise of Russian help, he led the first major rebellion against Turkish rule. The Russians, however, sat on their hands, the rebellion was put down with great ferocity, and Daskaloyannis, attempting to negotiate terms, was seized, dragged off to Chaniá, tortured, and skinned alive. His name lives on, not only on the statue, but also in, among others, the names of Chaniá's international airport, a ferry that plies along Crete's south-west coast, and a small hotel in nearby Loutró. ⏱ *1 hr.*

Returning to Hóra Sfakion, follow the coast east to Frangokástello. 26km.

❺ ★★ Frangokástello. This shell of a castle is misleadingly called Frangokástello—it's Venetian, not Frankish. As a memorial and a couple of statues

Commemorative statue at the Venizélos Graves.

Crete & the Ottoman Empire

The Ottoman wave from the east finally flooded Crete in 1645. Rebellions were inevitable, and the first big one took place in 1770 in the Sfakia region, where Daskaloyanis led a rebellion and was then, whilst trying to negotiate surrender, tortured and skinned alive. Further rebellions occurred regularly—all were ferociously put down. There was widespread support for the Cretans from ordinary people throughout Europe, but the great powers stayed out of it, afraid of further destabilising the already ailing Ottoman Empire. The end came in 1898 when Crete achieved its independence, and in 1913 it became part of Greece. The Turkish occupation left the same scars in Crete as it did throughout Greece—stories of massacre, humiliation, and cruelty abound. Furthermore, the Turks were not noted for their community investment—there's little surviving evidence of their rule, apart from a few mosques and minarets and the odd urban street with wooden balconies.

attest, this is where, on 17th May, 1828, a Greek called Hatzimichaelis Dalianis, determined to export the War of Independence from the mainland, led a Cretan rebellion against Turkish rule. In the inevitable defeat from hugely superior Turkish forces, Dalianis and most of the Cretans were killed. The statues are of Dalianis (on the left), and Nikos Deligiannakis, the most prominent of the Cretans, who survived and lived well into his seventies. This battle is the source of one of Crete's most intriguing ghost stories. On the anniversary of the battle, and for 12 days afterwards, so it's said, the spirits of the dead Cretans (called the Drossoulites, or 'Dew Men') can be seen marching

Wander the shell of frangokástello.

The Best Special-Interest Tours

Arkádi Monastery.

from the local church to the fortress, wreathed in mist. ⏲ *30 min.*

Return to Chaniá 80km.

Tour 2 begins and ends in Réthymnon. Round trip 260km.

❻ ★★★ **Réthymnon.** Réthymnon has the best crop of Turkish relics on Crete. There are numerous Turkish fountains dotted around the city (look at the one on the south side of the fortress—Smirnis/Koroneou—and the two on Patriarou Grigoriou, which strikes east from Koroneou) and lots of balconied Turkish houses, with ornate wooden balconies and doors and intricate mellow stonework. Even though it's now difficult to separate Turkish from Venetian architecture, a walk through the narrow lanes and alleys of the Old Town gives a really good impression of what Réthymnon was like during the Ottoman occupation. There are signs that the local authority is beginning to recognise the need to preserve some of the town's oldest Islamic buildings—both the large central Nerandzes mosque and the tiny Kara Pasha mosque (and its nearby fountain, next to Platía Iroon) were, at the time of writing, undergoing extensive renovation. ⏲ *1 hr. For detailed information on Réthymnon, see p 75 in Chapter 4.*

Take the National Road east. After about 6km, turn right, through Pigi and Loutra, to the monastery's free car park. 23km.

❼ ★★ kids **Arkádi Monastery.** The beautiful Arkádi Monastery is famous for its part in Crete's resistance to invasion. In 1866 a major rebellion saw most of rural Crete throwing off Turkish rule. However, despite intense resistance, massive Turkish military power kept the bigger towns subjugated. Seven hundred women and children fled the fighting in Réthymnon and took refuge in the monastery, which was garrisoned with nearly 300 armed resistance fighters under Lieutenant Dimakopoulous, plus members of the Revolutionary Committee, led by Abbot Gabriel Marinakis. The Turks laid siege with an overwhelming force of 15,000 men and 30 cannons. The fierce battle lasted 2 days, but the end was never in doubt. Rather than surrender, the survivors locked themselves in the gunpowder store and blew themselves and the attackers sky high. News of the massacre spread around the world through the recently invented telegraph, becoming one of the Ottoman Empire's most spectacular, and damaging, own goals. The Arkádi Monastery holds a very special place in the hearts of people throughout Greece—tourists are invariably outnumbered by Greeks paying their respects. ⏲ *1 hr. See p 128,* ❻.

Drive east to Perama, then follow signs for Melidóni. 27km.

Ottoman Crete

The Turkish pumphouse in Iráklion is now a café.

❽ Melidóni Cave. The cave, spectacularly worth a visit in its own right, was the legendary home of the bronze giant Talos who protected the Cretan coast from attack. In 1824, it sheltered over 300 local Cretans, mainly women and children, fleeing from the soldiers of Mehmet Ali, the pasha of Egypt brought in to help put down the rebellion. Provoked by the shooting of two emissaries sent into the cave to offer safe passage, Mehmet Ali first ordered the cave entrance to be blocked up, then, when this failed, the building of a fire to asphyxiate all those inside. A shrine near the cave entrance and a communal sarcophagus in the main chamber commemorate the event. ⏲ *1 hr. Admission 3€. Open daily, 9am–7pm.*

Drive 3km to the National Road, then east to Iráklion. 53km.

❾ ★ Iráklion. In Platía Kornarou, at the top end of Odós 1866, a delicate octagonal Turkish pumphouse, now a café, sits under the trees. Though heavily restored, it hasn't changed its appearance for centuries—you'll see it on many 19th-century engravings of the city. *For detailed information on Iráklion, see p 83 in Chapter 4.*

Go east on the National Road. After Mália follow signs left to Milatos. At the village, follow signs for 'Milatos Cave'. This leads you eventually to a right turn along a rocky dirt road. Don't worry—it's only 200m. When you get to the end, there's no sign but turn left. The cave is well marked on the right 2km up the mountain. Park on the road. 45km.

❿ ★ kids Mílatos Cave. Following a rebellion against Ottoman rule in 1823 sparked off by the War of Independence on the mainland, nearly 3000 Cretans, the story claims, sheltered in this cave. Promised safe passage by their Turkish besiegers, they surrendered, to be immediately massacred or sold into slavery. ⏲ *30 min. See p 147,* ❷.

Return to Iráklion on the National Road. 112km.

The Best Special-Interest Tours

Crete in **World War II**

1. Máleme
2. Hill 107
3. Mythos Bar
4. Galatás
5. Naval Museum, Chaniá
6. Allied War Cemetery & Soúda Bay
7. Askífou
8. Hóra Sfakíon
9. Three Brothers Tavérna
10. Préveli Monastery
11. Gialos Café/Snack Bar

Crete in World War II

Crete suffered two circles of hell during World War II—first the German conquest, then the occupation. Having seized Máleme airfield from the air, the Germans spread eastwards, then south. Despite individual heroism, particularly on the part of Cretan irregulars and ordinary soldiers, the Allied retreat was chaotic. Though many troops were evacuated from Hóra Sfakíon to Egypt, thousands remained stranded on the island. The subsequent occupation of Crete was one of the most blood-drenched in history. This tour starts near Chaniá and ends at Moní Préveli, 100km from Chaniá. You might divide the tour into 2 days, the first around Chaniá, the second from the Allied War Cemetery to Moní Préveli. START: **Máleme, just off the National Road about 15km west of Chaniá. Trip length 161km.**

❶ Máleme. Máleme airfield, on the east bank of the Tavronítis River, is no longer operational but remains a military installation and is closed to the public. But it has to be the starting point for any tour devoted to the Battle of Crete. On 20th May, 1941, following prolonged bombing and strafing from the air, thousands of German troops landed all around the airfield—by parachute and from gliders. Many of the gliders landed on the dry river bed below the bridge; one even crashed into the bridge itself. German losses were severe, and the New Zealanders defending the airport won an easy victory. In a macabre twist, the containers holding supplies that the Germans dropped had a dual function—they were coffin-shaped. As more German reinforcements landed, the defenders, with no support from Allied command in Chaniá and virtually no communications, were forced to retreat. The Germans secured the airfield perimeter, enabling German troop transports to use the runways. *15 min.*

From the airfield, drive along the coast road towards Chaniá. In Máleme itself follow signs to the right for the German War Cemetery. 2km.

❷ Hill 107. It was clear to both sides that Hill 107, rising to the south, was the key to control of the airfield. After a vicious battle, the Germans dislodged the Allied defenders and took the hill. With the bridgehead secure, troops and materials could flood in by air (British naval power prevented supply from the sea). In the 1960s, agreement

View from the German war graves cemetery, Máleme.

between the German and Greek governments allowed the German War Graves Commission (the Volksbund) to gather the remains of German soldiers from all over the island, and inter them in a newly established war cemetery on Hill 107, which opened in 1972. 🕐 *30 min. See p 117 in Chapter 6.*

3 kids **Mythos Bar.** Get down to the sea at Máleme and have a snack and a drink at the Mythos Bar, facing the beach. There's a kids' pool at the rear and a kids' menu. ☎ *28210 62046. $.*

Continue east along the coast road from Máleme, then, just before Chaniá, follow signs on the right to Galatás. 12km.

4 **Galatás.** After Máleme airfield and Hill 107, the Germans' next objective was the Agía valley (nicknamed 'Prison Valley' referring to the large white Agía prison). Running south-west from Chaniá, and overlooked by the heights of Galatás it was defended by an ill-equipped brigade of New Zealanders. Again, despite great bravery by the defenders, the Germans were victorious. To give the New Zealanders time to retreat in good order, a group of them, under the command of Colonel Kippenberger, counter-attacked on 25th May, briefly taking Galatás village square and inflicting heavy casualties. Galatás village hall contains a small museum with equipment and weapons from the battle (open most weekday mornings, but hours vary), and outside there is a memorial to the 145 New Zealanders who died during the counter-attack. Several days of chaotic fighting all over the area were followed by a general Allied retreat to the south coast on 28th–30th May, 1941. 🕐 *30 min.*

Drive into Chaniá, and park at the western entrance to the harbour, behind the fortress. 5km.

5 ★★★ kids **Naval Museum, Chaniá.** Crete's Naval Museum, housed in the fortress, has a graphic exhibition on the Battle of Crete—maps, weapons, equipment, models,

The Naval Museum in Chaniá.

and, in particular, photographs. Don't miss the picture of General Kreipe and his captors—British and Cretan (see p 138, ❸). As you return to the car, look out across the harbour. On the afternoon of 24th May, 1941 (the day before the action at Galatás described above), Chaniá was carpet-bombed by the Luftwaffe. The Germans avoided the harbour itself as they wanted to use it after Crete had fallen, but the rest of the town was in flames. But it's an ill wind, as they say—a local Cretan was seen diving into the harbour and rapidly skimming fish that had been stunned by the concussion of the bombs off the surface and scooping them up to three female companions on the quay. ⏱ *1 hr. For detailed information on Chaniá, see p 67 in Chapter 4.*

Drive east out of Chaniá, following signs for the Akrotiri peninsula. After the Venizélos Graves, follow signs for Soúda, the airport and the Allied War Cemetery. Park outside the gates of the cemetery. 6km.

❻ ★ **Allied War Cemetery & Soúda Bay.** Marked by a tall white cross and ranks of gravestones, the Allied War Cemetery lies at the extreme western end of Soúda Bay. Protected to the north by the Akrotiri Peninsula and to the south by the Malaxa escarpment, this 8km stretch of placid water is Crete's best natural harbour. But imagine the scene here, between 22nd and 26th April, 1941, when disorientated and demoralized Greek, British, Australian, and New Zealand troops disembarked after their defeat by the Germans on mainland Greece. Under constant attack by the German Air Force, Soúda Bay was a nightmare—dead men, wrecked shore installations, multi-hued oil-slicks staining the surface of the sea, and sunken ships, their

Memorial to the evacuation of Allied troops at Hóra Sfakion.

funnels and superstructures sticking up like skeletons out of the water. ⏱ *15 min. See p 122, ㉑.*

Drive east on the National Road (signposted Réthymnon) for about 32km. Turn right for Vrisses, then bear left as you get to the town. 50km.

❼ **Askífou.** The Askífou plateau, with its meadows, orchards, fields, and streams, was a welcome relief from the hard mountain terrain that the troops had climbed through to get there. Further defensive positions were set up at the entrance to the plateau, halting the German advance long enough for thousands of men to escape via its southern end. Some took the difficult route down the face of the escarpment, now the modern main road; others discovered that it was easier to get to the coast along the Ímbros Gorge. In Askífou, a small private

Driving in Crete

If you rent a car, here are some things to look out for:

- Contrary to popular belief, Cretans are courteous drivers. However, some drive very fast indeed, whilst others drive insanely slowly.
- Jay-walking in towns seems to be endemic, often because the pavement is obstructed by telegraph poles, restaurant tables and chairs, eccentrically parked vehicles, and so on.
- Traffic police are much in evidence—stick to speed limits, and don't drink and drive.
- You'll often see several people crammed onto a single moped—my record was two men, a woman, and a child, all on a 50cc Honda!
- Heavily laden donkeys and goats can be a hazard on country roads.
- Road signs are in Greek script, quickly followed by another with the same information in Latin script.
- Centre lines on roads are invariably sensible, so obey them—don't cross double lines to overtake.
- If turning across oncoming traffic on the National Road where there's no filter lane, pull over to the right and wait until it's all clear. Don't block traffic coming from behind.
- Don't acknowledge courtesy by holding out your hand palm outwards. This is, throughout Greece, a very rude gesture!

---

museum is stuffed with paraphernalia from the fighting. *30 min. See p 119,* **12**.

Continue south to Hóra Sfakion. 21km.

8 ★★ **Hóra Sfakion.** The exhausted troops ended up encamped around the little fishing port of Hóra Sfakion where they queued to be ferried to Allied warships lying just off the coast. By the end of the evacuation (and the final surrender of the island) on the night of 31st May/1st June, 1941, around 17,000 troops had been rescued, with 5000 left behind either to surrender or to join the resistance in the mountains. When the Germans arrived, they carried out savage reprisals against the local population for helping the Allied evacuation. Today, Hóra Sfakion is a charming little port at which the coastal ferry calls, with a new marina and a good selection of restaurants and cafés. But the memories of May 1941 are still there. As you drive down the hill into the town, look for a memorial on the left, dedicated to local people who were murdered by the Germans (there's a skull still visible in its base), and another on the quayside commemorating the evacuation. *30 min. See p 19,* **10**.

Préveli Monastery.

9 Three Brothers Tavérna.
Eat from the comprehensive menu at this tavérna, beautifully set on the rocks to the west of the town. As it's an Internet café you can also check your emails. ☎ *28250 83406. $.*

The final visit involves an exhilarating 50km drive eastwards along the coast, offering some of the most beautiful scenery and spectacular views on the island, to the Préveli Monastery.

10 ★★★ Préveli Monastery.
Climb the winding road up to the monastery to a striking modern memorial of statues of a Greek priest and an Allied soldier, both holding guns. The plinth, in English and Greek, pays tribute to the Abbot, monks, and local people who helped the 'English, Australian, and New Zealanders ... who were saved from the catastrophe'. The story behind it is this. In July 1942, a British submarine, *HMS Thresher*, put Commander Francis Pool ashore near Préveli Monastery. He was charged with finding and organising the evacuation of Allied troops left behind at Hóra Sfakion. He negotiated with Abbot Agathangelos Langouvardos for the monastery to be used as a holding station for soldiers waiting to be taken off the island by submarine. Over the following years, 5000 troops, who had been sheltered at great personal risk by families all over western Crete, were contacted, moved to the monastery, and evacuated to Egypt. ⏱ *1 hr. See p 131,* **15**.

11 Gialos Café/Snack Bar.
Have a drink and a swim, then return to the National Road at Réthymnon, and back to Chaniá/Máleme. *Plakias. No phone. $.*

Crete & The Arts

The Best Special-Interest Tours

1. Historical Museum
2. Museum Cafeteria
3. The Museum of Religious Art
4. The Tomb of Kazantzákis
5. The El Greco Museum
6. El Greco Café
7. Kazantzákis Museum
8. Labyrinth Music Workshop, Houdétsi
9. Thrapsanó

Crete & The Arts

For the artistic, Crete might seem to offer slim pickings. Yet it boasts two world superstars in Nikos Kazantzákis and El Greco, the 'Cretan School' of religious painting whose heyday was in 16th- and 17th-century Venetian Crete, and a flourishing tradition in music and in folk art, especially pottery and textiles. Kazantzákis (a personal hero) wrote like an angel, and is so much more than the author of *Zorba the Greek*. And El Greco might be an honorary Spaniard, but remember that he was a Cretan. Whole villages are given over to ceramics and textiles, and there's a lot of modern musical interest—part indigenous, part imported. And you'll come across folk-art in workshops, villages, and small museums right across Crete. START: **Iráklion. Trip length 124km.**

❶ ★★★ Historical Museum.

The best starting place for an arts-based tour is in Iráklion where the Historical Museum has some absorbing displays. Nikos Kazantzákis is covered in detail, including his desk and a reconstruction of his study, examples of his work, and a rich collection of photographs, well-labelled in English and Greek. The room dedicated to Doménikos Theotokópoulos (El Greco's real name) has the only two of his paintings that exist in Crete—the rest are in Spain. Also look for the section devoted to folk-art, particularly textiles. ⏱ *1 hr. See p 86,* ⓭.

❷ Museum Cafeteria.

Take refreshment in the little museum cafeteria, which looks towards the sea. ☎ *28102 83219. $.*

❸ The Museum of Religious Art.

Cretan religious painting and iconography is something of an acquired taste. But if you want to check it out, visit the Museum of Religious Art in the convent church of Agía Ekateríni—near Iráklion's cathedral. The biggest hitter of the Cretan School was Michael Damaskenos, who worked in the second half of the 16th century. His icons can be seen all over the Byzantine world, but six of the best are here in the museum. ⏱ *15 min. Agía Ekateríni, Platía. Admission 2 €. Mon–Sat 8.30am–1.30pm, plus Tues, Thurs, and Fri 5–7pm.* ⏱ *30 min.*

❹ ★ The Tomb of Kazantzákis.

The views are extensive, the gravestone simple, the inscription bound to make you think—'I hope for nothing, I fear nothing, I am

The tomb of Kazantzákis, Iráklion.

Thrapsanó is one of central Crete's main pottery making centres.

free'—a quotation from one of his books. Kazantzákis, famously critical of the church and a constant thorn in its side, was nevertheless granted a funeral service in Iráklion Cathedral, though no clerics accompanied the procession to the burial site here on the city's southernmost bastion. ⏱ *15 min. See p 85,* ❻.

The El Greco Museum is half an hour west of Iráklion, left off the National Road in Fodele. 27km.

❺ ★ kids **The El Greco Museum.** The museum is in the house where it is said El Greco was born, just outside Fodele. Though there's some dispute regarding this claim, the University of Valladolid in Spain clearly agrees with it, and contributed a plaque attached to Toledo rock now in the village square. ⏱ *30 min.*

❻ **El Greco Café.** Have a drink and a snack at the museum café. ☎ *28105 21500. $.*

Returning to Iráklion on the National Road, take the main road south past Knossós. Four to five km beyond Knossós, turn left and drive across the vineyard countryside to Mirtia. 40km.

❼ ★★★ **Kazantzákis Museum.** Based in the house of his grandparents, the Kazantzákis Museum is a fitting tribute to Crete's greatest writer. This fascinating man's life and times come alive through biographical information boards, busts, photographs, and paintings depicting him at various ages, copies of his books and plays in a variety of languages, models of stage set-ups, even some of his teapots. The more you know about him before your visit, the more you'll get out of it. ⏱ *1 hr. See p 138,* ❷.

El Greco (1541–1614)

Born in Iráklion in 1541, El Greco (real name Doménikos Theotokópoulos) moved from Crete to Venice, probably in his early twenties, to study painting in the studio of the great master Titian. By 1677 he had surfaced in Spain—first in Madrid, and finally in Toledo, where he lived until his death in 1614. El Greco is best known for his use of vivid colour, and as he got older, the elongated shape of the people. Though this was probably a stylistic trick, it has been speculated that it was the result of increasing astigmatism. Whatever the reason, El Greco's paintings, though very much a part of the Spanish Renaissance, look amazingly modern to 21st-century eyes.

Other Arts Attractions

Many villages specialise in ceramics and textiles—Margarítes, in Réthymnon province, for example, is a major pottery centre, whilst **Kritsá** near Ágios Nikólaos, and **Ágios Konstantinos** on the Lasíthi Plateau are good for textiles. Many Cretan towns have excellent folk-art museums (the one in Réthymnon is particularly good), whilst several 'tourist villages' have weavers and spinners at work, and their produce on sale. Finally, you can buy Cretan musical instruments direct from the makers. Try **Nikos Papalexakis** (email lyraboy1@yahoo.gr) in Réthymnon, or **Lampros Karandreas** (karandreas_lampros@yahoo.co.uk) in Ágios Nikólaos. Lyras begin at around 200€ for a 'starter' model; larger laoutos are anything from 800€ to 2000€.

Drive from Mirtia, through Agia Paraskies and Ágios Vasilios to Houdétsi. 10km.

❽ ★★ kids Labyrinth Music Workshop, Houdétsi. A brief guidebook entry can't do justice to the richness of musical experience at Ross Daly's Workshop. Anybody interested in traditional music from around the world can't fail to be captivated. ⏱ *1 hr. See p 139,* ❻.

Return to Agía Paraskies, then bear right off the Kastélli road to Thrapsanó. 15km.

❾ Thrapsanó. A pleasant village in its own right, Thrapsanó is one of central Crete's main pottery-making centres. The village square has pots and *pithoi* (large earthenware vases) all over the place, plus numerous pottery workshops, especially on the road to Evangelismos (drive past the church, then down the hill past the school). You can enjoy tours of most of the potteries, and several have factory shops. ⏱ *1 hr.*

Continue north through Evangelismos and Kastélli. At the National Road, turn right and return to Iráklion. 32km.

Woman weaving outside her shop, Ágios Konstantinos.

Oddball Crete

The Best **Special-Interest** Tours

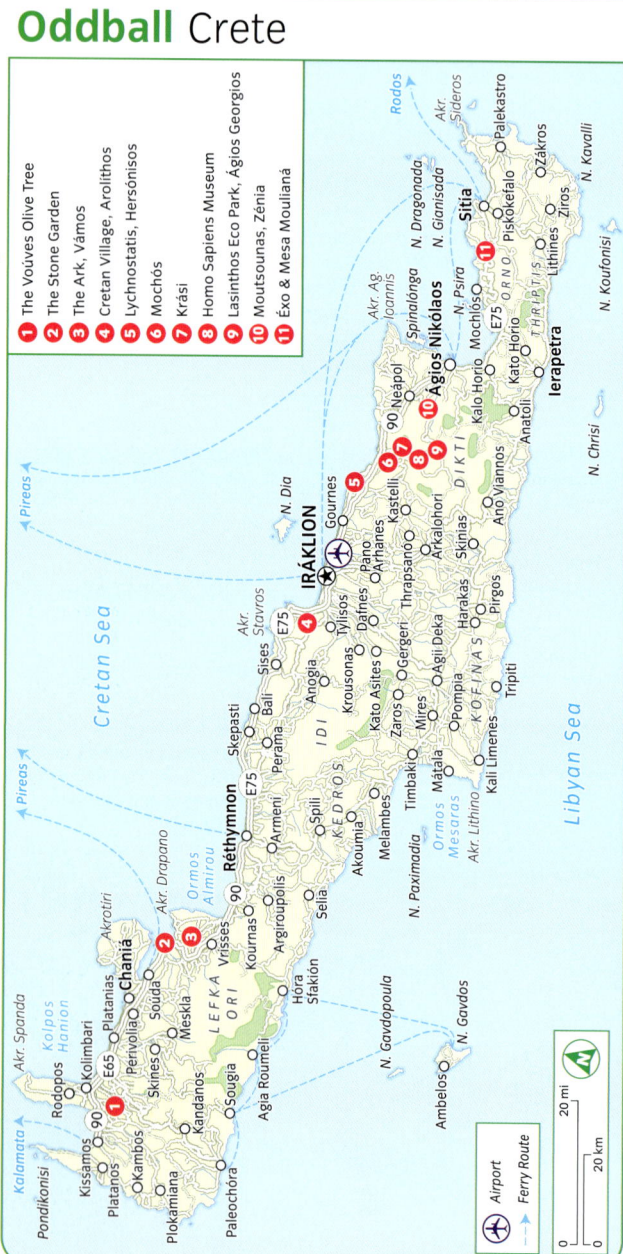

1. The Vouves Olive Tree
2. The Stone Garden
3. The Ark, Vámos
4. Cretan Village, Arolithos
5. Lychnostatis, Hersónisos
6. Mochós
7. Krási
8. Homo Sapiens Museum
9. Lasinthos Eco Park, Ágios Georgios
10. Moutsounas, Zénia
11. Éxo & Mesa Mouilianá

Oddball Crete

Travelling around Crete researching this book, I came across interesting things or places that didn't fit into any particular category. Some were simply one-offs that it would be a shame for you to miss. Others were obviously designed to attract visitors, each with its own café or tavérna. At first I thought the attraction came first, with the refreshments added later. But clearly in many cases the café or tavérna was already there, and the attraction was built as an afterthought to bring in more customers. With some, my first reaction was to laugh, then (whisper it) to mock. Yet I couldn't deny that they gave me absolutely unalloyed pleasure. Neither could I deny the sincerity with which they were offered. So here they are—the unusual and the oddball. They're too spread out for a day tour, so I've covered them from west to east and indicated their locations. They're brilliant!

Voúves in Chaniá Province, is north of Máleme off the National Road.

❶ kids The Voúves Olive Tree. Here is an attraction which clearly came before the tavérna that now stands next to it—the Voúves olive tree has grown where it now stands for 3000 years! With a circumference of 12.5 metres and a diameter of 4.6 metres, it is still, despite its great age, in rude good health. A branch was sent to the 2004 Athens Olympic Committee as a sign of peace and friendship. ⏱ *15 min. See p 117,* ❸.

The Stone Garden is near Kalives, 20km east of Chaniá.

❷ ★ kids The Stone Garden. Constructed over the last 15 to 20 years by the owner Giorgos Havaledakis, the Koumos Tavérna's stone garden is an odd mixture of stone artefacts—statues of strange animals, a chapel, a balconied house, archways and columns, and the tavérna, all built of rough field stones or decorated with them. There are also numerous pieces of old household equipment—a corn mill, several wells, an oven. Add a poem chiselled into a huge slab of stone, and you've

The Stone Garden's odd artefacts.

The Lychnostatis Open Air Museum.

got a very odd attraction indeed. ⏱ *30 min. See p 122,* ㉒.

Vámos is 27km east of Chaniá just off the National Road.

❸ ★★★ kids **The Ark, Vámos.** Lying like a green jewel on a hillside with the White Mountains in the distance, the Ark is a small and beautiful farm, with enclosures of ostriches. It also has horses, ponies, llamas, cows, pigs, goats, ducks, and geese, what appears to be a shrine to Hippocrates (the Medicine Park), a religious grotto (St John's Cave), a nice little children's playground, and a restaurant (ostrich omelet, ostrich sausages) and shop (with painted ostrich eggs). It even has its resident media celebrities—a monkey and a dog who have appeared on America's *CNN*. The monkey, grieving at the loss of a sibling, was adopted by the dog, which had been blinded in an accident—the monkey feeds the dog, the dog protects the monkey. ⏱ *1 hr. See p 123,* ㉘.

Just off the National Road 10km west of Iráklion.

❹ ★ kids **Cretan Village, Arolíthos.** Despite its recent construction (it opened in 1988) the Cretan Village gives a fair idea of many aspects of ordinary life in a

Komboloi (Worry Beads)

Though they look a bit like rosaries, Greek worry beads have no religious significance—they exist only to give you something to do with your hands. Consisting of beads in a wide range of materials—amber and coral are common, but so too are plastic, metal, and, if you've got the cash, precious stones—they are strung on a cord or chain loop about two hands' width long. There's usually a tassel and a single bead which is held between the fingers, a shield (the 'priest') where the two sides of the loop separate, and then the beads themselves. Komboloi can have any number of beads as long as it's odd. It's considered polite to fiddle with your komboloi quietly indoors, but outside, or in a cafenion you can sling them around a bit more flamboyantly. They are supposed to calm the nerves—those of the user, presumably, since their effect on everybody else in the vicinity is to drive them mad! Worry beads make ideal gifts—they are widely available in a price range from a few euros to a king's ransom. And they are very typically Greek. There are two komboloi museums, both on the mainland (See www.komboloi-museum.com and www.komboloi.gr).

traditional Cretan village—the cottages, narrow streets and alleys, workshops for ceramics, weaving and pottery, blacksmith's forge, household décor and much else, are condensed highlights of Cretan life. The Folk Museum on site is excellent. And this isn't just for the tourists—I was there with a Cretan school group. The village is a commercial concern, so there are rooms available, lots to buy in the shop, and a first-rate café and restaurant. ⏱ *1 hr. See p 133,* ㉒.

Take the National Road from Iráklion east, and Lychnostatis is just east through Hersónisos.

❺ ★★ kids **Lychnostatis, Hersónisos.** Lychnostatis also tries to give a concentrated introduction to Cretan life, though broader and slightly less commercialized than Arolíthos. Opened in 1992, it includes a farmer's and a merchant's house, a chapel, a windmill, oil and wine presses, a raki distillery, a shepherd's hut and a threshing floor, ceramic and weaving workshops, herb, flora and succulent gardens, and odd bits and pieces of equipment—an early pedalo, for example. The museum claims to have been built entirely using traditional methods, there's an introductory video and free guided tours. How authentic the various reconstructions are is difficult to say, but I found the whole experience informative and great fun. ⏱ *1 hr. Lychnostatis Open Air Museum, Hersónisos.* ☎ *28970 23660. www.lychnostatis.gr. Admission 5€ adults, 3€ students, 2€ children under 12. Open 9am–2pm Tues–Sun.*

Mochós is 14km south of Hersónisos in the hills.

❻ **Mochós.** This sleepy village has a shady square, a clutch of tavérnas and an attractive church. In 1986 its residents were shocked to hear that Olof Palme, the Prime Minister of

Working windmills at the Homo Sapiens Museum.

Visit local livestock from the Lasithi Plateau at Lasinthos Eco Park.

Sweden, had been assassinated as he walked home from the cinema in Stockholm. He was a popular figure in the village, regularly staying at his summer villa just behind the church. During the period of mourning after his death, the house (the Villa Palme) became a shrine, and the street in which it stands was renamed Odos Olof Palme (a street in Hersónisos was similarly renamed). Palme's murder remains unsolved.

Krási is a 10-minute drive south of Mohós.

7 Krási. Voúves boasts the oldest olive tree, but the village of Krási claims the oldest, and biggest, plane tree in Europe—2000 years of age, with a girth that can't be encircled by 12 adults with outstretched arms. Standing in the village square, it offers shade not only to customers of the village tavérnas, but also to the arcaded spring whose waters allegedly cure stomach complaints. ⏲ *15 min.*

Continue south for a further 15 min.

8 kids Homo Sapiens Museum. You can't miss the Homo Sapiens Museum with its six large white working windmills. It has, with reason, been called 'ludicrous', 'unsightly', and 'farcical' (*Rough Guide to Crete*). Yet there's something endearingly innocent about it. Purporting to tell the history of mankind, from earliest times to the present day, it's a ragbag of information, reconstructed huts, memorials, and artefacts. The whole place is built around a shop and a large tavérna—no doubt the reason for its construction. Yet the food and the coffee are good, and the views spectacular. In the car park we are entreated 'Please don't leave before you visit the Homo Sapiens Museum—you will remember it forever'. You certainly will! ⏲ *30 min.* ☎ *28970 51880. www.homo-sapiens-village.gr. Admission 2€. Daily 1 Apr–31 Oct 9am–7pm.*

Follow signs for the Lasithi Plateau from Neápoli. The Eco Park is just outside Ágios Georgios on the southern stretch of

the road that circumnavigates the plateau.

⑨ ★★ kids Lasinthos Eco Park, Ágios Georgios. One of Crete's most recent attractions, Eco Park began as a large tavérna with accommodation to which, in 2005, was added a 'traditional village' and a small collection of local animals. The owners wanted to bring in visitors for commercial reasons, but were also keen to preserve some of the traditional crafts and livestock of the Lasíthi Plateau. It's early days, but they seem to be succeeding.
⏲ *1 hr. See p 153,* ㉒.

About 10km before Neápoli and just after Zénia, look out for Moutsounas on the right.

⑩ kids Moutsounas, Zénia. Moutsounas is a café/minimarket which goes out of its way to get noticed. Across the road from the café is a weird and wonderful collection of stuff—children's playground equipment, a windmill (always popular in the Lasíthi region), one of those small three-wheeled putt-putts you still see around on the island, a mock wishing well, a small chapel. There's also a terrace with glorious views back down the mountain to the sea. Inside the building itself are souvenirs, clothes, paintings, photographs, worry beads, and a truly awesome range of booze—all home-brewed and distilled, much of it labelled 'No doctor' to emphasize the owner Manolis Farsaris's claims that drinking it keeps you healthy. Look out in the shop for ornamental wooden spoons—carved by the owner's father, who at the time of my visit was 102 years old. So perhaps those claims aren't so daft after all! *Zénia Village.* ☎ *28410 33860. AE, MC, V.*

The villages are on the main road from Ágios Nikólaos to Sitía, about 17km before Sitía.

⑪ Éxo & Mesa Moulianá. In late summer, there's a very peculiar sight at Éxo Moulianá and Mesa Moulianá. In the fields, and on every available rooftop in the villages, you'll see grapes laid out to dry. This is the area's main industry—growing grapes, and turning them into sultanas.

View an unusual collection of objects on display outside Moutsounas.

Family Crete

The Best Special-Interest Tours

1. Chaniá Town
2. The Stone Garden
3. The Ark
4. Georgioupolis
5. Lake Kournás
6. Loutró
7. Diadromés
8. Limnoupolis Water Park
9. Golden Fun Park
10. Hersónisos
11. Aquaworld, Hersónisos
12. Lychnostatis, Hersónisos
13. Star Beach, Hersónisos
14. Acquaplus
15. Crete Golf Club
16. Water City, Anopolis
17. Cretaquarium
18. Lasinthos Eco Park
19. The Diktean Cave
20. Homo Sapiens Museum

Crete is family friendly. When people in Crete ask if you have children, they're not just being polite—they really want to know. Cretans love kids. Wherever you go, children will be welcomed, indulged, pampered. Having said that, Crete is coming late to special provision for the little 'uns. Outside the main holiday areas, you won't find many attractions with children's itineraries, questionnaires, or explanations, or many restaurants with kids' menus, toys, crayons, or colouring-in books. So finding a balance of stuff to do for everybody can be tricky. Two areas of Crete do provide for the whole family—Chaniá and its hinterland in western Crete, and Hersónisos and surrounds in the east. So here are a few great places to visit in each of those areas. Many of these are worth a full day so are not organised into a tour.

Chaniá & Around

1 ★★★ **Chaniá Town.** Within Chaniá itself, the two things most likely to appeal to children are the **Naval Museum** (p 67, **3**), which has lots of child-friendly models and photographs, and the full-sized model of a **Minoan ship** on permanent exhibition in one of the Arsenali at the eastern end of the Venetian port. Whilst in Chaniá, teenagers can pick up their emails or check up on Facebook/MySpace at the **Notos** Internet café (Koundourioti St 31. ☎ 28210 98722. www.notoscafe.gr) or hang out, eat burgers, and listen to loud rock music at **Hippopotamos** (Sarpidonos 6. ☎ 28210 44120). *For detailed information on Chaniá, see p 67 in Chapter 4.*

The Stone Garden is near Kalives, 20km east of Chaniá.

2 ★ **kids** **The Stone Garden.** The Koumos Tavérna's Stone Garden is bound to fascinate children, not only because of the tortuous field-stone decorations, but also because there are usually animals for petting (sheep and goats, dogs and cats). If you get the chance, talk

A full-sized model of a Minoan ship on display in one of the Arsenali, Chaniá.

The Best Special-Interest Tours

Young ostrich at the Ark, Vámos.

to Giorgos Havaledakis, the interesting owner. He collected all the stone for the garden on forays into the White Mountains. Children will no doubt relate to his attitude to school—he likes to say that his favourite subject was playtime! 🕐 *30 min. See p 122,* ㉒.

Vámos is 27km east of Chaniá just off the National Road.

❸ ★★★ kids **The Ark.** The Ark is a major family attraction in this part of Crete. The animals, the playground, the pony rides, the views, things for sale in the shop, all appeal to kids. 🕐 *1 hr. See p 123,* ㉘.

Take the National Road 22km west out of Réthymnon to Georgioúpolis.

❹ ★★ kids **Georgioúpolis.** Behind the main square, a large children's play area—**Children's World**—offers a wide range of play equipment in a safely fenced, astro-turfed enclosure. Parents can grab a snack in the small tavérna whilst their children play on the swings, slides, see-saws, rockers, ball-pools, climbing frames and so on (*3€ per day, 15€ per week*). The whole family can choose from a range of Greek food, starting at around 5€. From just outside Children's World, the **Talos Express** tourist road train sets off for many of the attractions in the area—**Lake Kournas** (below), the glass-blowing factory at **Kokkinó Horió** (p 123, ㉖), and the **Ark** (above). Down at the little estuary harbour, you can hire canoes and pedaloes, and out on the river you might well see terrapins and loggerhead turtles. The other delights are also child friendly—the town square, the harbour, and the beach at **Kalivaki** (much safer than the town's main beach, and with model buildings). Georgioúpolis is worth a full-day visit, or even longer.

Take the road south out of Georgioúpolis—it's about 7km to Lake Kournás.

❺ ★ kids **Lake Kournás.** Another pleasant family pastime is taking a pedalo or canoe around the placid waters of Lake Kournás. There's a wide range of cafés and tavérnas for food and drink, and lots of wildlife to look out for—check out the comprehensive information boards at the lakeside. 🕐 *1 hr.*

Loutró is on the south coast, west of Hóra Sfakion.

❻ ★★★ kids **Loutró.** Loutró provides a wonderfully relaxed day out for families. First of all, there's the ferry ride—all the fun of going to sea packed into little more than 15 minutes. Then there's Loutró itself. Safe bathing, canoeing and boating, cafés and tavérnas, all in a quiet and pretty village with no traffic—the only way in is by boat or on foot.

Family Crete

Diadromés is just west of the National Road—about 4km south of Kalives.

❼ ★ Diadromés. Activities on offer at the outdoor centre of Diadromés include walking, mountain biking, horse riding, and supervised rafting and kayaking. For younger children there's a cheery playroom with lots of toys, and for all an Internet room, snack bar, and restaurant. Opened within the last few years, Diadromés is adding activities each year, and is a relaxing alternative to brasher entertainment. However, check what is available before setting out—water-based activities in particular change at short notice. ⏲ *1 day. Diadromés, Armeni.* ☎ *28250 41700. www.diadromeschania.gr. Sat and Sun 10am onwards. Credit cards not accepted.*

Limnoupolis is 8km south-west of Chaniá near Varipetro.

❽ ★★★ kids Limnoupolis Water Park. Limnoupolis has all the usual water features—swimming pools, crazy river, black hole, kamikaze, and a huge variety of multi-slides and tubes. There are special pools for young children, together with mini-cars and motor bikes, two bars, two restaurants (one fast food), and a shopping mall. ⏲ *1 day. Varipetro.* ☎ *28210 33246. www.limnoupolis.gr. Admission 17€ adults, 12€ children 6–12, free children 5 and under, adults over 65, and the disabled. May–October 10am–6pm.*

The Golden Fun Park is on the eastern outskirts of Chaniá.

❾ ★★★ kids Golden Fun Park. After the attractions of the comprehensive all-weather Golden Fun Park, travel west along the coast road for more kids' stuff—a full-sized go-kart track in **Kalamáki** (☎ 28210 33072, open 9.15am–3pm and 5.30pm–11pm) and, between Kalamáki and Plataniás, three snack bars with mini-golf, miniature go-karts and kids' rides—**Alaoum**, **Golf Land**, and **Fun Park Pantou**. Charges in all three are per activity—6€ per child in the play

Pedalos on Lake Kournás.

areas, mini-golf at 5€ for adults, 4€ for children, and go-karts 3€ for five minutes. ⏱ *1 hr upwards. See p 117,* ❶.

Hersónisos & Iraklion Province

❿ ★ kids **Hersónisos.** Given the reputation of the whole area as one spoilt by mass tourism, Hersónisos itself is an unexpectedly varied and interesting town—clean sandy beach to the north, tiny bays and sandstone cliffs to the south, a little harbour, boat trips along the coast, tourist road train around the town, decent shops, and a host of things for kids of all ages to do—swimming, mini golf, bungee-jumping, go-karting, horse-riding, all within walking distance of the town centre. *See p 14,* ❹.

⓫ ★★★ kids **Aquaworld, Hersónisos.** One of the best child-friendly attractions I've ever come across is right in the centre of town. Aquaworld's a gem, owned and run by English expat John McLaren. Starting with a handful of tanks in 1995, the aquarium expanded in size and scope as he rescued maltreated animals, unwanted pets, and creatures found by local children—terrapins, turtles, tortoises, lizards, and snakes, so that by today it has a wonderful cross-section of animals. And it's so unfussy—wherever safe, children are encouraged to handle the animals; photography is not banned (except for the octopi, who are shy); an African tortoise looking like a lumbering boulder has the run of the place; and once you've paid your admission, you can return as many times as you like, free, for the rest of your holiday. *Aquaworld Aquarium, Filikis Etirias 7, Limani.* 📞 *28970 29125. www.aquaworld-crete.com. Admission 6€ adults, 4€ children. 1 Apr–31 Oct 10am–6pm.*

Crete Golf Club.

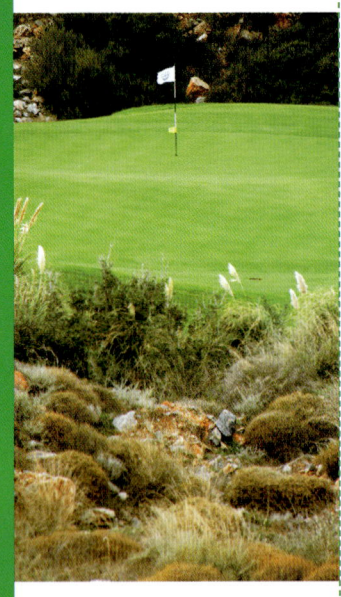

⓬ ★★ kids **Lychnostatis, Hersónisos.** This artificial 'Cretan Village' on the eastern outskirts of Hersónisos is odd, but interesting, with re-creations of different sorts of traditional buildings (houses, chapel, windmill, workshops, school), equipment (wine vat, distillery, threshing floor), gardens and so on. There's an introductory video, lots of displays, and, through the bottom gate, a little beach and café. It's a good way to get a taste of a traditional Cretan way of life, which is rapidly disappearing. ⏱ *2 hr. See p 55,* ❺.

⓭ ★ **Star Beach, Hersónisos.** On the same side of town as Lychnostatis, Star Beach is actually a hotel complex. However, the water park between the hotel and the sea is open to non-residents. The beaches, pools (and a toddlers' pool), water slides, and gym are free, though you have to pay for

Children will enjoy meeting the goats at the Lasinthos Eco Park.

other activities like water sports, diving, paragliding, pool, computer games, and Internet access. With free parking and plenty of bars, restaurants, and toilets, it's a very good family day out.

Acquaplus is on the Hersónisos to Kastélli road, 5km from the National Road.

⑭ ★★★ kids Acquaplus. One of two huge water parks (see also Water City below), Acquaplus is set into a hillside. Spreading over 40,000 square metres, this was the first water park on Crete. Activities include an adventure pool, aqua slalom, space bowl, lazy river, crazy river, black holes, kamikaze, hydro tube, and giant slides that snake down the hillside in profusion. The park has small pools and slides, playgrounds, and inflatables for younger children, and lots of shops and places to eat and drink. ⏱ *1 day.* ☎ *28970 24950. www.acquaplus.gr. Admission 20€ adults, 12€ children 5–12, free children under 5. Apr–Oct.*

⑮ ★ Crete Golf Club. Immediately across the valley from Acquaplus is Crete's only golf club. Visitors are welcome, as long as they have a handicap at a bona fide golf club at home. Gear can be hired and there's a driving range—an ideal day out for golfing families. ⏱ *1 hr–all day. See p 142,* ⑳.

Water City is off the National Road between Hersónisos and Iráklion.

⑯ ★★ kids Water City, Anopolis. This is the second water park in this area—and claims to be the largest in Crete. It has similar activities and facilities to *Acquaplus (see above). Anopolis.* ☎ *28107 81317. www.watercity.gr. Admission 21€ adults, 15€ children, free children under 4. 10am–6.30pm, mid-May–mid-Oct depending on weather.*

From Gournes follow signs to Cretaquarium.

17 ★★★ kids **Cretaquarium.** A pristine modern aquarium, built on what was once a US base (hence the antennae), the Cretaquarium is a fine addition to Crete's visitor attractions. ⏱ *2 hr. See p 143,* **21**.

Lasinthos Eco Park is 1km outside Ágios Georgios, on the road to Psichro.

18 ★★ kids **Lasinthos Eco Park.** Similar to Lychnostatis above, the Lasinthos Eco Park is an attempt to re-create different aspects of Cretan life in one place. It's particularly strong on crafts (pottery, wood carving, ceramics, weaving, wax working), and on the sorts of animals you might come across if you lived in a remote village. It also has a cafeteria, shop, and tavérna. ⏱ *1 hr. See p 153,* **22**.

Continue to the village of Psichro, and follow signs for the Diktean Cave. 4km.

19 ★★ kids **The Diktean Cave.** In the mountains, the Diktean Cave has two things that children will love—a donkey ride up a steep and

Entrance to the Diktean Cave.

rocky track to the cave entrance, and the cave itself, deep and dark but easily accessible via flights of steps. ⏱ *2 hr. See p 154,* **24**.

20 kids **Homo Sapiens Museum.** A large tavérna, a history of mankind, several working windmills, and wonderful views. Who could resist? ⏱ *30 min.* ●

4 The Best
Urban Tours

The Best of Chaniá

1. The Byzantine & Post Byzantine Collection of Chaniá
2. The Venetian Fortress
3. The Naval Museum
4. Galini Cocktail Bar
5. The Old City
6. Etz-Hayyim Synagogue
7. Harbour Square
8. Mosque of the Janissaries
9. The Archaeological Museum
10. Chaniá Cathedral
11. Skridlof
12. The Municipal Market
13. Arsenali
14. Maritime Museum of Crete Permanent Exhibition
15. Apostolis
16. The Lighthouse

Where to Stay

Amphora 17
Casa Delfino 18
Fidias 19
Hotel Contessa 20
Nostos Hotel 21
Porto del Colombo 22
Port Veneziano 23

Where to Dine

Anaplous 24
Ela 25
Fortezza 26
Hippopotamos 27
Notos Café 28

Previous page: Chaniá Naval Museum.

The Best of Chaniá

The capital of Crete's westernmost nomos (province), Chaniá is one of Crete's finest towns. Sometimes called 'the Venice of Greece' (for its architecture—it has no canals), the Venetians gave it a busy, boat-thronged harbour, a massive fortress, long-roofed boat-sheds (Arsenali), a lighthouse-tipped sea wall, mansions (some still in ruins after World War II), and a prosperous, laid-back feel. The capital of the island up to 1971, Chaniá still has a certain metropolitan swagger. It was the birthplace of one of Crete's most famous sons—Eleftherios Venizélos, the 1920s Greek prime minister—and was in Crete's front line during the 1941 German invasion. Given a tremendous pasting by the Luftwaffe, it has since then been restored and rebuilt. START: **The western end of the harbour, behind the Venetian fortress.**

❶ The Byzantine & Post Byzantine Collection of Chaniá.

Housed in a small Venetian chapel at the top of a flight of steps behind the fortress, the collection contains a small, clearly labelled display of coins, jewellery, icons, mosaics, sculptures, and other objects from the early Christian to the post-Venetian periods. Whilst its appeal is limited for the non-specialist, the beauty of the objects on display requires no background knowledge to be appreciated. It's worth a visit as a short-cut to what Cretans find important—note the local students sketching or tapping away on laptops. ⏱ *30 min. 82 Theotokopoulou St.* ☎ *28210 96046. Admission 2€ (3€ for combined ticket with Archaeological Museum). Tues–Sun 8.30am–3pm.*

Walk to the quayside, and in towards the centre of Chaniá, with the harbour to the left and fortress to the right.

❷ The Venetian Fortress.

Though not open to the public, you can get good views of the *Firka* (Turkish for barracks) from the quayside, and from inside the Naval Museum. Started in 1538 to protect the harbour entrance, a chain was stretched in times of trouble across the water to the lighthouse. The Turks used the fortress to house the town governor, and it was also a notorious prison—so where better to stage the ceremonial hoisting of the Greek flag when Crete became part of Greece in 1913? The fortress is currently being renovated.

Continue towards the centre. Look out for an anchor and a ship's screw. Enter the Naval Museum.

❸ ★★★ kids The Naval Museum.

This is one of my favourite Cretan museums. Housed in the last of the fortress buildings, it's packed with exhibits explaining Venetian ship-building methods, and exploring what Chaniá looked like in the past, together with many other odd corners of Crete's naval history. A comprehensive section deals with the

View of the Venetian Fortress.

A back alley in the Old City.

Battle of Crete. The views of Chaniá out of the east-facing windows glow like wall-mounted watercolours.
⏱ *1 hr. Akti Koundourioti. ☎ 28210 91875. Admission 3€. Nov–Mar 9am–2pm, Apr–Oct 9am–4pm.*

☕ **Galini Cocktail Bar.** On the quayside, and open 24 hours a day. Stop for a late breakfast, or for juice, cakes, and ice cream. ☎ *28210 91643. $.*

Take any of the alleys that lead up from the quayside.

The hub of the Old Town, Harbour Square.

5 ★★★ **The Old City.** Meander through the lanes and alleys of the Old City, crammed in between the remains of the ramparts and the quayside, where steps dog-leg up between crowded old houses, overhung by wooden balconies festooned with flowers. Some of these elegant old houses are among Chaniá's poshest hotels. Look out for the graceful Ranieri Gate.

Once through the Ranieri Gate, walk along Zambeliou to Kondolaki. Turn right, then right again. At the cross street you'll see the stone wall and entrance to the synagogue's courtyard in front of you. It's not easy to find, but do persist.

6 ★ **Etz-Hayyim Synagogue.** The only remaining monument to Crete's flourishing, 2400 year-old Jewish community, which perished in 1944 when all but one of Crete's Jews were herded onto a ship with around 500 captured Cretan partisans and sent to Auschwitz (they never made it—the ship was torpedoed by a British submarine). The synagogue was restored in 1999, and now is both a place of worship and a centre for Jewish culture.

The Best of Chaniá

The Mosque of the Janissaries was one of the first buildings erected by the conquering Turks in 1645.

🕐 *30 min. Parados Kondylaki.*
☎ *2821086286. Admission free. May–Oct 10am–6pm (prayers daily 9am).*

Walk back down Kondylaki to the quayside (stopping at Café Notos for a drink and to check your emails). Turn right for Harbour Square.

❼ Harbour Square. Undoubtedly the hub of life in the Old Town, Harbour Square (once Platía Sindrivani, now, officially, Eleftheríos Venizélos Square) is the haunt of shoppers, hawkers, and people-watchers. Clustered around a white marble fountain, the square has shops and tavérnas on three sides. The fourth side is open to the harbour, where tour boat-touts line up to offer their services.

❽ Mosque of the Janissaries. With its large dome surrounded by subsidiary domes, the Mosque of the Janissaries was one of the first buildings erected by the conquering Turks in 1645. It originally had a minaret, which was demolished between the two World Wars. Much photographed, it is now used sporadically as an event and exhibition hall.

Head away from the harbour up Halidon, Chaniá's main street.

❾ ★ The Archaeological Museum. The building in which the Archaeological Museum is housed, opposite the cathedral, started off as the Venetian church of the Monastery of St Francis, became a mosque during the Turkish occupation, and has since been a cinema and a military storehouse. Cool and tranquil even on the hottest and busiest of days, displays include mosaics, Minoan pottery, coffins, and clay tablets inscribed in both Linear A and B. The garden, next to the building's massive buttresses, is a relaxing place to sit, and contains a beautiful Turkish fountain. 🕐 *45 min. Halidon.* ☎ *28210 91875. Admission 2€, (3€ combined with Byzantine Collection). Tues–Sun 8.30am–3pm.*

Cross the street.

❿ Chaniá Cathedral. Chaniá's cathedral, the Church of the Three Martyrs, was built in the 1860s on the site of a soap factory (which itself was built on the site of an earlier church). The soap factory's owner, Mustapha Nily Pasha, had become Prime Minister of the Ottoman Empire and, to celebrate, he donated the land and enough money to build a church on the spot. The cathedral square's

The Arsenali on the quayside.

tavérnas and cafés are less crowded and marginally cheaper than those on the quayside.

Turn left out of the cathedral square, and continue up Halidon. Turn left down Skridlof.

⓫ Skridlof. Skridlof is renowned for its leather goods—here you will find all the handbags, purses, wallets, sandals, shoes, boots, and anything else you can think of that can be made of leather, on display on either side of this narrow alley. Prices can be surprisingly reasonable—there's a lot of competition.

Head east along Skridlof to Tsouderon.

⓬ ★★ The Municipal Market. Opened in 1913 to celebrate union with Greece by local hero Eleftherios Venizélos (at that time Prime Minister of Greece), the lofty, cross-shaped Municipal Market contains over 70 shops selling meat, vegetables, and fruit as well as a variety of souvenirs. Spend some time here, not only to buy stuff, but also to drink in the atmosphere.

Continue along Tsouderon past the minaret, then turn left along Daskaloyánis and Arholeon back to the inner harbour.

⓭ Arsenali. On the quayside, to the left, stand seven of the surviving *Arsenali*—long buildings designed to house ships completely undercover whilst they were being repaired. Beyond them is the **Megalo Neorio** (Great Shipyard), a large red-tiled building with two arched windows flanked by two smaller ones in the side facing the harbour. This was the oldest of the complex, and dates from 1585.

To the right, walk to the innermost end of the inner harbour to another two *Arsenali*. The one on the right houses the reconstructed Minoan ship.

Chaniá Shopping

There are tourist shops throughout the Old City, selling all the usual stuff. **Skridlof**—an alley to the south of the cathedral (see above)—specialises in leather goods of all types (look out especially for characteristic Cretan boots, though they're not cheap). Numerous shops sell sunglasses, bags, clothing, and embroidery along the two main shopping streets **Chalidon** and **Kondylaki**, and there's a wide selection of ceramics next to the Mosque of the Janissaries. **Sifaka** is famous for its cutlers, there's a large, cross-shaped indoor market off **Tsouderon**, and on Saturdays a farmers' market along **Minoos**, next to the eastern wall.

⓮ ★★★ kids Maritime Museum of Crete Permanent Exhibition. Starting in 2001, a team of experts under the leadership of Admiral Kourtis Apostolos set out to recreate a Minoan ship. Since none of the original ships survive (they sailed the Mediterranean 3500 years ago!), designs were taken from pictorial representations on frescoes and worked up digitally, to create a wooden model. From this, using materials and methods known to the Minoans, the 17-metre-long, 4-metre- wide ship was built. Consisting of a cypress-wood frame covered in linen cloth which was first coated in resin, and then lime, the ship (the *Minoa*) has sailed successfully, and is now on permanent display in Chaniá. ⏲ *30 min. Akti Enoseos. Admission 2€. Open 10am–4pm.*

⓯ Apostolis. By now it should be time for lunch, and you could do no better than this excellent fish restaurant on the quayside next to the Minoan ship exhibition. *Akti Enoseos.* ☎ *28210 4347012. $.*

The minaret-style lighthouse.

Continue along the harbour wall to the lighthouse.

⓰ The Lighthouse. When you get to the minaret-style lighthouse, there's not a lot to see. But the one-kilometre-plus walk along the harbour wall is exhilarating, and the views of Chaniá are out of this world. If you don't fancy the walk, a free ferry takes you across the harbour to the uniquely located Fortezza café/restaurant, built into the sea defences a couple of hundred metres from the lighthouse. (see *Where to dine* below).

Where to **Stay**

★★ Amphora OLD TOWN Meandering staircases, an inner courtyard, and the kind of off-kilter charm you'd expect from a medieval building. Front-facing rooms offer views across the outer harbour that would have inspired Canaletto. *2 Parados Theotokopoulo 20.* ☎ *28210 93224/6. www.amphora. gr. 20 rooms. Doubles 110€–130€. MC, V. Closed Jan–Feb.*

Amphora offers inspiring views across the harbour.

Port Veneziano on the quayside.

★★★ **Casa Delfino** OLD TOWN Top-end luxury in an immaculate 17th-century mansion in the heart of the Old Town. Suites are all different and have their own balconies. If it's good enough for the Queen of Spain (and Jean Paul Gautier)…! *Theofanous 9.* 📞 *28210 87400. www.casadelfino.com. 22 rooms. Doubles 186€–310€. AE, MC, V.*

Fidias TOWN CENTRE This cheap and cheerful hotel, in the back streets behind the cathedral, has a mix of singles, doubles, and shared multi-occupation. *Kal Sarpaki 6.* 📞 *28210 52494. 43 rooms. Doubles 20€–30€.*

★ **Hotel Contessa** OLD TOWN Beautiful medieval house with overhanging, half-timbered upper storey, deep in the heart of the Old Town. This was where, in the film, Zorba spent a dissipated couple of days. *Theofanous 15.* 📞 *28210 98566. www.contessa-hotel.com. 6 rooms. Doubles 80€–110€.*

Nostos Hotel OLD TOWN Comfortable rooms with traditional Cretan décor, pretty public areas, and striking views of Chaniá from the terrace, all in a picturesque 14th-century building that is said to have been an early Orthodox church. *Zambeliou 42–46.* 📞 *28210 94743. www.nostos-hotel.com. 12 rooms. Doubles 78€–115€. AE, MC, V.*

Porto del Colombo OLD TOWN With small, beautifully appointed rooms, this big old mansion, hidden away in the alleys behind the Venetian harbour, is said to have been the home of former Prime Minister, Eleftherios Venizélos. *Theofanous and Moschon.* 📞 *28210 70945. 10 rooms. Doubles 72€–103€.*

★ **Port Veneziano** INNER HARBOUR What this medium-sized modern hotel lacks in character it more than makes up for in location—right on the quayside at the eastern end of the Venetian inner harbour. Facing west, sunsets are spectacular. Most rooms have balconies overlooking the harbour. *Old Venetian harbour.* 📞 *28210 27100. www.portoveneziano.gr. 57 rooms. Doubles 105€–140€.*

Chaniá Nightlife

Chaniá's bars, restaurants, and tavérnas are concentrated around the Venetian harbour. One of the best for the younger set is **Hippopotamos** (📞 **28210 44120**), at the eastern end, or try **Klik Scandinavian Bar** (📞 **69471 22193**). Most of the all-night clubs and dance venues are along the coast west of the city. Try **Mylos Club** in Plataniás (📞 **28210 60449**, June–September), or **Destijl** in Agía Marina.

Where to **Dine**

★ **Amphora** OLD TOWN *CRETAN* The Hotel Amphora's street-level restaurant offers Cretan and Greek specialities in a coolly flagged room, open to the quayside and with views of the harbour. *2 Parados Theotokopoulo 20.* ☎ *28210 93224/6. www.amphora.gr. Entrées 3.50€–12€. MC, V. Midday–midnight. Closed Nov–Apr. Reservations recommended at peak times.*

Anaplous KASTELLI, EAST OF OLD TOWN *GREEK* One of several Chaniá restaurants occupying roofless mansions, Anaplous serves varied mezzedes and full meals, and there's often live guitar music. *Sifaka 37.* ☎ *28210 41320. Entrées 10€–20€.*

★★★ **Apostolis** INNER HARBOUR *GREEK FISH* This excellent traditional psarotavérna (fish restaurant), with old-fashioned wooden tables out on the cobbles, is highly reckoned by locals. *Akti Enoseos 6–10.* ☎ *28210 43470. Entrées 12€–30€. MC, V. Open 10am–1 to 2am.*

★★ **Ela** TOP END OF KONDYLAKI *GREEK* Set in the ochre ruins of a Jewish-built soap factory which has, at other times, been a school, a distillery, and a cheese factory, this charming restaurant often has live Greek music and specialises in casseroles and grilled meats. *Kondylaki 47.* ☎ *28210 74128. www.ela-chania.gr. Entrées 15€–35€. AE, DC, MC, V. Open 11am–1am.*

Fortezza SEA WALL NEAR LIGHTHOUSE *GREEK* A combined restaurant and café, the Fortezza is known not so much for its food as for its location—built into fortifications about half way along Chaniá's sea wall. If you can't be bothered to walk, their own little flat-bottomed ferry regularly runs customers back and forth across the harbour. *Old Harbour.* ☎ *28210 41550.*

★ **Hippopotamos** INNER HARBOUR *TEX-MEX* A cross between a fast-food restaurant and a music bar, this noisy hang-out for local young people provides budget food and loud rock, and closes only briefly in mid-morning. *Sarpidonos 6.* ☎ *28210 44120. Entrées 3€–9€. Open 10am–5am.*

Notos Café QUAYSIDE, OUTER HARBOUR *GREEK SWEETS* The ideal place to top-up your fluid levels, have a snack, and check your emails. A long-standing Internet café, it has four desktops and one laptop and, if you have your own laptop, WiFi. *A. Koundourioti Street 31.* ☎ *28210 98722. www.notoscafe.gr. 1€ for 15 min, 3€ an hour, and a small charge for printouts. Open 9am–midnight.*

The charming Ela Tavern.

The Best of **Réthymnon**

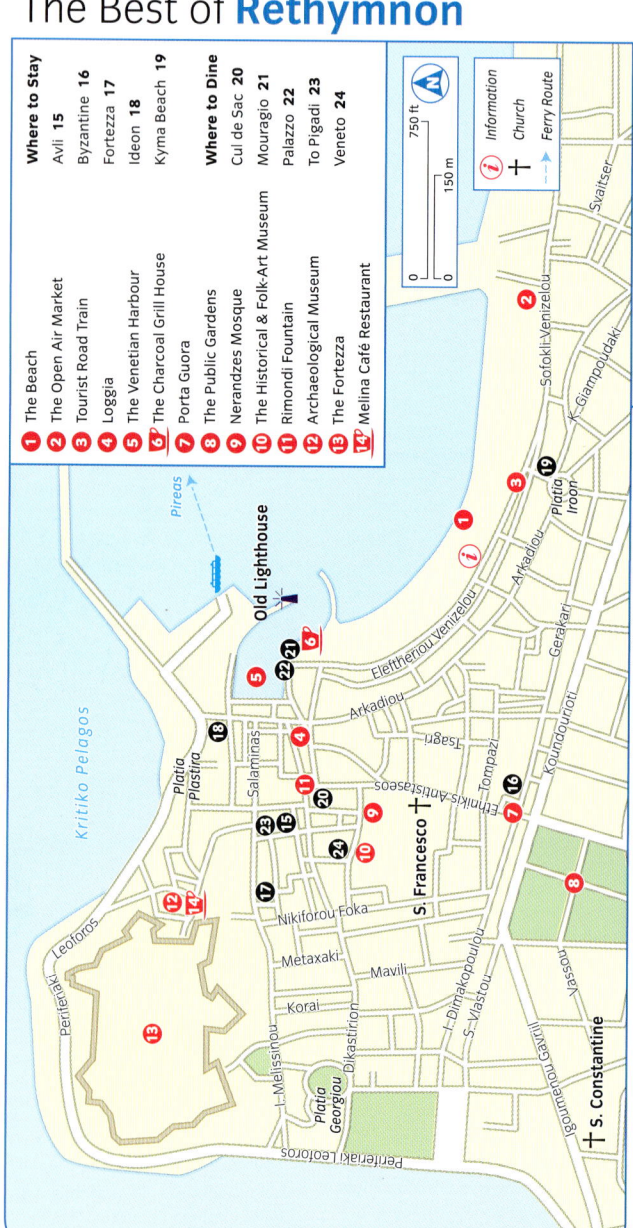

The Best Urban Tours

1. The Beach
2. The Open Air Market
3. Tourist Road Train
4. Loggia
5. The Venetian Harbour
6. The Charcoal Grill House
7. Porta Guora
8. The Public Gardens
9. Nerandzes Mosque
10. The Historical & Folk-Art Museum
11. Rimondi Fountain
12. Archaeological Museum
13. The Fortezza
14. Melina Café Restaurant

Where to Stay
- Avli 15
- Byzantine 16
- Fortezza 17
- Ideon 18
- Kyma Beach 19

Where to Dine
- Cul de Sac 20
- Mouragio 21
- Palazzo 22
- To Pigadi 23
- Veneto 24

i Information
✝ Church
→ Ferry Route

The Best of Réthymnon

Réthymnon, some 60 kilometres east of Chaniá, is, in many ways, similar to its western neighbour. It has a picturesque harbour and lighthouse, courtesy of the Venetians. It has an old quarter of narrow lanes, Turkish and Venetian houses, the odd mosque and fountain. It has excellent museums, cafés, bars, and restaurants, and a wide range of shops. Yet it has a character all of its own. Its reputation for learning goes back to the influx of intellectuals following the 15th-century sacking of Constantinople, enhanced more recently by the establishment of the Arts Faculty campus of the University of Crete, known for art, drama, music, and dance. Though Réthymnon is Crete's third largest city, it is accessibly small—its forty-plus thousand inhabitants could easily fit into most top-flight sports stadiums. And who can resist a place whose tourist literature boasts among its famous sons, 'Nick the Greek—poker player'! START: **Eleftherios Venizélos.**

The tour begins at the eastern end of Eleftherios Venizélos, the road that follows the curve of the beach into the city centre. Block-paving and regular benches make it an easy walk, though beware of road works!

1 kids **The Beach.** Heavily used by tourists and locals alike, the palm-fringed beach is so huge that you'll always find plenty of room. It's sandy, the swimming is good, there are several areas with 'tourist beach' facilities, joined to the promenade by boardwalks, and there's a profusion of bars, tavérnas, ice-cream parlours, and pizza joints across the road. It's perfect for a refreshing dip, either before your walking tour of the city or, even better, after it, to wash away the tiredness and the dust. Parts of the beach, though, are a bit dusty and scrubby—choose your spot well.

2 **The Open Air Market.** Open daily, this typically Greek market, which crowds into the area between the promenade and the marina, sells clothes, flowers, vegetables, fruit, cheese, olives, olive oil, and a wide range of household goods. Thronged with local people, it can't be bettered for atmosphere, nor as

Looking for clothes in the open-air market.

a place to put together an authentic Cretan picnic.

3 kids **Tourist Road Train.** From a starting point on Eleftherios Venizélos, tourist trains depart for a quick spin around the city. They take you down Arkadiou, one of the main shopping streets, into the city centre, around the fortress, alongside the sea, then back along the edge of the New Town. The trip is useful for orientation rather than as a substitute for proper sight-seeing. 6€ *age 15 and over,* 3€ *age 6–14,*

The attractive Venetian inner harbour is lined with tavernas and fish restaurants.

free aged 5 and under. Every half hour 10am–11pm.

Turn left off Eleftherios Venizélos, along any of the side streets, then right onto Arkadiou, with its smart shops—electronics, clothes, shoes, jewellery. Go to the end of Arkadiou.

❹ **Loggia.** Built in the mid-16th century by the Venetians, the open arcades of the handsome Loggia, once a club for the aristocracy, gave shade to its blue-blooded members whilst they gossiped and gambled. Now glassed-in, it offers occasional exhibitions, and, as the information office of the Ministry of Information and the Archaeological Museum, high-quality (and expensive) museum replicas. *Open 8am–3pm.*

Go along Petihaki, the short street that joins the ends of Venizelou and Arkadiou to the heart of Réthymnon—the Venetian harbour.

Where to Shop

Réthymnon has a wide range of tourist shops throughout the Old Town, and numerous classy jewellery shops—try **Mourtzanos 1907** on Arkadiou (28310 22363) or **Fere Silver and Gold** (28310 51011) either side of Paleologou. Leather is also well represented—**Xenia and Dolce**, on either side of Arkadiou (28310 27411) stock a wide range of coats, skirts, bags, belts, and other clothing. Traditional Cretan wines, foods, and herbs can be bought at **Agrotiko** on Titou Petihaki Square (www.agrotiko.gr) or **Avli Raw Materials** on Arampatzoglou (www.avli.gr). For hand-made Cretan musical instruments, visit the shop and workshop of **Nikos Papalexakis** on Dimakopolou, just beyond the Porta Guora (lyraboy1@yahoo.gr)—a lyra will set you back anything from 200€ to 1000€, a larger laouto twice that. There are street markets daily on **Andistasis**, and **Dimitrakaki** on Thursdays, and a big open-air market ten minutes' walk along the road beside the beach (Eleftherios Venizélos).

5 ★★ The Venetian Harbour.
Though now given over entirely to tourism, the tiny Venetian harbour is still one of the prettiest in the Mediterranean. The old stone quay, lined with tavérnas, fish restaurants, and colourful boats, curves tightly around to the Port Authority Building, the Customs House, and the immaculate 16th-century lighthouse. Depending on your itinerary, stop here for a coffee and a snack, or for a full meal.

6 The Charcoal Grill House.
If you're already feeling tired, take light refreshment at this tavérna, right next to the harbour. Outside it has a bank of three coin-operated massage chairs, to soothe away those aches and pains! *No phone.* $.

Walk back along Petihaki past the Loggia, then turn left up Souliou to Ethnikis Antistasseos, a long, pedestrianised street packed with tourist shops.

7 Porta Guora.
At the top end of Antistasseos stands the Porta Guora—a Venetian arch that is important as the only remaining part of the city walls, rather than for any intrinsic beauty. Indeed, it looks rather insignificant, and is much restored.

8 The Public Gardens.
Once a Turkish cemetery, the Public Gardens are much used by the elderly and mothers with toddlers, and dotted with drinking fountains and busts of public figures. They offer a pleasant place to rest up to the sounds of children playing in the nearby school, sit on a bench and eat a packed lunch, or have a drink in the little café. This is the venue for Réthymnon's Wine Festival in July where, for a nominal entry fee, you can wander around the tables set up around the gardens and sample wine from the producers to your heart's content (see p 160).

Doorway of the Venetian mansion housing the Historical and Folk Art Museum.

Return along Antistasseos.

9 Nerandzes Mosque.
Half way down Antistasseos, on the left, stands the Nerandzes Mosque, whose minaret provides one of the best views of Réthymnon. At the time of writing, alas, the mosque, minaret, and the square beyond were closed for renovation.

Turn off Antistasseos, past the mosque, up Vernadou to the Historical and Folk-Art Museum on your left.

10 The Historical & Folk-Art Museum.
The museum is worth visiting for both its architecture (it's housed in a wonderfully restored Venetian mansion) and for its strong flavour of traditional Cretan life. A display of **Battle of Crete** memorabilia (and, surprisingly interestingly, of coins) leads, through a peaceful courtyard garden and up a flight of steps, to the **Folk-Art Collection**, a riot of artefacts and photographs illustrating a broad range of Cretan crafts—basket-weaving, carpentry, pottery, baking, textile production,

A church-cum-mosque inside the fortress.

embroidery, agriculture, musical instrument-making, daggers, and a host of other everyday items. All are carefully exhibited and explained in Greek and English. Look out, too, for photographs of the renovation of the building. ⏱ *1 hr. Vernardou.* ☎ *2831 023398. Admission 3€ adults, 1.50€ concessions. Mon–Sat 9.30am–2.30pm.*

Return to Antistasseos, turn left, and walk down to tiny Petihaki Square.

⓫ Rimondi Fountain. Another reminder of Réthymnon's Venetian past, the Rimondi Fountain dates from 1629, and consists of a fragment of wall bearing four Corinthian columns in between which are three lion-heads spouting water. Not only is the fountain, with its mellow stone and weathered archway, a popular background for holiday snaps, it also marks the centre of the liveliest bar-and-restaurant region of the city.

Make your way along Arampatzoglou or Radamanthos to Nikiforou Foka, turn right, then climb up Katehaki to the fortress.

⓬ ★ Archaeological Museum. Housed in a building designed by the Turks to strengthen the main entrance to the fortress, then used as a prison, Réthymnon's archaeological museum contains a comprehensive collection of Minoan artefacts, especially sarcophagi, and numerous Roman remains. ⏱ *30 min. Réthymnon.* ☎ *28310 54668. Admission 3€ adults, 2€ concessions, free under 18s. Tues–Sun 8.30am–3pm.*

Right next to the museum is the entrance to the Fortezza.

⓭ ★★ kids The Fortezza. One of the most impressive fortresses in Greece, and said to be the largest ever built by the Venetians, Réthymnon's Fortezza (sometimes spelt 'Fortetza' to mimic the pronunciation) sprawls across the whole of the western side of the city. Designed to provide protection from pirates after a series of 16th-century raids, the fortress turned out to be something of a white elephant—when the Turks took the city in 1645, they simply by-passed it! Now consisting of massive walls enclosing a vast and dusty space dotted with conifers and cacti, crumbling military installations, barracks, and a church-cum-mosque, it is worth doing a complete circuit of the walls—the views are extensive, and the dusty silence and baking heat give an insight into what it must have been like to serve here as a soldier. ⏰ *1–2 hr. Admission 10€*

family tickets, 4€ adults, 3€ over 65s, free children/students/ disabled. Daily 9am–6.30pm (no entrance after 5.45pm).

14 **kids** **Melina Café Restaurant.** Ideally situated right next to the Fortezza for drinks or a full meal at the end of a long day's sightseeing. It has a terrace with extensive views of Réthymnon, a children's play area, and, inside, full airconditioning. *Corner of Chimaras and Katehaki.* 📞 *28310 21580. $.*

Where to Stay

★★★ **Avli** OLD TOWN   Avli has colonised several streets in the Old Town, providing a superb restaurant (see below), a wine bar, and a provisions shop, as well as the seven immaculate suites of the Avli Hotel. A full range of services and facilities (check out the website for a list) offer top-end luxury at top-end prices. *22 Xanthoudidou and Radamanthios St.* 📞 *28310 58255. www.avli.gr. 7 rooms. Suites 82.50€–139€ pp. AE, MC, V.*

★ **Byzantine** OLD TOWN   Tucked away in an alley just off Tesseron Martiron Square, a few metres from the Porto Guora, the Hotel Byzantine occupies an atmospheric old building, and offers simple rooms, most with baths, and a pleasant bar. Phone ahead—unexpected daytime calls in person sometimes go unheeded. *Vosporou 26.* 📞 *28310 55609. 8 rooms. Doubles 50€. MC, V.*

★★ **Fortezza** OLD TOWN   In the heart of the Old Town between the Rimondi Fountain and the fortress, the Fortezza is all clean modern lines and stylish understatement. With a pool, bar, restaurant, and airconditioning throughout (and free parking, a huge boon in Réthymnon), the Fortezza is a real find. *Mellisinou 16.* 📞 *28310 55551. www.fortezza.gr. 54 rooms. Doubles 70€–85€ w/breakfast. AE, MC, V.*

★ **Ideon** VENETIAN PORT   Handy for the Venetian port and the Old Town, the Ideon is, like the Fortezza,

Byzantine, tucked away in an Old Town alley.

The Kyma Beach Hotel.

clean and modern. It has a restaurant, cafeteria, bar, and pool. All rooms have airconditioning and balcony, and those in the annexe also have a fridge. Can be noisy, and check your room before committing—some are very small. *Platia Plastira 10.* ☎ *28310 28667. www.hotelideon.gr. 86 rooms. Doubles 59€–83€. AE, DC, MC, V.*

Kyma Beach ON TOWN BEACH The Kyma Beach Hotel is right on the beach, yet it's an easy walk into the city centre. It offers modern facilities, with all rooms air conditioned and double glazed (which keeps out the road noise) and balconied (most with sea views). There's an à la carte restaurant and bar, and a Goody's fast-food restaurant on the ground floor. *Agnostou Stratioti Sq.* ☎ *28310 55503. www.ok-rethymno.gr/Kyma-Beach-Hotel/EN/contact.html. 35 rooms. Doubles 75€–100€. DC, MC, V.*

Where to **Dine**

★★★ **Avli** OLD TOWN *CRETAN/MEDITERRANEAN* Set in a Venetian villa, and deservedly Réthymnon's most famous restaurant, the Avli is delightful indoors and out, with classy décor, barrel vaulting, multi-level courtyard terrace, abundant greenery, immaculately laid tables, and an inventive menu of both traditional and 'creative' Cretan cuisine. *22 Xanthoudidou and Radamanthios St.* ☎ *28310 58255. www.avli.gr. Entrées 10€–30€. AE, MC, V. Open 1pm–1am.*

Avli Raw Materials shop for traditional Cretan wine and food.

Booking advisable, especially at weekends.

★ **Cul de Sac** OLD TOWN *CAFÉ*
A cut above the average cafenion, the Cul de Sac has a good range of snacks, delicious coffee, immaculate toilet facilities, and is perfectly placed just opposite the Rimondi Fountain for watching the world go by. *Platía Petihaki, corner of Petihaki and Paleologou. Entrées 2.50€–6.50€. Open 9am till late.*

Mouragio VENETIAN HARBOUR *FISH* One of the string of restaurants lining the quayside in the Venetian harbour, Mouragio is heavily used by locals. The fish is very fresh—a waiter rushed out with a net while I was there and caught one off the quayside! *Old Venetian harbour.* ☎ *28310 26475. Entrées 7.50€–18€. AE, MC, V. Open Apr–Oct 11am–midnight.*

★★ **Palazzo** VENETIAN HARBOUR *GREEK* Overlooking the Venetian harbour, but not easy to find (down the alley that leads from the Loggia to the quayside), the Palazzo has a stylish roof terrace overlooking the harbour, above the quayside bustle. *The Old Port.* ☎ *028310 25681. Entrées 15€–50€. AE, DC, MC, V. Open Apr–Oct 10am–1pm or 2pm. Reservations necessary for roof terrace.*

★ **To Pigadi** OLD TOWN *GREEK* Near the Rimondi Fountain, To Pigadi (The Well) does good quality,

Roof terrace over-looking the harbour at Palazzo restaurant.

traditional Greek food at reasonable prices in a 16th-century house. Good wine list, and nice terrace with (yes) a well. *Xanthoudidou 31.* ☎ *28310 27522. www.pigadi-crete.com. Entrées 13€–25€. DC, MC, V. Open Wed–Sat 10am–3pm, 6pm–1am, all day Sundays.*

★★ **Veneto** OLD TOWN *MEDITERRANEAN* Opposite the Folk-Art Museum in the vine-draped alley of Epimenidou, the Veneto is pretty as a picture. Set in the rooms, courtyards, and terraces of an old Venetian manor house, a wide Mediterranean menu is on offer, with a wine list containing a colossal 100 Greek labels. *Epimenidou 4.* ☎ *28310 56634. www.veneto.gr. Entrées 12€–22€. MC, V. Open Apr–Oct 6pm–midnight. Reservations recommended.*

Where to go at Night

The main night life is in the bars and restaurants of the Old Town, around the Venetian harbour and the streets around the Rimondi Fountain. Principal discos are in hotels to the east of the town, and there's a wine festival in the Public Gardens in late July.

The Best of **Iráklion**

The Best Urban Tours

1. Archaeological Museum
2. The Museum of the Battle of Crete & National Resistance 1941–1945
3. Platia Venizelou/Platia Nikiforou Fokas
4. The Bembo Fountain
5. Statue of Erotokritos & Arethoúsa
6. The Tomb of Kazantzákis
7. The Morosini Fountain
8. San Marco Basilica
9. The Loggia
10. Ágios Títos
11. El Greco Park
12. Fresh
13. Historical Museum
14. The Natural History Museum of Crete
15. The Venetian Harbour
16. Venetian Fortress (The Koules)
17. Y Vardia

Where to Stay

- Atlantis 18
- Kastro 19
- Kronos 20
- Lato 21
- Mirabéllo 22

Where to Dine

- Flocafe 23
- Ippokampos 24
- Loukoulos 25
- Pagopoleion 26
- Parasies 27

† Church
✉ Post Office

The Best of Iráklion

Far and away Crete's biggest city, and its capital since 1971, Iráklion is visited more because of its airport and its position near the island's premier tourist attraction—Knossós—than because of any intrinsic delights of its own. Indeed, it comes in for a comprehensive guidebook kicking for its noise and traffic, dust and dirt. Even its own tourist literature admits to 'architectural chaos'. And yet. It has numerous pedestrianised streets and alleys to escape the traffic. It has the best collection of Minoan artefacts in the world. It has intriguing reminders of the Venetian occupation—an attractive harbour with boat yards, a mighty, thoroughly restored fortress, imposing city walls, fine civic buildings. It offers insights into Cretan arts—from painter El Greco to one of the giants of modern Greek literature—*Zorba the Greek* author Nikos Kazantzákis. It has the up-to-date and beautifully situated Natural History Museum of the University of Crete. Don't write off Iráklion—it's worth at least a day's exploration. START: **The Archaeological Museum.**

❶ ★★★ Archaeological Museum. Possessor of the most comprehensive Minoan collection in the world, the Archaeological Museum is currently being refurbished. As a result, at the time of writing only a tiny fraction of the exhibits were on show. Even so, they are worth seeing—look out particularly for the huge double-headed bronze ceremonial axe, the boar's-tooth helmet, the statue of a bull, a variety of fascinating mosaics, the ornately decorated larnax or coffin, statuettes of people and animals, clay plaques showing fine Minoan buildings. When the reorganisation is complete, this museum will be a spectacular world superstar. But, I was told it would be 'at least two or three years' before it's likely to open. ⏱ *30 min. Xanthoudidou St.* ☎ *28102 79000 (or 28102 79086). 4€ during renovations. Tues–Sun 8am–7.30pm, Mon 1pm–7.30pm (closes 5pm Nov–Mar).*

❷ The Museum of the Battle of Crete & National Resistance 1941–1945. Next door to

Platia Venizelou is a good place to start an exploration of the area.

The tomb of Kazantzákis.

the Archaeological Museum is another devoted to the Battle of Crete and Greek resistance to the subsequent occupation of the island. Although legends and explanations are sadly in Greek only, the cases of exhibits and the haunting photographs of men and women who were active in the resistance speak for themselves. ⏱ *15 min. Corner of Doukos Beaufort and Merambelou.* ☎ *28103 46554. Admission free. Mon–Fri 9am–2.30pm.*

From Doukos Beaufort turn right to Platía Eleftherias. Full of undistinguished 20th-century architecture and eucalyptus and palm trees, the square is the focus of the modern city. Walk west along busy Dikeosini or Daidalou, or narrow Korai, lined with smart cafés, to Iráklion's Old City.

③ ★★ Platía Venizelou/Platía Nikiforou Fokas. Much quieter, more traditional, and more interesting than the newer parts of the city, the centre is clustered around Platía Venizelou and Platía Nikiforou Fokas. It's a good place to start an exploration of the area.

Walk up Odos 1866, past the market stalls. At the end of the road, on Kornarou Square, there are two monuments worth seeing.

④ The Bembo Fountain. Erected in 1588 by the Venetians from Roman bits and pieces, the Bembo Fountain stands next to a little kiosk added by the Turks, now a café. The two make an interesting tableau.

⑤ Statue of Erotokritós & Arethóusa. In the square itself is an impressive modern statue of Erotokritós and Arethóusa, the central characters of the famous 17th-century Cretan epic (over 10,000 verses!) poem written by Kornaros (1553–1613), *Erotokritós.*

The Loggia, once a meeting place for wealthy aristocrats.

Ágios Titos is worth visiting for its flamboyant history.

Cross the square and continue south along Evans. Turn right at the archway. Continue for 300m then climb the steps to the top of the Martinengo Bastion.

6 ★ The Tomb of Kazantzákis. Nikos Kazantzákis was one of Greece's greatest writers. Raised just south of the capital, he chose this spot on Iráklion's southernmost bastion for his tomb because of its views north across the city to the sea. On a gravestone which is moving in its simplicity is his epitaph (which he chose before his death in 1957)—'I believe in nothing, I hope for nothing, I am free'. *See p 49*, **4**.

Return to Platía Venizelou.

7 The Morosini Fountain. Built in 1629 (when Francesco Morosini was Venetian governor), and surrounded by cafés and shops, the fountain is a focal point for life in the city, and is frequently used as a meeting point. Now adorned with lions rather than the original figure of Neptune, it explains the local name for Platía Venizelou—Lion Square.

8 San Marco Basilica. On the square, just as 25 Augoustou starts to drop down to the Venetian Port, stands San Marco Basilica, built by the Venetians as a cathedral, converted into a mosque by the Turks. It is now used as an occasional exhibition centre. Together with the Morosini Fountain, the steps of San Marco offer a convenient place for foot-weary tourists to rest, gorge on street food or ice-creams, and watch the world go by, free of charge. *Platía Venizelou*.

9 The Loggia. Farther down 25 Augoustou is the Venetian Loggia—originally built in 1541 as a shady meeting place for wealthy aristocrats, and remodelled in 1628 by Morosini. Used as an arsenal (and badly damaged) by the Turks, it took 18 years to restore in the 1960s and '70s, and is now Iráklion's Town Hall.

10 ★★★ Ágios Titos. Worth visiting for its flamboyant history and for the serenity of the little tree-dotted square that it dominates, Ágios Titos was built around 961 to celebrate the re-conquest of Iráklion from its Arab rulers for the Byzantine Empire.

Statue in El Greco Park.

It was remodelled into a Roman Catholic church during the Venetian occupation, rebuilt several times after fire and earthquake, became a mosque under the Turks, and finally returned to being an Orthodox church in the 1920s. It was named for St Titus, one of St Paul's disciples, whose head sits in a chapel-reliquary to the left as you enter. The head spent the Turkish occupation in Venice, and was only returned to Iráklion by order of the Pope in 1966. I don't know where the body is! ⏱ *30 min. Ágios Titos Sq.*

Cross 25 Augoustou and enter El Greco Park, a little green haven in the city centre.

11 El Greco Park. A good place for a rest, and perhaps refreshment. There's a supermarket directly across the park for snacks or picnic items, and walls and benches in the park on which to sit whilst you eat them.

12 Fresh. A modern café much favoured by locals, with big-screen TV and spiral staircase up to the toilets—good if you'd rather not picnic. *No phone. $.*

Exit the far end of the park along Minotavrou, and walk down to the main harbour road. Turn left to the Historical Museum.

13 ★★★ Historical Museum. Housed in a renovated mansion facing the sea, the Historical Museum is something of a hidden gem. It covers Byzantine and Venetian artefacts (ground floor), El Greco (first floor), and Kazantzákis, the Battle of Crete, folk-art, and union with Greece on the second floor. Exhibits are well displayed, all labelling is in English and Greek, and there's a neat little cafeteria with balconies. ⏱ *45 min. 27 Venizelou Sofokli.* ☎ *28102 83219. www.historical-museum.gr. 5€ (concessions 3€), free children 12 and under. Mon–Sat 9am–3pm (closed Sun and public holidays).*

Turn left out of the museum, and follow the coast road for 500m to the next stop.

Where to Shop

Iráklion offers the best shopping in Crete, with all the big retail names you'd expect in a capital city. **Odos 1866** is home to the city's market, **Dedalou** to the higher-end shops, and **Kalokerinou** to more affordable textile emporia. For shoes, head for **Averof**. Good quality Byzantine icon reproductions can be bought at **Stergiou** in Evans Street (☎ 28102 24987) and at **XS Icons** in Odos 1866 (☎ 28102 85187), but they're not cheap. For recorded Cretan music go to **Aerakis** on Dedalou (☎ 28102 25758).

14 ★★★ kids **The Natural History Museum of Crete.** Though established in 1980, many tourist maps still don't show this museum. It covers all habitats and regions of Crete in an engaging, hands-on way. For example, in the children's **Discovery Centre** there's a plane tree whose hollow interior hosts the Plane tree cinema (showing a film about the wildlife that would normally surround it), a 'cave of mystery' (stalagmites and stalactites, bats), 'secrets of the earth' (a simulated archaeological dig), and a 'night camp' (nocturnal animals). There's a café, and a botanical garden at the rear. ⏱ *minimum 1 hr. Knossou Avenue.* ☎ *28102 82740/ 28103 24366 www.nhmc.uoc.gr. Children 3€, free accompanying adults. Mon–Fri 8.30am–2.30pm, Sun 10am–3pm. Closed Sat.*

Return east to the Venetian harbour.

15 ★★ **The Venetian Harbour.** Since the modern port with its ferries and cargo ships lies to the east, the Venetian harbour contains only fishing boats—each painted blue and white, with a little wheelhouse, bow-mounted winch, and awning at the stern—and the odd small pleasure craft. There are also several Venetian boathouses (or *Arsenali*), most isolated from the traffic flow by sheets of corrugated iron. The one exception forms part of the pedestrian sidewalk of the main road.

16 ★★ kids **Venetian Fortress (The Koules).** At the end of the left-hand sea wall of the harbour squats the massive, beautifully restored Koules. It's open to the public, offering grand views along the coast and across the city. There are few finer sights, on a windy day, than the waters of the Mediterranean breaking at the feet of the huge fortress walls and crashing across the car park. ⏱ *30 min.* ☎ *28102 44215. 2€. Tues–Sun 8.30am–3pm.*

17 ☕ **Y Vardia.** Part of the same block as the Coastguard and Port Authority building, this large tavérna sits right on the dock. Excellent food and pleasant views. *No phone. $.*

If you want to shorten this gruelling itinerary, skip numbers 6 and 13—they both have parking, and can be visited by car.

Blue and white fishing boats in the harbour.

The Best of Iráklion

Where to **Stay**

Hotel Lato is well placed for the harbour and city centre.

★★★ **Atlantis** CITY CENTRE This luxurious, largely business, hotel is five minutes' walk from the harbour, the Archaeological Museum, and Venizélos Square, and has a roof garden, pool, and all the services you'd expect. Parking is available. Rooms are quiet and breakfasts excellent. It is no longer one of the Grécotel chain, though is often described as such. *Igias 2.* 📞 *28102 29103. www.aquilahotels.com. 160 rooms. Doubles 70€–165€ w/breakfast. AE, DC, MC, V.*

★★ **Kastro** CITY CENTRE Between El Greco Park and the Historical Museum, the Kastro has comfortable rooms with airconditioning and all facilities in a central location at reasonable prices. But it's not easy to find, and parking in the area is difficult. *22 Theotokopoulou St.* 📞 *28102 85020. www.kastro-hotel.gr. 38 rooms. Doubles 60€–85€ w/breakfast. Children aged 0–2 free, aged up to 12 flat rate if sharing parents' room. AE, MC, V.*

Kronos VENETIAN HARBOUR Just up from the Venetian harbour, the Kronos is a good, basic, modern hotel. All rooms are airconditioned and have a small balcony. The hotel is on a busy street, so expect street noise. Standards of cleanliness were very acceptable during my visit, but reviews from others have been mixed. *2, Sof. Venizelou Str. and M. Agarathou.* 📞 *2810 282240. www.kronoshotel.gr. 32 rooms. Doubles 62€–70€.*

★★★ **Lato** VENETIAN HARBOUR With its modernist layout and décor, terrific rooftop ('Herb Garden') and main ('Gourmet') restaurants, steam room and gym, airconditioning and WiFi, the Lato is a top-of-the-range hotel well placed for the harbour, museums, and city centre. Staff when I was there were particularly friendly and helpful. *Epimenidou 15.* 📞 *28102 28103. www.lato.gr. 58 rooms. Doubles 91€–263€. AE, MC, V.*

Mirabéllo VENETIAN HARBOUR Next door to the Kastro, the Mirabéllo has had mixed reviews. However, though it can't compete with hotels of similar price in other parts of Crete, for one in the centre of the capital city, its tariffs are very reasonable and the rooms I saw were acceptably clean and tidy. *Theotokopoulou 20.* 📞 *28102 85052. www.mirabello-hotel.gr. 25 rooms. Doubles 55€–68€. MC, V.*

Where to **Dine**

Flocafe CITY CENTRE *CAFÉ* Part of a chain of coffee shops found all over Greece and Cyprus, Flocafe is one of several cafés along Korai, and offers a range of club sandwiches, baguettes, and mini-pizzas, as well as cakes, ice-creams, puddings, and drinks. The service is first class—despite being busy, iced water is put in front of you within seconds of sitting down, and your order taken and filled within minutes. *Korai. www.flocafe.gr. Entrées 5€–8€. Open 8am–2am.*

★★★ **Ippokampos** OPPOSITE VENETIAN HARBOUR WALL *FISH* On two floors, with views of the harbour from upstairs, the Ippokampos is an excellent fish restaurant. Unpretentious yet highly reckoned by locals, and therefore very busy—they don't take reservations, so you might have to wait your turn for a table. *Sofokli Venizelou junction with 25th Augst.* ☎ *28102 80240. Entrées 5€–11€. Open Mon–Sat midday–11.30pm.*

★ **Loukoulos** CITY CENTRE *ITALIAN/ INTERNATIONAL* No pizza joint this—the Loukoulos is up-market and pricey. With lovely décor, a pleasant little courtyard, and excellent food this is definitely a cut above. Specialties include wild boar and lobster cooked in a wood-burning oven. The restaurant is also known for its wide range of pasta. *Korai 5.* ☎ *28102 24435. www.loukoulos-restaurant.gr. Entrées 15€–35€. AE, DC, MC, V. Open midday–5pm and 6pm–1am.*

★★ **Pagopoleion** CITY CENTRE *CAFÉ/BAR/RESTAURANT* A stylish modern café/restaurant set in a

Ippokampos for excellent fish dishes and views of the harbour.

converted ice-factory and right next to Ágios Titos church. Immaculate toilets, interesting menu (general Mediterranean as well as more narrowly Greek), huge wine list—the Pagopoleion has the lot. Look out for weekend afternoon buffets. *Platía Ágios Titos.* ☎ *28102 346028. www.icefacktory.gr. Entrées 12€–26€ AE, DC, MC, V. Open midday–2am.*

Parasies CITY CENTRE *GREEK* Just behind the Historical Museum, the décor is modern and cool-but-comfortable, the main courses largely meat based, the salads fresh, the vegetables organic. Good wine list. Much used by locals, who rate the restaurant's grilled meats very highly. *Historical Museum Square.* ☎ *28102 25009. Entrées 30€–50€. AE, V. Open midday–midnight.*

The Best of **Ágios Nikólaos**

1. Tourist Road Train
2. Tourist Information Office
3. Folk-Art Museum
4. The Bottomless Lake
5. Du Lac
6. Kitroplatia
7. Palazzo
8. The Archaeological Museum
9. Panagia Kera
10. Lató
11. Kritsá

Where to Stay
Angelos 12
Coral 13
Hermes 14

Where to Dine
Avli 15
Barko/Palazzo 16
Itanos 17
Pelagos 18

The Best of Ágios Nikólaos

Capital of Crete's eastern Lasíthi region, **Ágios Nikólaos** is enviably located on hills surrounding an attractive bay, given individuality by the unique and allegedly bottomless lake around which the town centre is built. Though feeling the most touristy of the island's four largest towns, Ag Nik (as it's often called by visitors) is short on perceptible Minoan, Venetian, or Turkish influences, with no castle, old harbour, or minarets. So there's little sightseeing to be done—it's more a case of strolling around the town and enjoying the ambience. There are five beaches within reach of the town itself, it's the centre of a wide range of excursions, and is well placed for the spectacular Gulf of Mirabéllo. This tour comes in two parts—a figure-of-eight tour of Ágios Nikólaos itself, and a short detour (by car or by tourist road train) to the craft village of Kritsá. START: **The car park at the ferry dock.**

Walk off the dock and bear right, along Akti I Koundourou facing the outer harbour towards the town centre.

1 kids **Tourist Road Train.** Take Ágios Nikólaos's 'Little Train', whose 'Tour 1' gives a good 35-minute introduction to the geography of the town. There are two other tours—one up to the hills to the north, towards Eloúnda (useful if you don't have time for a proper tour, see p 148, **4**), and a third out to the village of Kritsá (if you don't have time for the tour described on p 95, **11**). *12 Thermistokleous St.* ☎ *28410 25420. 7€.*

Continue to the bridge across the mouth of Lake Voulismeni. You are now at the centre of Ágios Nikólaos.

2 **Tourist Information Office.** Greek tourist information offices can be very half-hearted, but Ágios Nikólaos's is a good one. Directly opposite the bridge, it stocks a good range of pamphlets, maps, brochures etc, for both the municipality and for the surrounding area. *21 Akti I Koundourou St.* ☎ *28410 22357. www.aiosNikolaos.gr.*

3 ★ **Folk-Art Museum.** Virtually next door to the Tourist Information Office, in one of Ágios Nikólaos's

Ag Nik's Ups & Downs

Since its heyday as the port for ancient Minoan Látó, Ágios Nikólaos became totally unimportant during the Roman and Byzantine periods, was briefly resurrected by the Venetians, then largely ignored by the Turks. When it was first chosen as the capital of Lasíthi Province, in 1905, it was a hamlet with a population of 95. Since then it has passed through a stage—now thankfully ended—as resort-of-choice for the boozy, youth-dominated mass-package trade, to become an amiable seaside town dominated by bars, restaurants, and tourist shops.

The Bottomless Lake, lined with restaurants and boats.

oldest buildings, the Folk-Art Museum is small but beautifully formed. It has a good selection of examples of Cretan popular art—textiles, needlework, carpentry, jewellery, and so on—together with (inevitably in Crete) guns, musical instruments, coins, and other everyday objects. ⏱ *15 min. 1 K. Palaeologou St.* ☎ *28410 25093. Admission 4€. Daily 10.30am-2.30pm, 6pm-8pm. Closed Sundays.*

Walk back across the bridge and bear left to the lake.

View to Kitroplatia.

④ ★★ **The Bottomless Lake.** Lake Voulismeni is commonly called the Bottomless Lake, though its depth has been measured at a less-than-infinite but still impressive 70 metres. Prone to stagnation, it was connected to the sea by the Turks in 1867. Lined with restaurants (and their touts) on the left and boats on the right, with hotels and more restaurants (and a chapel) facing you among the trees on the cliffs that curve around the lake, **Omirou**, the lakeside street, is a picture—it's the peaceful heart of this busy holiday town. Stop for a coffee or a meal and look out for the electric flash of kingfishers. Then walk all the way around the lake—about ten minutes—until you get back to the bridge.

⑤ **Du Lac.** A good stop for a drink is at the Café du Lac, 28th Oktovriou St, up the steps from the lake, or, if it's time for a more substantial meal, in the Restaurant du Lac which is part of the same block, but on the lakeside. ☎ *28410 22711. $.*

Climb the steps, then turn right up pedestrianised, tree-lined 28th

Vantage point with the mountains of the Gulf of Mirabello providing the backdrop.

Oktovriou, a shopping street parallel to Omirou. At the top is Platia Venizelou, a glorified traffic roundabout with a war memorial in the middle. Continue down Venizelou Street to the town beach.

6 Kitroplatia. The south-east-facing part of Ágios Nikólaos is the location of the town's main beaches. Having arrived at the clean and sandy town beach, or **Ammos**, you can turn right and walk along the coast to the **Municipal Beach Club** (free, despite its name), and a couple of kilometres beyond that, **Almyros** (probably the best beach but a fair distance to walk). If you turn left at Ammos Beach, you can follow Akti Nearchou past the Marina (a nice muddle of un-chic working boatyards) to get, via a paved path, to neat, pocket-sized **Kitroplatia**, my own favourite, tucked in between two small headlands, lined with cafés and restaurants. Beyond it, the road takes you past a vantage point containing a modern statue (a fin? a tentacle? the prow of a boat?) back to the ferry

Where to Shop

Ágios Nikólaos is dominated by cafés, bars, restaurants, and tourist shops, but there's some excellent shopping if you know where to look. Upmarket jewellery and watches can be bought at **Vicky M** on Kounourou St (☎ **28410 83011**), accurate copies of ancient pottery at **Atelier Ceramica** (☎ **28410 24075**) on Palaelogou St (the road up to the Archaeological Museum), and modern icons at the **Byzantio** workshop on 28th Oktovriou St, (☎ **28410 26530**), opposite the Post Office. **East Mediterranean** (☎ **28410 29322**, on Venizelou Square) stocks a wide range of Cretan wine, spirits, olive oil, herbs, and honey, and for quality crafts—embroidery, ceramics, leather goods etc—the short trip out to the village of **Kritsá** is well worth taking.

Buy quality handicrafts, including lace in Kritsá.

port. The mountains that run along the southern coast of the Gulf of Mirabéllo provide a craggy backdrop.

7 Palazzo. Get refreshment at this café on Kitroplatia beach then have a swim. *$*.

Return to the bridge in the town centre. The second part of the figure-of-eight tour, the north-eastern part of Ágios Nikólaos, begins here. Retrace your steps along Omirou, but continue around the lake and you get some of the best urban views in Crete. At the main road up from the bridge (Palaelogou), turn left and climb the hill.

8 ★ The Archaeological Museum. On the right at the top of the hill, Ágios Nikólaos's Archaeological Museum, though not in the same league as Iráklion's, is still worth a visit, as it contains finds from all over eastern Crete. Numerous artefacts come from places visited elsewhere in this book—Zákros (p 152), Móchlos (p 31), Mália (p 29) and Oloús (p 148), for

Wind Turbines

Problem: Crete experiences huge surges in demand for electricity, created by the summer influx of visitors. Further problem: Crete has only one power station. Interesting fact: Crete is one of Greece's windiest islands. Solution: the hundreds of wind turbines you'll come across in eastern Crete. Yes, that's why growing armies of these white, wildly waving monsters are marching across the landscape. Whether you think them elegant or a blot on the landscape is a matter of personal taste. But without them, power cuts would be a far greater problem than they are. And this solution to the island's energy problems isn't new—look out for the dozens of ruined windmills (or, on the Lasíthi Plateau, working ones) you'll come across all over eastern Crete.

example. It's typical of the small local museums that have sprung up all over Greece, with attractive well-labelled displays on a less intimidating scale than the big-city ones—a pleasure to visit. ⏲ *30 min. 74 Konstantinou Palaelogou St.* ☎ *28410 24943. Admission 3€ adults, 2€ concessions. Tues–Sun, Jul–Oct 8am–5.30pm, Nov–Mar 8.30am–3pm.*

Cut right down any of the side streets where alleys and/or steps lead steeply and picturesquely down to the sea. At the coast road (Akti S. Koundourou) turn left for the Municipal Beach of Ammoudi, or right for the pleasant walk back to Ágios Nikólaos's central bridge.

The second part of the tour is a short side-trip to Kritsá—by car, or by the Tourist Road Train's Excursion 3. Allow 2–3 hours.

9 ★★ **Panagia Kera.** Before reaching the one-way system in Kritsá itself, look out for a bus stop pull-off on the right, bearing a large brass plaque. Park and follow the signs past the tourist kiosk, café/bar and shop to the Byzantine church of Panagia Kera. It has the most famous set of Byzantine frescoes in Crete. The church itself doesn't follow the usual Byzantine pattern—huge buttresses have extended the normal church shape into a sort of triple triangle. Very distinctive and very attractive. ⏲ *30 min. Open 8.30am–3pm. Admission 2.35€.*

Continuing towards the centre of Kritsá to the one-way system, the site of ancient Lató is signposted off to the right. Follow the road until you arrive at the gates across the entrance to the site—it's about 2km.

10 Lató. Built by the Dorians, and under occupation throughout the classical period, this large ruined hilltop city has spectacular views all around. ⏲ *1 hr. Admission 2€. Tues–Sun 8.30am–3pm (ticket office closes 2.30pm).*

11 ★★ **Kritsá.** The traditional village sits on a hillside. Widely known for its handicrafts, its sloping streets are lined with shops selling embroidery, olive wood artefacts, pottery, ceramics, leather goods, olive oil, wine, herbs, and souvenirs. Though village merchandise isn't cheap, the fact that it's from Kritsá is said to be a guarantee of its quality. And although the village has become commercialised, there is still no doubting its authenticity, from the tiny central platía, church, and village notice board to the numerous (largely older) people staffing the shops or sitting out in the sun.

Where to **Stay**

Angelos SEAFRONT A small family-owned hotel, the Angelos offers clean rooms with airconditioning, fridge, and balcony at very reasonable rates. Its location couldn't be better—overlooking the sea, a five-minute walk north of the town centre. The ground floor minimarket (owned by the same family) is ideal for filling that fridge with drinks and snacks. *16 Koundourou* ☎ *28410 23501. 12 rooms. Doubles 35€–45€. V.*

Coral SEAFRONT Overlooking the sea but an easy five-minute stroll from the town centre, the Coral is the budget version of its sister hotel the Hermes (see below). Facilities are a little more basic than those at the Hermes, but all rooms have

Du Lac is a hotel, restaurant and café in one.

★★★ **Du Lac** LAKESIDE In a prime position on the lake right in the very centre of Ágios Nikólaos, the Du Lac is a three-in-one. At the lakeside is its highly regarded restaurant (see p 97), above that is the Café du Lac, opening onto shady, pedestrianised 28th October St, and above that is the hotel itself—reception is in the café. All rooms are en-suite, with airconditioning, fridge, and balcony, whilst the more spacious studios have a separate small kitchen. Breakfasts can be provided by the café and restaurant just downstairs. *17, 28th October St. ☎ 28410 22711. www.dulachotel.gr. 24 rooms. Doubles 50€–60€. AE, DC, MC, V.*

airconditioning, mini-fridge, and balcony, there's a rooftop pool and bar, a restaurant, and access to the small pebble beach and sun-terrace across the road. *Akti Koundourou, ☎ 28410 28363. www.mhotels.gr. 165 rooms. Doubles 87€–148€. AE, DC, MC, V.*

★★ **Hermes** SEAFRONT Virtually next door to the Coral, and owned by the same company, the Hermes is more upmarket (and more expensive). After a five-year renovation, facilities are excellent, with pool and garden on the roof (with panoramic views of the Gulf of Mirabéllo), two restaurants and bars, airconditioning, WiFi, mini bar, balcony in all rooms, fitness centre inside the hotel and dive centre outside. *Akti Koundourou. ☎ 28410 28363. www.mhotels.gr. 218 rooms. Doubles 87€–148€. 10% reduction for booking direct via Internet. AE, DC, MC, V.*

Where to **Dine**

★★ **Avli** TOWN CENTRE *GREEK* Tucked away in a back street behind the Folk Museum, this traditional, family-run Cretan tavérna does superb *mezzedes*, main courses, and local wine from the barrel, all served in a little courtyard/garden. Phone ahead—opening times are for guidance only! Reserve in July and August. Or just wait for a table. *12 Odos P Georgiou. ☎ 28410 82479.* *Entrées 8€, 12€ with wine. Open midday–3pm, 7pm–late Apr–Oct.*

★★ **Barko/Palazzo** KITROPLATIA BEACH*MEDITERRANEAN* This stylish restaurant (Barko) and café (Palazzo) on Kitroplatia beach offers a wide selection of beautifully presented *mezzedes*, pasta, fish, and meat in classy surroundings. *Kitroplatia Beach. ☎ 28410 24610.*

Where to go at Night

Ágios Nikólaos has a lively nightlife. Cafés, bars, and restaurants are open till late, and the numerous cocktail bars are thronged with young people until the wee hours—try the **Moritz**, the **Aegean**, **Ellinadiko,** or **Lotus** (details of all these are on www.cafeclub.gr). For dancing try **Mambo** (once Lipstick—they often change their names) in Stalos village west of Chaniá; for raucous fun the **Sorrento**, 23 Kounourou or the **Aquarius Pub and Sports Bar**, 4/6 Koundourou ☎ 28410 23732. But there are hundreds—just walk around the lake or the port and find one to your taste.

www.barko-palazzo.gr, email info@barko-palazzo.gr. Entrées 20€–60€. MC, V. Open 9am–after midnight. Reserve in high season and at weekends.

★ kids **Du Lac** LAKESIDE *GREEK/INTERNATIONAL* One of a string of restaurants facing the lake along Omirou, Du Lac is reckoned by locals to be the best. Service is quick and friendly, the food is fresh though not cheap, there are snacks and a children's menu. *Omirou.* ☎ *28410 22414. www.dulac-restaurant.com. Snacks from 3€, meals 5€–28€, 5.50€ children. AE, DC, MC, V. Open 8am–midnight or later.*

Pelagos restaurant.

The Best Urban Tours

Parking in Crete's Cities & Towns

Parking in Crete's larger towns or cities can be a nightmare. But remember, parking in Crete is relatively cheap.

Chaniá
Come into the town from the National Road, and grab any on-street parking you can. You'll find a fair amount, free, even around the Venetian port. Otherwise, head for the free area beside the fortress at the western end of the harbour—a five-minute walk into town.

Réthymnon
Entering the town, turn right at the end of the Public Gardens into the left-hand lane and queue for the main car park. If full, follow the traffic around to the left, drive parallel to the coast, bear left back to the coast and left along the beach. Park anywhere. Other options are the car park next to the open-air market; next to the port or the car park beyond the fortress—a fair hike into town!

Iráklion
On-street parking all over the city but the best bet is just east of the Venetian harbour. It's 2.50€ a day and only five minutes' walk into the centre. If you miss the entrance, carry on to the next roundabout, double back and try again.

Ágios Nikólaos
Lots of on-street parking. But for ease, head for the big free car park on the ferry dock. Cross the bridge, and follow the one-way system around. It's easy!

★★★ **Itanos** TOWN CENTRE *CRETAN/GREEK* Just off Platía Venizelou, the Itanos is a delight. Don't be put off by the photographs of food at the entrance—inside is a traditional, cool, Greek eating place, with high ceilings and no-nonsense tables. The food is unashamedly Cretan—kid with artichokes, beans and spinach, snails, moussaka, casseroles, and soufflés. Vegetarian options, and home-made house wine and raki. *1 Kyprou.* ☎ *28410 25340. Entrées 5€–13€. Open Apr–Oct 11am–11pm. Nov–Mar 11am–6pm.*

★★★ **Pelagos** TOWN CENTRE *FISH* One of Ágios Nikólaos's top fish restaurants, the Pelagos is set in an elegant early 20th-century mansion behind the Folk Museum. Though not cheap, the food is fresh—you can see the fish on ice in a small fishing boat in the flower-decked gardens. Meat dishes also. *Koraka and Katehaki 10 .* ☎ *28410 25737. www.pelagos-restaurant.com. Entrées 15€–20€. MC, V. Open Mar–Oct 28 midday–2am. Reservations recommended in August.* ●

5 The Great Outdoors

The Great Outdoors: Best **Beaches**

1. Georgioúpolis
2. Almirída
3. Falásarna
4. Elafonísi
5. Paleochóra
6. Réthymnon
7. Bali
8. Frangokástello
9. Palm Beach
10. Agía Pelagía
11. Tombruk
12. Mátala
13. Eloúnda
14. Ágios Nikólaos
15. Vái
16. Káto Zákros

Previous page: Coming out of Imbros Gorge.

Whatever your reason for visiting Crete, you are likely to spend at least some time on the beach—and Crete has more beaches than any other Greek island. Here is my pick of the bunch.

Chaniá Region

1 ★★ **kids** **Georgioúpolis.** A terrific urban beach, with all the facilities and showers you could need and waiter service from nearby hotels. Don't swim, though, when the red warning flag is flying. The beach north of the river is better for kids. Leave the town square and descend the hill to the river. Cross the bridge, and take the first right. The beach is a few hundred metres on, beyond a tavérna recognizable from its models of famous Greek buildings outside.

2 ★ **kids** **Almirída.** The gently shelved curve of sand next to the village is lined with cafés and tavérnas and much used by locals. Windsurfers, kayaks and catamarans are available for hire. Many of the cafés/restaurants offer British/American food and traditional Cretan options.

3 ★ **Falásarna.** On Crete's extreme north-west coast with spectacular sunsets, Falásarna lies at the bottom of a series of hairpin bends on the road from Plátanos. It's a sandy beach in a nice setting, with crystal-clear water and a few restaurants and cafés popular with locals, especially on Sundays. You need your own transport—the bus service is very sketchy.

4 ★★ **kids** **Elafonisi.** One of Crete's most famous beaches, Elafonisi is about 5 kilometres off the main road. Elafonísi itself is actually a small island, reached by wading from the main beach through shallow water. The beaches—mainland and island—are idyllic, with dazzlingly white sand, azure waters, interesting rock formations, and weed-fringed pools. An almost tropical paradise which, despite its remoteness, attracts crowds, especially during high-season weekends.

5 ★ **Paleochóra.** A small town sitting astride a narrow peninsula, Paleochóra has two totally different beaches—a stony one facing east and a sandy one facing west— 200

The North beach of Georgioúpoli is better for kids.

Réthymnon Region

6 ★★★ Réthymnon. You can't miss the town beach in Réthymnon, stretching eastwards for miles from the Venetian port. Wooden walkways take you across baking sand from the café- and restaurant-lined promenade. Though parts can be dusty and dirty, there's a lot of sand to choose from—pick your spot carefully!

7 ★★★ kids Balí. One of my favourite places in Crete, Balí lies at the bottom of a hill just off the National Road between Réthymnon and Iráklion. A little fishing village which has adapted to tourism in a big way, it's as pretty as a picture, and climbs up the hillsides above three small coves separated by headlands. The first cove has a pebble beach dominated by the swish Bali Beach Hotel, the second is the sandy town-beach proper, next to the little harbour, and the third—Paradise Beach—lies beyond and is the best for swimming.

8 ★★ Frangokástello. This sandy beach with safe bathing lies in the shadow of a ruined Venetian castle (park on the walls). Try the super café/tavérna on the beach. Owner Nectario runs it in the summer and grows and processes olives in the winter for the tavérna's olive oil.

9 ★ kids Palm Beach. Rightly considered one of Crete's most beautiful beaches, it isn't saved from high-season crowds by the difficulties of getting to it. At the foot of the cliffs dominated by Préveli Monastery, the sandy cove is surrounded by a dense palm forest. There are pools and waterfalls upstream, a small bar, and you can hire canoes and pedaloes. You can get to the beach from the cliffs above (park below the monastery), or more easily by boat from Plakiás or Ágia Galini. But be warned—it gets horribly crowded during the high season, and litter is a real problem.

Iráklion Region

10 Agía Pelágia. A busy little seaside town a short drive down from the National Road, Agía Pelágia has a good sandy beach between two rocky headlands, two hotels and lots of tavérnas, clean water, and safe swimming.

Frangoákastello beach, in the shadow of a ruined Venetian castello.

⑪ Tombruk. East of Iráklion, just past the airport, Tombruk is the nearest thing the capital has to a city beach. Three or four first-class tavérnas attract local crowds at weekends, and though there can be problems with flotsam, it tends to collect at the east end of the beach, leaving the rest of the sand clean.

⑫ ★★ kids Mátala. Facing west and equidistant from Réthymnon and Iráklion, Mátala is best known for the labyrinth of hollowed-out caves that dot the sandstone headland at the north end of the beach. It was these caves that attracted hordes of young people in the 60s, who slept in the caves and on the beach, played music, misused substances, and generally had a ball—the names Cat Stevens, Bob Dylan, and Joni Mitchell are often mentioned. It's now an agreeable, tavérna-lined, sand-and-shingle beach with a lifeguard tower, deckchair and umbrella hire, and a few colourfully-dressed young people selling jewellery.

Lasíthi Region

⑬ ★★ Eloúnda. Eloúnda has two very different beaches. Right next to the picturesque harbour is the sandy municipal beach, skirted by a tree-lined promenade and children's playground. A kilometre or so to the south, the oddly attractive causeway to the remains of ancient Oloús offers, at intervals, little sandy bays where you can swim, plus more extensive beaches at the end, around a cluster of stone windmills.

⑭ ★★ Ágios Nikólaos. Ágios Nikólaos, too, has a choice of beaches (see p 91 in Chapter 4). Each of the four has its own delights, but for cleanliness and convenience I'd go for **Kitroplatia**,

The sandy beach at Agia Pelágia.

the archetypal Greek urban beach, surrounded by tavérnas.

⑮ ★ kids Vái. Another of Crete's world famous beaches, Vái, in the relatively remote extreme northeast, owes its celebrity to its pale golden sand and forest of palm trees. If you can visit outside July and August it's well worth the trip, but at the height of the season you're lucky to see the sand for all the sunbathing bodies, and tavérnas and cafés are heaving and expensive.

⑯ ★ Káto Zákros. With its end-of-the-world feel, you probably wouldn't visit Káto Zákros if it wasn't for the Minoan Palace. But, although in itself it's nothing to write home about, the beach at Káto Zákros has an atmosphere all its own. Right next to the cluster of tavérnas and rooms-to-let that form the village, pebbles shelve down to impossibly blue water below arid red cliffs. A good place to stop for food, or even overnight.

Best **On Land**

The Great Outdoors

1. The Samariá Gorge
2. The Imbros Gorge
3. The Zákros Gorge
4. The Rodopou Peninsula
5. Loutró
6. Thrónos
7. Spili
8. Plakiás
9. Zaros
10. Lasithi Plateau
11. The Crete Golf Club
12. Avidou
13. Georgioupolis
14. Hersónisos
15. Karteros
16. Pitsidia
17. The Ark
18. Lasinthos Eco Park
19. Cretaquarium
20. Yoga Plus

Crete is one of Greece's most popular destinations for walking and trekking. Though you might feel that the climate is too hot for summer walking, this isn't the case—walks are often at high altitude, and Crete's frequent winds (p 110) help to cool things down. Routes 1 to 3 are probably Crete's best known and most popular; 4 to 10 are up-and-coming hiking areas—look out for local tourist board publications such as *Nature and Culture Routes of Lasíthi,* or ask local people at tourist offices, restaurants, or hotels for detailed directions.

❶ ★★★ The Samariá Gorge.

Crete's signature walk drops down from just south of Omalos on the fringes of the White Mountains to Agía Rouméli beside the Libyan Sea. It's spectacularly beautiful, has much of interest to see, including a range of wildlife, the deserted village of Samariá about half way down, and the so-called Iron Gates—cliffs almost 300m high on either side of the trail (though locals say they were only named the Iron Gates recently). Though rugged, the path is well maintained and clearly marked (and, polished by a million feet, very slippery, so wear rubber soles). Having said that, there are major disadvantages. The Samariá Gorge walk is long—16km with a descent of about 1200m. It's a tough challenge, even for experienced walkers—helicopters and donkeys are held in reserve to rescue the unfit, the unlucky, and the ill prepared. The Gorge is also difficult to get to. You have to make your way to the entrance by bus or taxi from wherever you're staying (parking is severely limited and often chaotic), then, after completing the walk, catch a ferry along the coast from Agía Rouméli to Hóra Sfakíon, then a bus or taxi back to base. You could book onto an excursion—they pour into the Gorge from all over Crete—so you're dropped off right at the entrance, and picked up in Hóra Sfakíon. But this is the third disadvantage—most tour buses arrive at roughly the same time, so it can become very congested. If you decide to go (during the high season Saturday is the best day), start early, take a water bottle (it can be replenished from the river and springs on the way down), wear stout shoes, a hat, and plenty of sun-screen, and take food—there's nowhere to eat until you get to the coast. Visit the informative website if you intend to walk the gorge. ⏱ *4–8 hr. www.west-crete.com/ samaria-gorge.htm. Admission 5€, free under 15. Open May–Oct 7am– sunset, depending on weather. Can also be closed at short notice if wet and/or windy.*

The last few yards of the walk through the Imbros Gorge.

The Great Outdoors

❷ ★★★ kids The Ímbros Gorge. The Ímbros Gorge, about 20km east of Samariá, is a better bet for the less intrepid. It's half the length, less than half the price, and much more accessible. It is also free of crowds most of the time. The gorge walk begins 2 kilometres south of Ímbros. The well-signposted entrance lies on a path that drops down to the left from the main road beside the Tavérna Porofarango. Though not as spectacular as its brother to the west, the Ímbros Gorge is picturesque and, though very narrow in parts, is exhilarating walking. At 8km, it's doable in two to three hours, even stopping to examine the flora and fauna and admire the views. The gorge ends at the village of Komitades. You can park at the Tavérna Porofarango, walk down through the gorge, then get a bus or taxi from Komitades back to the car. Alternatively, park in Komitades, get a bus or taxi to the gorge entrance, do the walk, and arrive back at the car. At the bottom of the gorge, both the Tavérna Ímbros and the Tavérna Komitades have information about bus times and taxi firms. Have a drink or a meal at whichever of the three tavérnas (one at the top, two at the bottom) you choose. ⏱ *2–3 hr. Admission 2€. Open Apr–Oct 7am–sunset.*

❸ ★★★ The Zákros Gorge. The Zákros Gorge offers visitors to the eastern end of Crete the chance to enjoy the delights of ravine-walking without the long traipse to the more famous Samariá Gorge in the west. It's also a lot shorter (4km) and a great deal more user-friendly. Don't be put off by its alternative name—the Valley of the Dead. It's several thousand years since anyone was buried here! Apart from the descent to the floor of the gorge, the walking is relatively easy, the views spectacular, and the flora and fauna plentiful. From the village of Ano Zákros (Upper Zákros), take the road to Káto Zákros (Lower Zákros). After about 2.5 kilometres, park next to the sign 'Footpath Zákros Gorge' and follow its directions along the dirt track (see p 152, ⓰). From the end of the dirt track (through a wooden door in a fence), a path drops steeply down to the gorge floor (take care here), then along the left-hand side of the ravine. Caves high on the sides of the ravine were

Start of the Zákros Gorge walk.

Bike safari on the Lasithi Plateau.

used by the Minoans for burying their dead. At the bottom of the gorge turn left to the Palace of Zákros (see p 30, ❾) and Káto Zákros village itself. After a meal and a swim, catch the bus or take a taxi back to the car. ⏱ *2 hr. Admission free. Open 24/7/365.*

❹ **The Rodopou Peninsula.** Virtually free of surfaced roads, the Rodopou Peninsula offers extensive opportunites for exploration on foot (see p 118).

❺ ★★★ kids **Loutró.** There is, inevitably, good walking around Loutró, since walking is the only way of getting to the village on land. In particular, the walk from Loutró to Anópoli, then through the Aradena Gorge back to the coast at Marmara, is special, but only the very fit and experienced should try it. Once in Marmara, you can walk back to Loutró (if you're still able to stand), or catch the ferry. *See p 120,* ⓯.

❻ **Thrónos.** Thrónos is rapidly becoming a centre for organised hikes into the Amári Valley and up onto Mount Psiloritis. *See p 129,* ❽.

❼ ★ kids **Spíli.** Apart from being an attractive village in its own right, Spíli lies at the heart of a network of footpaths and mule-tracks that penetrate the surrounding hills. *See p 130,* ⓭.

❽ **Plakiás.** North of the town are paths that offer the chance to explore the Kourtaliotiko and Kotsifou gorges. *See p 131,* ⓱.

❾ ★ **Zaros.** A walk to and through the Gorge of Zaros starts at the monastery of Ágios Nikólaos just west of the village. *See p 141,* ⓮.

❿ ★★★ **Lasíthi Plateau.** The whole plateau is criss-crossed with footpaths, blessedly mostly on the flat. Look out particularly for the stretch of the E4 Pan-European footpath from Ágios Georgios to Psiro, then across to Káto Metochi. *See p 153 in Chapter 6.*

⓫ ★ **The Crete Golf Club.** This is currently Crete's only 18-hole golf course. A fine course with extensive views opened in 2003, it was designed by Briton Bob Hunt to minimise its impact on the local environment. With its compact layout and desert terrain, less accurate golfers will find themselves in trouble if they stray from the fairways and greens! At 67€ for a round, it's not cheap, but then there's little competition. Twilight golf from 5pm is more cost-effective

Activity Holidays

If, rather than doing your walking independently, you'd prefer a **walking** break organised by a specialist company, check out the following websites: www.hfholidays.co.uk; www.exploreworldwide.com; www.responsibletravel.com; www.worldwalks.com; www.hidden-greece.co.uk; www.headwater.com.

For canyoning (crossing gorges using ropes and climbing equipment) and caving there can be few better places on Earth than Crete. www.cretanadventures.gr/en/act_caving.html and www.blueaegean.com.

Climbers come for the three mountain ranges that divide the four regions of Crete—the White Mountains (Lefka Ori), the Psiloritis (Idi) Mountains, and the Dikti Mountains. All rise to well over 2000 metres, and offer opportunities for hill-walking and rock-climbing. www.climbincrete.com.

(42€), but you'll struggle to get a full round in before the light goes. The club has all that you'd expect of a tournament-class course—a comfortable club house with bar/restaurant, locker rooms and pro shop, a driving range, and practice greens. Equipment—buggies, trolleys, and clubs—can be rented quite reasonably, and there's a handicap limit of 28 for men and 36 for women (and no fibbing—an hcp certificate is essential!). *The Crete Golf Club, Hersónisos.* ☎ *02897 026000. www.crete-golf.gr*.

Horse Riding

There are numerous riding stables offering lessons at all levels and rides, from canters on the beach to day tours of countryside and mountains. The following selected sites are within reach of most holiday areas in Crete.

⓬ **Avidou.** Based in the hills above Hersónisos, but with stables in Georgioúpolis, contact Unicorn Trails on www.unicorntrails.com. Also in Avidou, try Odysseia Stables; www.horseriding.gr.

⓭ **Georgioúpolis.** Zoraidas is located between the square and the river (www.zoraidas-horseriding.com).

⓮ ★ kids **Hersónisos.** On the eastern edge of Hersónisos, try www.hersonisos-horseriding.com.

Horse riding at Hersónisos.

Learn to cook with healthy local produce.

⑮ Karteros. Just east of Iráklion, try www.ippikos.gr.

⑯ Pitsidia. If you're in Mátala, go north-east to Pitsidia for www.melanouri.com.

Wildlife

Crete is one of the best places in Greece to see wildlife. Its size and topography means a full range of habitats, with a wide variety of plants, animals, and birds. The best way to bone up on the island's flora and fauna is to visit the **Natural History Museum of Crete** in Iráklion (see p 87, ⑭). For the non-specialist, the stars among Crete's birds are the eagles and vultures—up in the mountains and high plateaus, look out for Golden Eagles, Lammergeiers, and Eurasian Griffon Vultures, all with enormous wingspans. Mammals include the wild goat or kri-kri, and, off the coast, dolphins and Sperm Whales (for dolphin and whale watching, try www.interkriti.net/minicruise), whilst the most notable amphibians are the terrapins and, in particular, the Loggerhead Turtles (see box on p 114). As for farm animals, several places in Crete have collections which you can visit—⑰ ★★★ kids **The Ark**, near Vámos (see p 123, ㉘), for example, or the ⑱ ★★ kids **Lasinthos Eco Park** on the Lasíthi Plateau (see p 64, ⑱). Finally, creatures of the undersea world can be observed directly, either by snorkelling/diving, or from one of the glass-bottomed boats, or in captivity at the excellent ⑲ ★★★ kids **Cretaquarium** *(see p 64, ⑰).*

⑳ Yoga Plus. For those who want to learn or practise ashtanga yoga,

Lasinthos Eco Park on the Lasíthi Plateau.

Cretan Winds

Something that impacts on many outdoor activities—Crete is very windy! Just as Inuits have many names for snow (disputed, I know), in Crete each wind has its own name. From due north, going clockwise:
North: Vorias (Meltemi in summer), Boreas, Tramontana
North-east: Vorias Anatoliko, Gregorio, Grego
East: Anatolikna, Levante, Ageliotes
South-east: Notios Anatolikos, Sirocco, Souroko, Euros
South: Notios Ostra
South-west: Notios Ditikos, Garbis
West: Pounente, Ditikos, Zephyros
North-west: Vorias Ditikos, Maistro, Schiron
Northerly: Etesians/Meltemi.
And don't think that these winds are gentle breezes—the Notios Ostra, for example, blowing in from North Africa, can keep people indoors for days, with temperatures of 40°C or more, and everybody knows about the Meltemi in July and August—it can throw patio furniture around as if it's made of balsa wood.

Yoga Plus, in Ágios Pavlos on Crete's south coast, offers a series of courses. *www.yogaplus.co.uk/yogaplushomepage.html*.

Other Activities
Apart from walking, other activities are gaining ground in Crete:

Cooking. Crete's famously healthy diet makes it a wonderful destination for a food-based holiday. *www.cookingincrete.com*.

Cycling. Cycling as a holiday activity is really beginning to catch on in Crete. The island's rugged landscape is ideal for mountain biking,

Get off the beaten track with a guide-led jeep safaris.

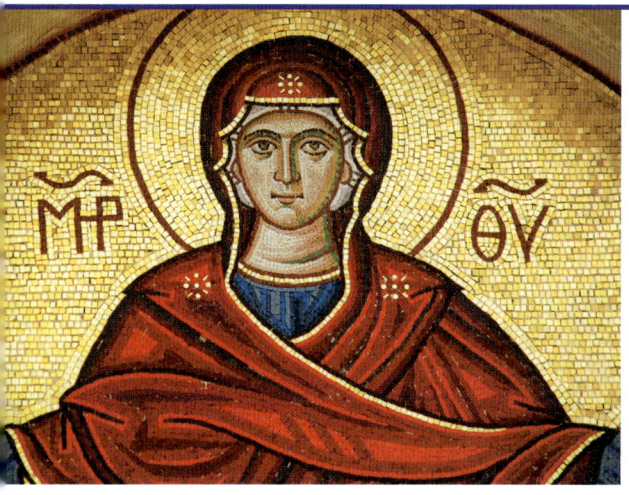

Mosaic above a church door.

and large plateaus such as the one that gives its name to Lasithi province provide more sedate, less hilly road cycling. Check out: *www.cycling.gr; www.hellasbike.net; www.footscapesofcrete.com/mountainbikingincrete.htm; www.olympicbike.com; www.cyclegreece.gr; www.greeka.com/greece/greece-mountain-biking.htm.*

Jeep Safaris. A guide-led jeep safari is a good (if rather environmentally dubious) way of getting off the beaten track, and fleets of jeeps are appearing in many parts of Crete. *www.cretejeepsafari.eu; www.blueaegean.com/Alternate%20Tourism/jeep_safaris.htm; www.kavi.gr/Packages/Outdoor_Activities_en/Jeep_Safari; www.crete-holidays.net/jeep_safari_eng.html.*

Paragliding. 45 Cretan paragliding sites are listed on the ICNA website *www.icna.gr.*

Rafting. Though limited by the lack of water in many parts of Crete during the summer, upland torrents provide exciting rafting (descending in large inflatable rafts usually with six to eight paddlers and a professional guide) or monorafting (single inflatable boats with one guide to 6 to 8 boats) throughout the year. *www.infohub.com/travel_packages/canoeing_kayaking_rafting_greece_197.html.*

Religious Tourism. Crete's great wealth of early Christian and Byzantine art and architecture has led to an increasing influx of religious tourists—not only Cretans themselves and other Orthodox Greeks intent on pilgrimage, but also Russian Orthodox people from eastern Europe and non-Orthodox Christians wanting to admire the island's wealth of ecclesiastical buildings or follow in the footsteps of St Paul. Many secular admirers of Byzantine art and architecture, too, want to visit the numerous Byzantine churches, both large and small, on the island, for their architecture, décor, and colourful icons and frescoes. You can, of course, visit Byzantine sites under your own steam, but it is also possible to join specifically religious tours. *www.christiantours.gr.*

Best **At Sea**

- **1** Paleochóra
- **2** Sougia
- **3** Agia Roumeli
- **4** Hóra Sfakion
- **5** Plakiás
- **6** Ágia Galini

Best At Sea

With its long coastline, clear water, and frequent winds, it's no wonder that Crete has become one of the foremost countries in Europe for many water-based activities and sports. Beaches in the most popular tourist areas have boat and canoe hire, and many offer water-skiing, windsurfing, jet-skiing, and parascending. Similarly, virtually every port and harbour has its lines of quayside kiosks selling excursions by boat. Some are glass-bottomed to observe the aquatic world that thrives beneath the surface. Many excursions include drinks, a picnic, and bathing on the way—simply browse the hoardings, read the brochures, compare what's on offer and the prices, fight off the touts, and choose.

Ferries. A delightful way to travel is on one of Crete's south-coast ferries—they're cheap and reliable. A regular service links ❶ ★ **Paleochóra**, ❷ **Sougia**, ❸ **Agía Roumeli**, ❹ **Hóra Sfakion**, ❺ **Plakiás** and ❻ ★ **Ágia Galini**. From the north coast regular ferries link Crete with the mainland and with other islands. *www.cretetravel.com/To_and_from_Crete/Ferries_Crete.html.*

Water Sports

Diving. There are diving schools all over Crete, many of them attached to hotels. Wherever you're staying, the following list should include a dive centre near you:

Agía Pelágia: Amoudara and Mália: www.diversclub-crete.gr.

Ágios Nikólaos: www.divecrete.com.

Chaniá: www.blueadventuresdiving.gr

Hersónisos: www.scubakreta.gr

Hóra Sfakion: www.notosmare.com

Iráklion and around: www.eurodiving.gr

Plakiás: www.scubacrete.com and www.seadream-divers.com

Réthymnon: www.diving-center.gr

Sailing. Sailing can involve anything from an afternoon in a hired dinghy to an extended trip in a flotilla sailing around the coast. Small dinghies can usually be rented off the beach, but for anything more complicated (and expensive) you

Yachting off the coast of Ágios Nikólaos.

Saving the Loggerhead Turtles of Crete

The beaches near Réthymnon have been the birthplace of Loggerhead Turtles for millions of years. However, tourist development is causing a dramatic decline in the number of nesting turtles. During the nesting season, a team of international conservation volunteers can usually be seen protecting egg-laying adults and day-old hatchlings, especially on the sandy beaches east of the town. The volunteers carry out night beach patrols to prevent interference and ensure the beach is free from tourist clutter. They mark and monitor new nests, then 2 months later undertake dawn beach patrols to protect emerging hatchlings from over-eager tourists, and light and sound disorientation from nearby developments. Volunteers also hold information and slide shows at beachside hotels and have an information stand in the centre of Réthymnon. The best time to see adult Loggerhead Turtles is at night between June and August; hatchlings can be seen making their way to the sea at night and early morning between August and October.

To learn more about the turtles and find out how to become a volunteer, visit www.archelon.gr, visit the Réthymnon information booth, or read *Wildlife and Conservation Volunteering* by Peter Lynch, published by Bradt guides, Feb 2009.

need to go through a specialist company. Particularly suitable for all ages and levels of expertise, and for singles, couples, and groups, flotilla holidays can be socially inclusive and very reasonably priced. My personal recommendation, offering a wide range of different sorts of sailing holidays is www.sunvilsailing.co.uk. *Also try www.sail-the-net.com/yacht-charter/destinations/mediterranean/greece/crete.html; www.cosmosyachting.com/yacht-charter-greece-island-crete.htm.*

Check out the companies where you are staying:

Almirida (website's in French): www.ucpa.com/centre_sportif/almirida.htm UCPA

Ierapetra: www.ierapetra.net/nautilos

Mirthios: www.kalypsodivingcenter.com

Plakiás: www.dive2gether.com

Réthymnon: www.atlantis-creta.com ●

Dive centre and swimming platforms in Ágios Nikólaos.

6 The Best
Regional Tours

The Best Regional Tours

Chaniá Region

1. Golden Fun Park
2. German War Cemetery
3. The Olive Tree of Vouvés
4. Goniá Monastery
5. Afráta
6. Afráta Beach
7. Elafonisi
8. Paleochóra
9. Portofino
10. Kándanos
11. Vrisses
12. Askífou Plateau
13. The Ímbros Gorge
14. Hóra Sfakíon
15. Loutró
16. The Blue House
17. The Venizélos Graves
18. Koukouvayia Café
19. Stavrós
20. Monastery of Agia Triáda
21. Allied War Cemetery & Soúda Bay
22. The Stone Garden
23. Kalíves
24. Almirida
25. Dimitris
26. Kokkinó Horió
27. Vámos
28. The Ark

Where to Stay

Daskalogiannis Hotel 29
Grecotel Kalliston 30
Hotel Pal Beach 31
Kalíves Beach Hotel 32
S.A. Guest Houses 33

Where to Dine

East of Eden 34
The Good Heart 35
Koumos, Stone Garden 36
Ostria 37

Previous page: Church of the Panyia, Fodele.

Chaniá Region

Chaniá region contains some of Crete's most varied and interesting holiday experiences, from barren mountains to sandy beaches, gorges to plateaus, big holiday resorts to tiny villages. It's the backdrop against which the tragedy of the Battle of Crete was played out during World War II. It has Crete's best walking. It has lots for kids, and it is served by the island's only major airport outside the capital. All tours start in Chaniá. All can be done in a day, though you might want to spread things out over several days.

Tour 1: West Coast (Round trip 210km)

Follow the old coast road (not the National Road) west out of Chaniá—signposted Plataniás/Kastélli Kissámou. Before reaching the town limits, look out for the Golden Fun Park on the right. 1km.

❶ ★★★ kids Golden Fun Park. A well planned and run all-weather park that appeals across the age ranges with bumper boats, mini-golf, go-karts, trampolines, inflatable slides, a bouncy castle, indoor play area, a room of arcade games, five pool tables, and an eight-lane bowling alley. Refreshment is available in a café and snack-bar—pizzas, sandwiches, toasties (4€–8€), and there's a large and friendly staff. ⏱ *1 hr–all day. Káto Daratso.* ☎ *28210 32132. www.goldenfunpark.gr. Admission 5€ each for indoor and outdoor (includes 1 drink), plus additional charges for bowling, mini-golf, pool. Internet access 2€. Open 10am–11pm for play areas, check website for individual activities.*

Continue for 17km along the coast road, through to Máleme. There are lots of beaches, cafés, hotels, and restaurants along this stretch of coast.

❷ ★ German War Cemetery. Signposted from the main coast road, the German War Cemetery stands above Máleme airfield, which was where the Germans, at huge cost in lives, established a bridgehead from which they conquered the island. Four and a half thousand young men lie buried here on what is now a peaceful hillside overlooking the sea, but which was, in 1941, the scene of indescribable carnage. ⏱ *30 min. See p 43,* ❷.

Take a 6km detour south to Voúves a kilometre or so after Tavronitis.

❸ kids The Olive Tree of Voúves. At a thumping 3000 years, the Voúves olive tree is probably the oldest in the world. Imagine—it had already passed its thousandth birthday when Jesus was a boy! ⏱ *15 min. See p 53,* ❶.

This famed olive tree in Voúves is said to be over 3,000 years old.

The pleasant beach at Afráta.

Back at the coast, drive through Kolimbari onto the Rodopou Peninsula, heading for Afráta. 5km.

4 Goniá Monastery. Pleasantly set in its own gardens, the monastery is worth a quick visit. Look out for the Turkish cannonball still lodged in one of its walls. This was where German bodies from all over Crete were assembled before being reinterred in the German War Cemetery in the early 1970s. ⏱ *15 min. Open mornings and late afternoons.*

5 ★★ Afráta. A further 3km brings you to Afráta, a hamlet with a couple of tavérnas (see below) and, at the bottom of a long hill, a pleasant, if rocky, little beach. The road stops here—for advice on exploring the rest of the Rodopou peninsula, look at www.cretanvista.gr. If you do decide to walk, that'll see off the rest of the day.

6 Afráta Beach. A short drive down from the village brings you to Afráta Beach, a pebbly cove between rocky headlands. Have a swim, and get refreshments from the seasonal kantina. *No Phone. $.*

Drive back to the National Road past Kastélli Kissámou, then turn south parallel to Crete's west coast. Wooded mountains, sea views, pretty villages—it's a far cry from the tourist strip either side of Chaniá. At Kefali, bear right to Elafonisi. Total distance 70km.

7 ★★ kids Elafonisi. Fine pink-tinged sand, warm opaline water, all protected from the open sea by a low-lying island (Elafonísi itself) to which you can wade, this is close to paradise. Though remote, summer crowds drive here, or catch a boat from Paleochóra. National Park status keeps away the worst excesses of development, and therefore of facilities, but you can get food and drink at a handful of seasonal kantinas.

Take the road to Sfakia and join the main Paleochóra road there. 32km.

8 ★ Paleochóra. Sitting astride a small peninsula, Paleochóra is an attractive small town with two beaches—one sandy (facing west), the other pebbly—a few shops, lots of cafés and restaurants, and the remains of a castle.

9 Portofino. Overlooking the pebbly, east-facing beach, the Portofino does good pizzas in a proper oven. ☎ 28230 41114. $.

Drive north to Kándanos. 17km.

10 Kándanos. A force of Greek irregulars held up the pursuing German army for two days here in World War II and as punishment the whole village was wiped out 'Never to be rebuilt' as the German plaque has it. The village *was* rebuilt, which is no doubt why the plaque is allowed to remain, next to one celebrating the bravery of the Cretan defenders.

Tour 2: To the South Coast (Round trip 156km)

Drive east on the National Road (signposted Réthymnon) for about 25km. Turn right for Vrísses. In the town, turn left and park. Walk back across the bridge into town. 32km.

11 ★ Vrísses. There's nothing specific to stop for in Vrísses, yet with its wealth of old plane trees, the rushing water of the river (when it hasn't dried up), the tavérnas

The green patchwork of the Askifou Plateau.

An entrance to the Ímbros Gorge.

thronged with locals, it's a good place for a coffee or a meal. Look out for the statue of a kri-kri, the mountain goat native to Crete.

From Vrísses, the road climbs up into the impressive White Mountains. White? Yes—snow in winter, bare limestone for the rest of the year.

12 Askífou Plateau. After an exhilarating 12km climb, the road tops a rise, and suddenly the Askifou Plateau stretches out below you like a lush green quilt cupped by the arid peaks surrounding it. The ruins of a Turkish castle sit atop a conical hill, and, in Askífou village, signs invite you to inspect the private 'War Museum 1941–1946' (opening times vary, no admission charge but donations welcome). Most of today's tour follows the route taken by the Allied forces fleeing the victorious Germans in 1941. *See p 45,* **7**.

Once across the plateau, climb up into the mountains. After 6km, look out for the Café-Tavérna Porofarango on the left.

The Best Regional Tours

⑬ ★★★ kids The Ímbros Gorge. The entrance to the Gorge slopes steeply down from just below the tavérna. It's more manageable than the celebrated Samariá Gorge to the west (8km rather than 16km), less crowded, cheaper (2€ rather than 5€), and easier to manage. *For detailed information on managing the walk, see p 106,* ❷. ⏲ 2–3 hr. Admission 2€.

Continue south via a series of hairpin bends to the coast. At the bottom of the hill, sweep around to the right and drive down into Hóra Sfakion. 15km.

⑭ ★★ Hóra Sfakion. Clustered around its little harbour, Hóra Sfakion is every inch the small Cretan fishing village and seaside town. But it's a lot more than that. Two monuments bear witness to its place as the Dunkirk of the Battle of Crete. From here, under constant Luftwaffe attack, 10,000 – 12,000 British, Australian, and New Zealand troops were evacuated to Egypt. The monument commemorating this heroic event stands prominently next to the harbour; the one to the even more heroic local people who helped the Allies, and died in the subsequent Nazi reprisals, stands half way down the hill into the town. Not that World War II was the only violence suffered by the town and the region. Sfakion is notorious for its family vendettas—one such feud led, over the years, to 90 deaths, ending as recently as 1960. *See p 46,* ❽.

Park near the harbour, and buy a ferry ticket for Loutró (4€) at the kiosk). The boat goes from Hóra Sfakion to Paleochóra, stopping at Loutró, Agia Roumeli, and Sougia.

⑮ ★★★ kids Loutró. One of the prettiest of the south coast villages, Loutró is a fifteen-minute hop along this beautifully barren coast. A crescent of white cuboid houses with blue doors and shutters arches around a bay beneath ochre cliffs. Restaurants line the pebble beach, and holidaymakers paddle canoes or splash about in the clear water. You'll be accompanied off the ferry by supplies carried on wheelbarrows or little motorised carts—the only mechanised transport. Access to the village (except for a long hot hike from Hóra Sfakion) is exclusively from the sea.

The coastal town of Hóra Skakion.

Chaniá Region

The picturesque village of Loutró.

16 The Blue House. One of the many tavérnas that line the beach at Loutró. Have a swim, then eat. ☎ 28250 91127. $.

Tour 3: The Akrotiri & Drapano Peninsulas (Round trip 100km)
From Chaniá, follow signs east towards the airport. As you climb the hill out of the town, look out for signs for the Venizélos Graves off to the left. 6km.

17 ★ The Venizélos Graves. Eleftheríos Venizélos (1864–1936), Prime Minister of the whole of Greece on numerous occasions from 1910 to 1933, chose to be buried at the scene of one of his greatest triumphs. His grave, and that of his son Sophocles (1894–1964), sit in landscaped parkland which also contains a church and a statue of the raising of the Greek flag. It's a popular Cretan day out, and there are several popular cafés next to the monument. ⏱ 1 hr. See p 38, ❸.

18 Koukouvayia Café. Just below the graves, a lively café with terrace overlooking great views across Chaniá. A good place to have drinks and crepes. ☎ 28210 27449. $.

Beyond the Venizélos Graves, turn left off the main airport road, following signs to Stavrós. 12km.

19 Stavrós. No more than a half-hour drive from Chaniá lies a series of popular beaches along Akrotiri's west coast, culminating in the one at Stavrós. This is the pick of the bunch so, in summer, the most crowded. The mountain that partially encloses the almost circular bay is where the final scene—the collapse of the mine—in *Zorba the Greek* was filmed.

Old corn mill equipment, a few of the random things on display at the Stone Garden.

Glass ornaments on sale in Kokkinó Horió.

Retrace your route for 3km then follow signs left for Agia Triáda. 8km.

㉠ ★ Monastery of Agia Triáda. A superb example of Cretan Venetian-style architecture from the 17th century, Moni Zangarolo, as it is sometimes called, is the nearest monastery to the holiday areas around Chaniá. A working religious settlement, its stonework is ruddy gold in colour, intricate in design, and set among peaceful olive groves and fields. ⏱ *15 min. Admission 2€. Open 9am–7pm.*

Return past the airport, following signs for Soúda and the Allied War Cemetery. 17km.

㉡ ★ Allied War Cemetery & Soúda Bay. Superbly set at the end of Soúda Bay and beautifully maintained, the ranks of plain white headstones surrounding a large cross look out across the natural harbour where, in 1941, Allied warships were under constant attack from German dive bombers. As with the German War Cemetery, the youth of the fighting men buried here is almost unbearably poignant. *See p 45,* ❻.

Drive through Soúda to the National Road then, about 5km east, follow the signs to Kalami. You are now on the old coast road. Head for Kalives. As you enter the village, turn right at the IN.KA supermarket, drive under the National Road, then turn left and left again. About 10km.

㉢ ★ kids The Stone Garden. A delightful oddity, this. Built in the grounds of the Tavérna Koumos, it consists of a cave, chapel, house, museum, shepherd's hut (the koumos), tables, chairs—all built from knobbly stones collected in the White Mountains by owner Giorgos Havaledakis. There are (real) sheep, goats, and puppies, and pieces of arcane agricultural equipment. All free for the price of a drink or some food. *See p 53,* ❷.

Return to the main road and turn right into Kalives for 1km.

㉣ Kalives. Despite determined villa-building, Kalives is still unspoilt, with a good range of shops and a pleasant beach. A nice place to stop for a coffee (or even for a few nights) is the Kalives Beach Hotel (see below).

Follow the signs for Almirída. 3km.

㉔ ★ kids Almirída. Something of a British ex-pat enclave, Almirída has a sheltered Blue Flag beach with a row of highly reckoned tavérnas on and just behind it—most grow their own vegetables and catch their own fish. You can hire boats and windsurfers in the village. *Pre-book on ☎ 28250 31443).*

㉕ Dimitris. Stop for lunch at this excellent fish tavérna on the beach at Almirída, with a lot of its food home-grown. But do also browse the other restaurants on the beach, especially Psaros, Thalami, and Lagos—they're all very good. *☎ 28250 31303. $.*

From Almirída, climb up through Plaka towards Kokkinó Horió. 2km.

㉖ ★ kids Kokkinó Horió. Literally 'red village', referring presumably either to its geology or its politics, Kokkinó Horió was used for the village scenes in the film *Zorba the Greek*. Just before arriving in the village, look out for an ivy-covered building with a mountain of broken bottles outside it. This is the glass-recycling plant of Andreas Tzompanakis, where you can watch the glass-blowers at work, or buy rather retro glass ornaments. *Open 8am–8pm. Glass-blowers at work 8am–midday, 1–3pm.*

Continue south to Kefalas, then bear right for 5km to Vámos. 11km.

㉗ Vámos. The regional capital, Vámos is at the heart of Cretan agri-tourism—the attempt to combat rural depopulation by replacing departing young people with tourists. Vámos S.A., formed by local people in 1995, rents out a variety of beautifully renovated houses, and also runs a tavérna, an Arts Café, a shop, and a travel agency. *(Check out www.vamossa.gr, and below).*

In the village, ask directions to the Ark—it's rather complicated!

㉘ ★★★ kids The Ark. Just outside Vámos is another of Drapano's quirky attractions—The Ark. It's an ostrich farm with a shop and a restaurant that sells ostrich omelettes and ostrich sausages. But it's also a petting zoo, with ponies, cows, llamas, deer, pigs and poultry, a playground, and a picnic area. And there's a religious dimension—the site includes a grotto of St John, a large religious icon, a monument to Hippocrates, and a chapel. The whole site is pleasantly wooded, and hangs below awe-inspiring views of the White Mountains. *⏱ 1 hr. Kivotos. ☎ 69791 06886. Admission 2€, children 1€. Refunded if you spend more than 10€ in the park. Opening times vary. Phone ahead.*

Proceed west to the National Road to return to Chaniá.

Pet ponies at the Ark near Vámos.

Chaniá Region

Where to **Stay**

Children's play area at the Kalives Beach Hotel.

★★ **Daskalogiannis Hotel**

LOUTRO   A comfortable little hotel, the Daskalogiannis offers cool, clean bedrooms, all with balconies looking out across the bay. The café has outside tables and chairs next to a small boat dock, and Internet facilities. *Loutró Sfakia, Chaniá.* ☎ *28250 91514. http://loutro.com/daska.htm. 11 rooms. Doubles 45€–65€ w/breakfast. AE, DC, MC, V. Open Apr–Oct.*

★★★ **Grecotel Kalliston** NEA KYDONIA

On the beach side of the coast road west of Chaniá, just under 5km from the centre of Chaniá (the bus stops directly across the road), the Grecotel Kalliston is a medium-sized hotel with the feel of a much bigger one. Three restaurants, two bars, three pools, a full programme of kids' and adults' activities, sport, and night time activities. *Glaros, Nea Kydonia.* ☎ *28210 34400. www.grecotel.com. 127 rooms. Doubles 120€–304€ w/breakfast. AE, DC, MC, V. Open Apr–Oct.*

Hotel Pal Beach PALEOCHORA

One of 15 small hotels advertised by the local Hotel Owners Association (www.paleochora-holidays.gr), the Pal Beach provides clean and pleasant rooms on two floors facing the beach. All rooms have balconies, fridge, and fan. In-hotel facilities are limited to a snack-bar, but all the town's facilities—cafés, restaurants, shops, banks, etc—are within easy walking distance. *Paleochóra.* ☎ *28230 41512. www.palbeach.gr. 52 rooms. Doubles 70€–96€ w/breakfast. Credit cards accepted, but with a lot of paper work. Open Apr–Oct.*

★★ **Kalives Beach Hotel** KALIVES

Within walking distance of Kalives's cafés, restaurants, and shops, the Kalives Beach is beautifully located where the river Xydas runs into the sea. The hotel has private access to a sandy beach (across a footbridge), and a hotel terrace with river and sea views. *Kalives Apoloronou.* ☎ *28250 31285. www.kalyvesbeach.com. 100 rooms. Doubles 120€–140€. AE, DC, MC, V. Open early Apr–end of Oct.*

★★ **S.A. Guest Houses** VAMOS

A mixture of traditional houses renovated to a high standard (an inn, a wine store, a doctor's house, an olive oil mill), and new houses built on traditional lines, dotted around the Vámos area. No hippy austerity here—all have full mod cons and a pool or access to one. Involvement in local activities—walking, cooking, harvesting—is an option, but not compulsory. *Vámos Apokoronou.* ☎ *28250 23251. www.vamossa.gr. Doubles 65€–180€. Open all year except for Christmas period.*

Where to **Dine**

Koumos, Stone Garden.

★★ **East of Eden** MÁLEME *CRETAN* This is what the Greeks do best—a family-run tavérna with lots of indoor seating for the winter, and outdoor tables on a terrace and on the beach itself for Crete's long summer. Food's excellent (and very reasonable), service is fast, and kids have acres of beach to play on, and a wooden slide inside. When we were there, a power cut brought out the best in the staff—until generators could be deployed, they carried on serving what they could cook without electricity, by the light of the headlights of a cluster of cars. *Pirgos Psilonerou.* 28210 62083. *Entrées 7€–15€. Open May–Oct 'All day long'.*

★★★ **The Good Heart** AFRATA *CRETAN* A typical, small, family-run village tavérna/ouzeri, the Good Heart (Kali Kardia) is the next best thing to eating in somebody's house. The owners raise their own chickens, rabbits, and goats, make their own wine, and food is served on a flower- and vine-bedecked terrace with multi-coloured gourds hanging from the trellis. Don't be put off by the English-transport-café- type menu—ask what's good, and order it. Some chicken and rabbit meals take a long time—be prepared to wait, or phone ahead. *Afráta.* 0824 22077. *Entrées 6€–12€. Open 9am–late.*

Koumos, Stone Garden KALIVES *CRETAN* Set in an eccentric wonderland made of rock, overlooked by the distant grey bulk of the White Mountains, expect traditional good food here. There are farmyard animals to feed, and the owner, one of the local characters, is very laid back—when we were there he was busy, so he let us make our own coffee. *Kalives Apokoronou, Chaniá.* 28250 32257. *Entrées 9€–20€. Open 10am–late.*

Ostria PALEOCHORA *GREEK* The Ostria is a large restaurant across the road from the sandy beach, with a good range of Greek dishes, well-cooked and plentiful, and prompt service. At the back, a little folk museum contains household implements—a loom, a fiddle, textiles, and much more. The owner has a cage of birds to keep inquisitive children entertained. *Paleochóra.* 28230 41986. *Entrées 7€–19€. Open midday–1am.*

The flower and vine bedecked terrace at the Good Heart.

Réthymnon Region

The Best Regional Tours

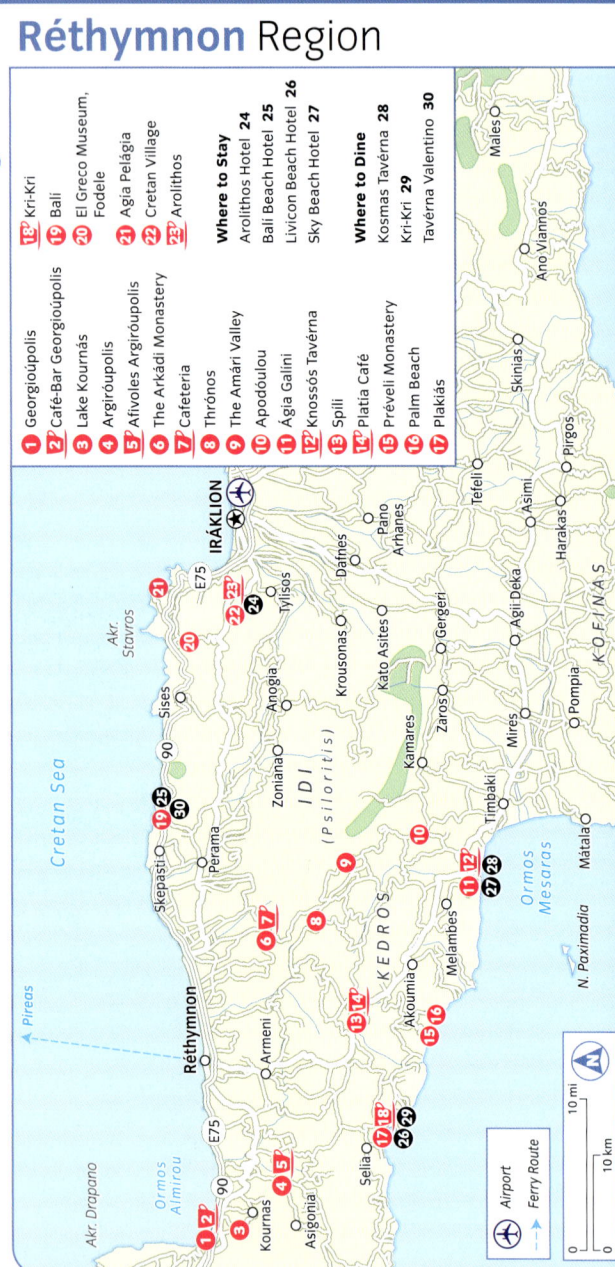

1. Georgioúpolis
2. Café-Bar Georgioúpolis
3. Lake Kournás
4. Argiroúpolis
5. Afivoles Argiroúpolis
6. The Arkádi Monastery
7. Cafeteria
8. Thrónos
9. The Amári Valley
10. Apodóulou
11. Ágia Galini
12. Knossós Tavérna
13. Spili
14. Platia Café
15. Préveli Monastery
16. Palm Beach
17. Plakiás
18. Kri-Kri
19. Bali
20. El Greco Museum, Fodele
21. Agia Pelágia
22. Cretan Village
23. Arolithos

Where to Stay
Arolithos Hotel 24
Bali Beach Hotel 25
Livicon Beach Hotel 26
Sky Beach Hotel 27

Where to Dine
Kosmas Tavérna 28
Kri-Kri 29
Tavérna Valentino 30

Réthymnon region is, in many ways, similar to Chaniá region. It has a substantial mountain range (Psiloritis), good inland walking (the Amári Valley, the area around Spíli), attractive south coast resorts (Plakiás, Ágia Galíni) and some of Crete's best-known monasteries (Arkádi and Préveli), each associated with two of Crete's greatest struggles against invasion. All tours start in Réthymnon and can be done in 1 day though you might want to linger and spread things out over several days.

Tour 1: West of Réthymnon (Round trip 68km)

Drive west from Réthymnon along the National Road. Come off at Georgioúpolis and drive into the town where there's ample parking. 22km.

❶ ★★ kids Georgioúpolis. The town marks the beginning of a long sandy beach (I measured it at over 10km) lined at the town end with hotels and cafés which will serve refreshments on the sand. There are treacherous currents, though, so watch out for warning flags. Between the beach and the square is the starting point for a tourist road train (the Talos Express) offering tours of local beauty spots. Beyond the square, the road runs down to the river, a bridge, fishing boat moorings, and a booth where you can hire pedaloes and canoes. The river is reedy, a prime spot for seeing loggerhead turtles and terrapins. For safer bathing than at the town beach, cross the bridge and turn right for **Kalivaki** beach—safe, sandy, and with views of a pretty little chapel on the breakwater. *See p 60,* ❹.

❷ Café-Bar Georgioúpolis. Used by locals as well as visitors, this is a good place to stop for refreshment—drinks, breakfasts, snacks—and watch the world go by. *On the main square. No phone. $.*

Follow the signs out of Georgioúpolis for 7km to Lake Kournás.

❸ ★ kids Lake Kournás. Crete's only freshwater lake has a little community of tavérnas, cafés, and shops selling ceramic ware at the lakeside. You can hire pedaloes (7€) and canoes (4€), and there's a wealth of wildlife—fish (especially eels), frogs, turtles, birds, insects—with information boards to tell you what to look out for. There's even a local folk tale that tells how the lake was a village flooded by God because of the sins of its inhabitants, with the only virtuous villager—the priest's daughter—spared by being turned into a water-sprite. *See p 60,* ❺.

Pedalos for hire at Lake Kournás.

Beyond Kournás, follow signposts for Argiróupolis. The road climbs prettily between trees and streams. Beware potholes! 14km.

4 ★★ **kids** **Argiróupolis.** First comes the lower village, where five tavérnas climb the steep banks of rushing streams under huge chestnut, plane, and walnut trees. All have a good reputation for fish and meat dishes, and all have built-in water features—water wheels, bells, cascades, tanks of live fish. Stop here for lunch (see Tavérna Afivoles below), then go to the upper village. Sleepy, traditional little **Argiróupolis** has extensive views and a checkered history—look out for the Dorian/Roman remains of ancient Lappa, another church (**Agía Paraskevi**) which has a Minoan child's sarcophagus as the step into the churchyard, a handsome Roman mosaic, and a reservoir built by the Emperor Octavius in 27 BC—still, apparently in use. Ask at Lapa Avocado Beauty Products, (right, through the archway, and it's on your left) for a free plan of the village with everything marked. Or book a donkey tour *(Stelios or Joanna on ☎ 28310 81070).*

5 **Afivoles Argiróupolis.** Stop at this or indeed any of the tavérnas in the lower village for a snack or for a full meal. ☎ *28310 81011/82452.* $.

A local man from Argiróupolis.

Return to the National Road via Episkopi. 25km.

Tour 2: Arkádi Monastery, the Amári Valley, & the South Coast (Round trip 162/224km, depending on your return route)
Take the National Road east. After about 6km, turn right, and drive (through Pigi and Loutró,) the 17km to the monastery's free car park.

6 ★★ **kids** **The Arkádi Monastery.** Venerated as the ultimate symbol of Cretan resistance to the Turks, the Arkádi Monastery is a mellow building attractively set in the mountains with a tragic, if uplifting, story. In 1866 a Cretan rebellion was put down with ferocity by the Turkish occupiers. Civilians escaping from Réthymnon fell back to the monastery. Three hundred armed Cretans, protecting over 700 sheltering women and children, were besieged by 15,000 Turkish troops with 30 cannons. The defenders fought heroically but when it became clear on the second day that defeat was imminent, the Cretans locked themselves into the gunpowder store where they blew up themselves and their tormentors. Wander around the Venetian monastery church, the arched cloisters, the monks' cells, store rooms, and food treatment rooms. There's a shop selling icons and other religious items, and a small museum.

The cloisters of the Arkádi monastery.

Look out for the piece of shrapnel lodged in the blasted olive tree that stands in the courtyard outside the church, the roofless gunpowder store where the explosion occurred, and, on the way back to the car park, the old windmill which is now the 'Heroes Memorial', with busts of the Cretan leaders outside, and, within, the skulls of over 60 of the defenders, showing damage caused by bullets, swords, or the final explosion. See p 40, **7**. ⏱ *1 hr. No phone. Admission 3€. Open 8am–7pm, all year.*

7 **Cafeteria.** Take refreshment at the monastery cafeteria, just across the car park. *No phone. $.*

Turn left out of the car park onto the road to Thrónos. Some maps mark it as a dirt road. It's not—it's new tarmac! 8km.

8 **Thrónos.** Standing at the head of the Amári Valley on a hill that does indeed look like a throne, Thrónos was originally Minoan Sybritos—you can see the ruins of its acropolis by following a path behind the church.

Turn left towards Fourfouras.

9 ★★ **The Amári Valley.** You are now travelling along the Amári Valley, through villages surrounded by vineyards and olive groves, dominated by the grey Psiloritis Mountains to your left. In this burgeoning hiking area, the bustle and noise of the coast seem a million miles away. Take a 5km detour to Amári itself, whose steeply raked roofs, wood-fire chimneys, and Venetian clock tower are more like the Italian Alps than the heart of Greece's hottest island. Back on the main road, drive through Fourfouras (fill up with petrol if you're low) and Nithavris, after which the road splits. Turning right will bring you to the west Amári villages, scene of one of the worst German atrocities during World War II. In reprisals after the kidnapping of General Kreipe (see p 138, **3**), the villages were destroyed and their male occupants massacred. The buildings you see date entirely from after the war.

White buildings on the cliffs at Ágia Galíni.

❿ Apodóulou. For a more uplifting trip back into history, go straight on to the village of Apodóulou, and ask a local to point out the ruins of the House of Kalitsa Psaraki. The daughter of a local official, she was one of a group of girls abducted by the Turks during the Greek War of Independence and sold into slavery in Egypt. In Alexandria slave market, she and her companions were spotted by Scottish traveller, Egyptologist and all-round good chap, Robert Hay, who bought their freedom, shipped them back to Britain, and paid for their education in England. Inevitably, he and Kalitsa fell in love and they married (in 1828), and lived happily ever after.

Continue south to the coastal town of Ágia Galíni. From Thrónos to Ágia Galíni—30km.

⓫ ★ Ágia Galíni. Ágia Galíni, with its white buildings, small harbour, flowers, sandstone cliffs, and palm trees, is an attractive town, though crowded in the summer. There's a beach just around the headland from the harbour—a 5-minute walk along a path past World War II gun emplacements. There are excursions from the harbour to dolphin-watch, to visit the Paximadia Islands, or along the coast to Palm Beach and the Préveli Monastery (see below).

⓬ Knossós Tavérna. Ágia Galíni has a comprehensive range of cafés and restaurants for a midday meal. The Knossós has good Cretan food and great views of the harbour. ☎ *69390 52232*. $.

Drive north-west to Melambes. It's an occasionally pot-holed road with extensive views of the mountains ahead and back towards the coast. Join the main road to Réthymnon and head for Spíli. 30km.

⓭ ★ kids Spíli. Built into a rocky hillside, Spíli has a clearly defined village square where water cascades out of the cliff face below a pleasant tavérna terrace and runs along a trough to emerge from the mouths of 25 lion-head spouts. A network of alleys and steps climbs steeply beyond the square. Like the Amári Valley, hiking is a growing attraction in the area—hence the walkers cooling their feet in the icy water.

14 Platía Café. If you didn't stop for refreshment in Ágia Galíni, try the Platía, which has a shady terrace overlooking the lion-head spouts. *No phone. $.*

Continue towards Réthymnon for about 3km then turn left towards Asomatos . Look for signs to Moni Préveli on the left. The road climbs through rugged mountain scenery, past the atmospheric ruins of the lower St John's monastery. 21km.

15 ★★★ Préveli Monastery. Préveli Monastery's fame stems from the central part it played in helping Allied soldiers, mainly Australians, to escape after being left behind after the evacuation from Hóra Sfakíon (see p 46 in Chapter 3). Just before you get to the monastery there's an impressive statue of a gun-toting Greek Orthodox priest standing beside a similarly armed Allied soldier. Plaques in Greek and English mark the successful hiding during the war of 5000 troops (many of whom were taken off by submarine), and also salute the bravery of the Abbot Agathangelos Langouvardos. The monastery itself is one of Crete's most beautiful. Set on its promontory high above the sea, it has a small museum and a café which serves snacks and drinks. *30 min. Admission 3€. Open 25th Mar–31st May 8am–7pm; 1st Jun–31st Oct 8am–1.30pm and 3.30–6.30pm; Sundays and holidays 8am–6pm.*

16 ★ kids Palm Beach. Star of many Cretan holiday brochures, Palm Beach really is lovely to look at, though, in high season, not so beautiful to know. A sandy cove where the river that carved out the Kourtaliotiko Gorge empties into the Libyan Sea, the water is deep blue, the beach heavily shaded by palm groves and oleander bushes. It's not easy to get to—there's a car park half way down the hill from the Préveli Monastery, but it's a stiff climb from there—and your best bet is by boat from Ágia Galíni.

Return to the main road, and turn right towards Plakiás. 12km.

17 Plakiás. The final stop on this tour is the prosperous small resort of Plakiás, a haven of small hotels and good restaurants. There's a handful of shops, a small harbour with fishing boats, a beach, good

A battle of Crete monument outside Préveli Monastery.

Fisherman working on his boat in Bali harbour.

walking, and short cruises along the coast.

18 Kri-Kri. End the day with a swim at Plakiás, food at the Kri-Kri or just a drink at the Avra or the Gialos between the main street and the sea. (See p 135).

Drive up through Mirthios, then turn left along the stunning coast road to Hóra Sfakion, or go right for 38km on the main road back across the island to Réthymnon and the National Road.

Tour 3: East of Réthymnon (Round trip 150km)

Drive east along the National Road. After about 32km, turn left to Balí.

19 ★★★ kids Balí. This delightful, thriving fishing village seems to have balanced the traditional (small fishing boats, fishermen mending their nets, tavérnas overlooking the small harbour, church) with the needs of holiday-makers (two sandy beaches separated by a headland, a choice of small hotels and restaurants, mountain-views, scuba diving, paragliding and fishing, small-scale discos, excursion boats, and a road train). It gets very crowded in July/August, but if you can visit outside these months, Balí is paradise.

Return to the National Road, continue east for about 20km, then follow signs for Fodele. In the centre of the village turn right, following signs for the museum (1km).

20 ★ kids El Greco Museum, Fodele. El Greco (1541–1614) is far and away Greece's most celebrated painter (though he did most of his work in Spain). There's some dispute about his actual birthplace, but nevertheless the village of Fodele claims him as its son. The house where he is said to have been born has been sympathetically restored, there's a good selection of copies of his paintings, back-lit to bring out the vividness of their colours, and a bust of the great man (actual name Domenicos Theotokopoulos) next to the entrance. ⏱ 15 min. *Municipality of Gazi, Fodele.* ☎ 28105 21500. *Admission 2€. Tues–Sun 9am–5pm May–Oct.*

Bust of El Greco at his birthplace museum in Fodele.

Continue along the National Road, then off to Agia Pelágia. 11km.

21 Agía Pelágia. A handsome resort with sandy beaches and good restaurants, Agía Pelágia is popular with foreign holidaymakers, but also with Cretans from nearby Iráklion.

From the National Road, continue east almost to the outskirts of Iráklion, then follow signs to the village of Arolithos. 18km.

22 ★ kids **Cretan Village.** On the right, just before you get to Arolíthos, the privately owned Traditional Cretan Village offers a sort of 'essence of Crete' at which it might be easy to smile, but which is actually rather successful. Flag-stoned lanes meander downhill between terraced cottages and shops, craftsmen ply their trades and sell their wares, there are potted plants and flowers everywhere, and there's a church, a bakery, and a well-presented folk museum. *Village:* ⏱ *1 hr.* ☎ *28108 21050. www.arolithosvillage.gr. Free admission. Museum:* ⏱ *30 min. Admission 3€ adults, 1.50€ concessions. Mon–Fri 9am–8pm, Sat and Sun 10am–3pm.*

Beach life at Agia Pelágia.

23 **Arolíthos.** Eat at the Arolíthos Restaurant or chill out and enjoy the views at the Arolíthos before returning to Réthymnon. *Cafenion* ☎ *28109 21050. $.*

Return to Réthymnon on the National Road (66km), or, if you've got time, on the old road through Perama (84km).

The privately owned Traditional Cretan Village.

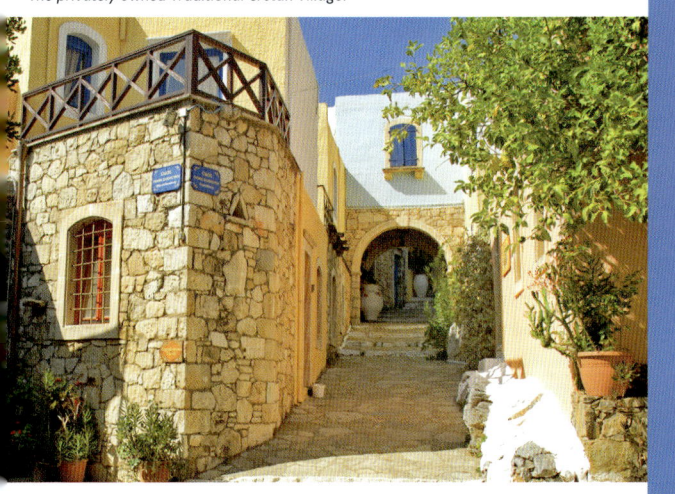

Where to **Stay**

★★ Arolithos Hotel AROLITHOS
The Arolithos Hotel offers well-appointed rooms decorated in Cretan style scattered throughout the 'traditional village'. All rooms have fridge and air conditioning, most have balcony or terrace, and open fires in winter. There's a swimming pool, and food is available in a café/bar and in the restaurant. An agreeable alternative to tourist hotels and villas. *Iraklion,* ☎ *28108 21050. www.arolithos.com. 34 rooms. Doubles 80€–120€ (but check for offers). AE, MC, V.*

★ Balí Beach Hotel BALI   Right in the centre of beautiful Balí, the hotel is perched on the little headland that separates the village's two beaches. There are views of Balí and the coastal mountains, the hotel has a swimming pool, direct access to the beach, roof garden, restaurant, and three bars, and all rooms have balconies with sea views, fridge, and air conditioning. *Bali,* ☎ *28340 94210. www.balibeach.gr. 125 rooms. Doubles 50€–100€. AE, DC, MC, V. Open 1st May–late Oct.*

★ Livicon Beach Hotel PLAKIAS
The small, family-run Livicon hotel sits right on the beach, a two-minute walk from all the village's bars and restaurants. Rooms are clean and uncluttered, there's a useful kitchenette area (fridge, hotplates, sink), and all rooms have balconies or terraces, the ones at the front with sea views. It's no-frills—there's a café/bar on the ground floor in which you can have breakfast, a cupboard full of guns, and that's about it. A real find. *Plakiás.* ☎ *28320 31216. 10 rooms. Doubles 30€–40€. Open Apr–Oct.*

Sky Beach Hotel AGIA GALINI
Even compared with the bewildering choice of hotels in Ágia Galíni, the Sky Beach, which cascades down the hillside from the main road to the sea, has a lot going for it. It's just outside the town proper, and is therefore much quieter than most, yet it has a beach, a shop, and a tavérna right on the doorstep. And it's only a five-minute footpath walk around the headland into town. Studios and apartments are basic, but large, airy and clean, and all have air conditioning, balcony, and kitchenette. There's a small café in the hotel. *Ágia Galíni.* ☎ *28320 91415. www.skybeach.gr. 11 rooms. Doubles 100€. V.*

Swimming pool at the Bali Beach Hotel.

Where to Dine

★★ **Afivoles Argiróupolis** ARGIROUPOLIS *CRETAN* One of a group of five tavérnas set beside rushing waters under the trees in the lower part of Argiróupolis, it offers a full range of Cretan and other traditional Greek dishes, with tables set on terraces surrounded by waterfalls and water features. *Argiróupolis. ☎ 28310 81011/82452. Entrées 6€–18€. Open 10am–4pm at weekends till end of June, July–Sept open all week 10am–late. But do phone and check in advance.*

kids **Kosmas Tavérna** AGIA GALINI *CRETAN* A family-run tavérna with largely Cretan food, though with the odd international (eg Thai) dish thrown in. Much of the cooking is done in olive-wood-burning ovens, and the restaurant itself is full of photos, paintings, antique furniture, and odds and ends which convey a real feeling of Cretan life. And—a rarity in Greece—small toys and colouring books are provided to keep the kids amused. *Kosmas and Ines Linoxilakis, 74056 Ágia Galíni. ☎ 28320 91222. www.kosmas. Agiagalini.com. Entrées 5€–17€. MC, V. Open midday–3pm, 5.30pm–midnight.*

★ **Kri-Kri** PLAKIAS *CRETAN* Named after the native Cretan mountain goat, the Kri-Kri is popular with locals as well as holidaymakers. Meat is cooked on charcoal, and excellent pizzas in a proper pizza oven. The service is fast and efficient, the food good, the location central. There are lots of flowers and potted plants under a wooden canopy. And if the bill's a little slow in coming, don't be too quick to complain—it'll be because they are preparing a little freebie—in my case a glass of raki with a little dish of kiwi fruit and orange. *Kri-kri Tavérna, Plakiás. ☎ 28320 31123. Entrées 4€–11€. MC, V. Open midday–1am. Apr–Oct.*

Kri-Kri Taverna in Plakiás, named after the native Cretan mountain goat.

★★ **Tavérna Valentino** BALI *CRETAN* There can be few tavérnas more perfectly placed than the Valentino—right on the beach in the center of Balí. There's a good range of Greek food (including substantial vegetarian options), cooked in locally produced olive oil, the menu's in Greek, English, French, and German (with pictures, but don't be put off), and the beach is right next to the restaurant—fidgety kids can simply play on the sand. Indeed, the Valentino harvests the sea with its own fishing boat—you can't get fresher fish than that! And the views are delightful. *Geropotamos, Balí ☎ 28340 94501. Entrées 5€–22€. V. Open midday–midnight.*

Iráklion Region

The Best Regional Tours

1. Palace of Knossós
2. Kazantzákis Museum, Mirtiá
3. Kreipe Monument
4. Archánes
5. The Proedrio
6. Labyrinth Musical Workshop
7. Minos Winery, Peza
8. Górtys
9. The Cafeteria/Tourist Shop
10. Festós
11. Agía Triáda
12. Mátala
13. Lions
14. Zarós
15. The Limni Tavérna/Café
16. Hersónisos
17. The Palace of Mália
18. Kalyba Tavern
19. Acquaplus Water Park
20. Crete Golf Club
21. Cretaquarium

Where to Stay
22. Aldemar Royal Mare Hotel
23. Eleonas Hotel
24. Idi Hotel
25. Nikos Hotel

Where to Dine
26. Kavouri
27. Lykastos
28. Votomos Tavérna

Apart from having Crete's capital city and its biggest airport, Iráklion region has other attractions. The jewels in its crown are undoubtedly its Minoan sites—most of the renowned palace sites are within an hour's drive of the capital. It also has the world's biggest museum of Minoan antiquities. Iráklion region has the bulk of Crete's vineyards, currently being promoted by well-organised wine-roads, plus many attractions related to the arts. Finally, east of Iráklion is one of Crete's main holiday areas with hotels, villas, beaches, and tourist attractions. And although Greece's largest island, Crete is still small, and Iráklion region is central so those staying in Iráklion province can visit any part of the island. All tours begin in Iráklion, though finding the right road out of the capital can be difficult. Ask directions at your hotel.

Tour 1: Knossós & Around (Round trip 66km)

Get onto the National Road south of the capital, and follow signs to Knossós. As you approach the entrance to the site, (about 6km from the city centre) there are several car parks. Use the one with spaces for coaches, or park right outside the gates if there's room. 8km.

❶ ★★★ kids Palace of Knossós. Rightly the most famous Minoan site in the world, Knossós has its controversies. In particular, Sir Arthur Evans, who excavated the site early in the 20th century, has been criticised by other archaeologists for both his overly dogmatic interpretations and for his perhaps fanciful reconstructions. That said, it's a wonderful site which electrifies the imagination—as you walk around, bear in mind that this huge and sophisticated palace was built and occupied over a thousand years before the time of Plato and Aristotle. Wooden walkways make moving around easy, and detailed information boards explain the layout and use of the different sections. Professional guides are available (10€ per adult), but you're better off looking around at your own pace, especially

Discover the most famous Minoan site in the world at Knossós.

Entrance to Minos Winery, Peza.

if you've read up about the site beforehand (*See p 13,* ❶). ⏱ *2 hr.* ☎ *28102 31940. www.ancient-greece.org/archaeology/knossos.html. Admission 6€. Open 8am–6pm (gates close 5.35pm).*

Continue south from Knossós. Past an aqueduct turn left, following signs to Mirtía, and the Nikos Katantzákis Museum. 14km.

❷ ★★★ **Kazantzákis Museum, Mirtía.** In a colourful square dotted with potted plants and modern sculpture, the Kazantzákis Museum has a wealth of information and artefacts relating to Greece's greatest writer. Mirtía is worth a visit in its own right—it's a substantial and very pretty Cretan village. *See p 13,* ❷. ⏱ *30 min–1 hr.* ☎ *28107 41689. www.kazantzakis-museum.gr. Admission 3€ adults, 1€ children. Open Mar–Oct 9am–7pm daily, Nov–Feb Sundays 10am–3pm. If no signs of life, knock!*

Return the way you came, along a scenic road surrounded by vineyards. Back at the main road, turn left. Two kilometres later, turn right to Archánes and park immediately. Don't miss the modern monument on the intersection. 15km.

❸ **Kreipe Monument.** The monument to the kidnapping of General Kreipe is a brutal concrete monolith with the top partly broken off and bearing a scribble of steel wire, sitting on a mound surrounded by low bushes. The commander of the German occupying forces, Kreipe was on his way to Headquarters at the Villa Ariadne, next to the Palace of Knossós, on 26th April, 1944, when he was kidnapped by a joint guerrilla force of Cretans and Brits. After many adventures, he and his captors were smuggled off the island to Egypt. It was a massive propaganda

Where to go at Night

Because it's not really a holiday town, nightlife in Iráklion is more about local people than tourists. Most of such action as there is takes place around the pedestrianised squares of the Old City—**Platía Venizelou** and **Platía Nikiforou Fokas**. For the disco scene you'll have to travel outside the city, west to **Ammoudara**, or more particularly, east to **Hersónisos**—try **Amnesia** (www.amnesiaclub.gr), **New York** (www.new-york.gr), or **Cameo Club** (www.cameoclub.gr). But there are loads more, and they come and go.

coup for the Allies and the Cretans, but despite a note left in the General's abandoned car saying that the kidnap was the work of British commandos alone, it still led to horrendous reprisals when the infuriated Germans destroyed a series of villages in the Amári Valley, killing all their male occupants.

Continue along the road towards Archánes. 5km.

4 Archánes. Not only is Archánes a likeable, typical Cretan town (paved platía with churches, some attractive old mansions), it also has a highly reckoned **Archaeological Museum** with some recent Minoan finds from the region. *15 min. 28107 52712, www.crete-kreta.com/archaeological-museum-archanes. Telephone before visiting the museum. Free admission. Open 8.30am–3pm Tues–Sun.*

5 The Proedrio. The Proedrio, in a handsome mansion across the road to the library/town hall, combines good coffee with a pleasant ambience. *No phone. $.*

Carry on out of the village and follow signs for Houdétsi. 7km.

6 ★★ kids Labyrinth Musical Workshop. In the centre of Houdétsi, a large house in lawned grounds contains, somehow surprisingly, a centre for world music. Established in 1982 by Ross Daly, an Irish *lyra* (a Cretan stringed instrument) virtuoso, it now attracts musicians from around the world. There are concerts, recitals, and seminars, musical instrument- making workshops, and a museum with over 200 musical instruments. *30 min–several hr. Houdétsi, Nikos Kazantzákis Municipality. 28107 41027. www.labyrinthmusic.gr. Admission 3€. Open 9am–3pm, 5.30–8pm.*

Drive back towards Iráklion on the main Pirgos–Iráklion road. Stop at the Minos Winery, in Peza. 5km.

7 Minos Winery, Peza. Just one of the host of regional vineyards which have joined the 'winemakers' network' pledged to promote Iráklion province's wines, the Minos Winery offers introductory videos, guided tours, wine tastings, a small collection of old wine-making equipment, and a well-stocked shop. If you are really into wine, get hold of the *Wine Roads of Heraklion Prefecture* booklets, either at one of the participating wineries, or from tourist information offices, which outline the excellent itineraries and give full details of what each vineyard offers. *1 hr. Minos-Miliarakis Winery, Peza Pediados. 28107 41213. www.minoswines.gr. Free admission. Open Mon–Fri 9am–4pm, Sat 10.30am–3pm. Sun by appointment.*

Ancient remains of the city of Górtys.

The Best Regional Tours

Tour 2: The Road to Mátala (Round trip 146km)

South-west of Iráklion turn off the National Road towards Agia Varvara and the south (signposted 'Mires'). After Siva a new road runs to Agia Varvara, a rural town notable mainly for its 'navel of Crete'—a huge conical rock topped by a chapel. The road then winds down onto the Messara Plain. Drive through Agii Deka ('Ten Saints') towards Mires. Ancient Górtys straddles the road just outside the village. 44km.

8 ★★ Górtys. The city of Górtys, although originally established in Minoan times, reached the height of its power under the Dorians (from the 8th century BC until just after the time of Christ), and the Romans, when it became the capital from which they ruled Crete and much of Egypt and North Africa (67 AD until the 9th-century Saracen invasion). Most famous for the detailed Dorian *law code* inscribed on one of its walls, it is the place where Hannibal stayed briefly after his defeat by Rome. It was also where Christianity came to Crete when Titus was sent here by St Paul to convert the island. Look out, too, for the Górtys plane tree, which, according to myth, is where Zeus made love to Europa after abducting her from the mainland. There's a large car park, a shaded café, and shop. *See p 18,* **5**. *30 min. T.K. 70012, Agii Deka.* ☎ *28920 31144. Admission 4€ adults, 2€ over 65, free under 18. Open 8am–8pm daily, 10th Apr–31st Oct.*

9 The Cafeteria/Tourist Shop is a pleasant place to browse and enjoy a cold drink and a snack. *No Phone. $.*

Carry on through Mires, then take a left turn off the main road to Festós. 16km.

10 ★★ Festós. Festós is worth visiting not only because of the importance of its **Minoan Palace**, but also for the views across the Messara Plain. It's an agreeable walk to the site, and there's a substantial tourist pavilion selling snacks and drinks and the usual postcards and gifts. As you descend the steps into the site, look out for the impressive Grand Stairway, and the covered palace remains.

Beach and caves at Mátala.

Iráklion Region

You'll hear the chink of hammers on chisels—the archaeological work goes on. *See p 18,* ⑥. ⏱ *30 min.* ☎ *28920 42315. Admission 4€ adults, 2€ over 65, free under 18. Open 8am–6pm daily.*

Turn right out of the car park, then follow signposts for 3km to Agía Triáda.

⓫ ★★ **Agía Triáda.** Agía Triáda is something of an enigma—nobody is really sure what it is. Perhaps a small palace, perhaps a summer retreat, it is almost unparalleled in the richness of Minoan artefacts that were found here—especially three magnificently decorated cups and a number of frescoes (all now in the Iráklion Archaeological Museum). *See p 29,* ⑤. ⏱ *30 min.* ☎ *27230 22448. http://odysseus.culture.gr/. Admission 3€ (combined ticket with Festós 6€). Open Nov–Mar 8.30am–3pm, Apr–Oct 10am–4.30pm.*

Return to the fork just before Festós and turn right. The road descends to the Messara Plain, then across to Mátala. 10km.

⓬ ★★ kids **Mátala.** Mátala is one of Crete's best-looking seaside towns. This is where Zeus, disguised as a bull, came ashore with Europa on his back (myth). It was also the port for Górtys (fact). It has a wide sand-and-pebble beach between two yellow sandstone headlands. The one on the right is a honeycomb of caves which it is thought were hollowed out during Roman/early Christian times, possibly as tombs. They have since been used as habitation, as ammunition stores, and in the 1960s as temporary living accommodation for hordes of hippies. At various times Bob Dylan, Joni Mitchell, Cat Stevens, and the Rolling Stones came to drop out and turn on at this 60s El Dorado. There are lots of tavérnas and cafés right on the beach, and some cut

The tree-fringed Votomos lake.

interestingly into the left-hand headland. *See p 103,* ⑫.

⓭ **Lions.** One of the best of a number of good restaurants on the beach at Mátala is Lions. If it's too early, don't worry—there are good eating choices in Zaros. ☎ *28920 45108.*

Return towards Iráklion the same way as you came, but just after Mires, turn left, following signs for Zaros. The road climbs steadily through mountain scenery. 28km.

⓮ ★ **Zaros.** If Mátala is El Dorado, then Zaros, high in the mountains and built on a beautiful lake, is Shangri-La. Half way along the meandering main village street turn right (signpost *The Lake*) up a tiny lane to the clear, tree-fringed **Votomos Lake.** If you get to the far end of the main street, and the famous water-bottling plant (Zaros water is all over Crete) you've gone too far: turn back, and look out for another tiny sign—this time saying *Limni*, to the left. Zaros really is an oasis in the aridity of the Psiloritis range. There are several excellent mountain hotels and restaurants (see below). It 107, ⑨.

Tour the impressive Minoan palace at Mália.

15 The Limni Tavérna/Café ☎ 28940 31338 ($) on the lake in Zaros, or the Votomos Tavérna ☎ 28940 31302, (see p 145) just before you get to the lake, are both excellent choices for lunch or an evening meal.

Return to Iráklion via Agia Varvara. 45km.

Tour 3: East of Iráklion (Round trip 80km)
Drive east along the National Road to Hersónisos. 24km.

16 ★ kids Hersónisos. Hersónisos is usually depicted as the worst kind of Mediterranean holiday-industry sprawl, but I liked it, and the surrounding area. In terms of family attractions, it's hard to think of a better place to go. Hersónisos has a harbour with a Greek church and small boats, lots offering sea trips. There's a tourist road train that gives a good overview of the area (10€ for a 1-hour trip—tickets at the harbour), and a much nicer beach than I'd expected. Indeed, the whole coastline—all sandstone bluffs, little bays, sandy beaches, and waving palm trees—is very attractive. There's a good little aquarium run by a Brit (**Aquaworld**, p 62, 11), an extensive free amusement park (**Star Beach**, p 62, 13) and one of those kitsch museums of traditional Cretan life, **Lychnostatis**, that shouldn't work but does. *See p 55 in Chapter 3.*

Drive east out of Hersónisos towards Ágios Nikólaos on the National Road. 14km.

17 ★ The Palace of Mália. It's ironic that Mália, of the all-night partying, deafening discos, and lager louts reputation, has just beyond it one of Crete's most impressive Minoan palaces. The information centre has graphic models to show what the palace must originally have looked like, and throughout the site the context maps and information boards make for a very user-friendly visit. *See p 29, 6. 30 min–2 hr. Admission 4€. Open 8.30am–3pm Tues–Sun.*

18 Kalyba Tavern. Just beyond the palace site, and on the beach, the Kalyba Tavern makes for a good swim-and-refreshment break. *No phone. $.*

Return west along the Old National Road. At Hersónisos turn left towards Kastélli. A 5km drive south brings you, on the right, to Acquaplus Water Park. 15km.

19 ★★★ kids Acquaplus Water Park. One of Crete's best water parks, with all the slides, flumes, and just about every other water feature you'd expect, set into the side of a valley. *See p 63, 14.*

Immediately after the water park, the 500m drive to Crete's only golf course snakes off to the right.

20 ★ Crete Golf Club. Maintaining an 18-hole golf course on

Museum of traditional Cretan life – Lychnostatis.

Greece's hottest island can't be easy, yet they've managed it. With a driving range too! Climbing up the valley side opposite the Acquaplus Water Park, it would seem like a perfect family day out—parents drop the kids off at the water park, then play a round before picking them up. But no—the club says it has far more whole families booking in for a full round (see p 63, ⓯.)

From the Old National Road, turn left towards Iráklion, then at Gournes, follow signs for Cretaquarium. 14km.

㉑ ★★★ kids **Cretaquarium.** Barely three years old, the Cretaquarium is a fine introduction to the marine life of Crete. The memory of the slowly revolving moon jellyfish, beautifully lit, will live with me till I die. There's a cafeteria and a comprehensive shop. *Cretaquarium, Gournes.* ☎ *28103 37788. www.cretaquarium.gr. Admission 8€ adults, 6€ concessions (inc. children 5–17), audioguide 2€. At time of writing closed for installation of 25 new tanks. Check website before going.*

Where to **Stay**

★★★ **Aldemar Royal Mare Hotel** HERSONISOS More of a resort than a hotel, the Aldemar Royal Mare Hotel takes up a huge site between the main Iráklion road and its own secluded blue flag beach. With 341 rooms, 43 deluxe suites, 29 freshwater swimming pools, seven international-standard clay tennis courts, a world class spa, a large children's club area, a variety of common rooms (Internet, games etc) and more bars, restaurants, and shops than you can shake a stick at—you could have a terrific holiday without showing

The Aldemar Royal Mare Hotel's blue flag beach.

your nose outside. *Limin Hersonissou.* ☎ *28970 27200. www.aldemarhotels.com. 384 rooms. Doubles 96€– 388€ per night w/breakfast (minimum booking a week) MC, V. Open Apr–Oct.*

Eleonas Hotel ZAROS The Eleonas Hotel consists of a group of lodges clustered around a swimming pool and restaurant, just beyond the lake in the cool upland village of Zaros. There's good walking nearby (the Agiou Nikolaou Gorge), horse riding, archery, mountain biking, all in unspoilt countryside on the lower slopes of Mount Psiloritis. All lodges have open fires, air conditioning, fridge, and so on. *Zaros.* ☎ *28940 31239. www.eleonas.gr. 11 rooms. Doubles 85€– 95€ w/breakfast (reductions for week/fortnight) MC, V.*

Idi Hotel ZAROS More of a traditional hotel than the Eleonas, the Idi has 34 rooms in the main building and 25 bungalows dotted around the wooded grounds. All have air conditioning and balcony or terrace. For a smallish inland hotel, the Idi does very well for facilities, with swimming pool, fitness centre, sauna, tennis courts, together with tavérna, restaurant, and a bar. Don't be put off by the derelict swimming pool at the front of the hotel— there's a new one to the rear. There's a trout farm and fish restaurant next door. *Zaros.* ☎ *28940 31301. www.idi-hotel.com. 59 rooms. Doubles 55€–80€. MC, V.*

Nikos Hotel MATALA A small, family-run hotel with good, clean basic rooms and a shady tavérna, centrally located near the beach and the village centre. All rooms have balcony and fridge. *Messara, Mátala.* ☎ *28920 45375. www.matala-nikos.com. 20 rooms. Doubles 45€. Open Apr–Oct.*

Where to Dine

★ **Kavouri** HERSONISOS *CRETAN* A busy restaurant with a good range of traditional Cretan dishes—their specialty is leg of lamb cooked slowly in the oven. There's a colourful, if narrow, pavement terrace, decked out with large urns and bits of agricultural machinery, all under gourd-bedecked vines. Service is friendly and efficient. *Archeou Theatrou, Hersónisos.* 📞 *28970 21161. Entrées 5.50€–10€. MC, V. Open 1pm–midnight or later. May–Oct.*

Limni Tavérna/Café ZAROS *CRETAN* Traditional tavérna right on the water of Zaros's lake, with extensive terraced decks for summer dining and an airy high-ceilinged, rustic-wood room for winter. Fresh trout from the lake is a specialty. *P. Zaridakis, I Limni, Zaros.* 📞 *28940 31338. Entrées 10€–23€.*

Lions MATALA *CRETAN* On entering the Lions, you are likely to be whisked into the kitchens in the traditional way, to see what's on offer. Food is Cretan and of good quality, and you should get a table even in the height of summer—it's deceptively big, on three levels. *Lions Restaurant/Café, Mátala.* 📞 *28920 45108. Entrées 7€–18€. MC, V. Open 10am–late. Apr–Oct (or even Nov if weather is good).*

Lykastos ARCHANES *CRETAN* A small tavérna which occupies a converted old house right on the main square, Lykastos is known mainly for the range of its mezzedes and grilled meats—especially the lemon rabbit and chicken. Wash it down with a carafe of the house white wine from a local co-operative. *Main Square, Archánes.* 📞 *28107 52433. Entrées 3€–5€.*

Votomos Tavérna ZAROS *INTERNATIONAL* To get to the Votomos Tavérna, which is attached to the Idi Hotel and next to an old water mill, you have to walk past numerous large fish tanks full of trout. With the languorous movements of the fish and the sound of the waterfall that feeds the tanks, you couldn't ask for a more idyllic setting for a meal. And the fish could scarcely be fresher! The menu offers a range of Greek and international dishes, with meat and fish to the fore. *Zaros.* 📞 *28940 31302. Entrées 6€–22€. MC, V. Open 11am–2am.*

Views over Zaros's lake at the Limni Tavérna.

The Best Regional Tours

Lasíthi Region

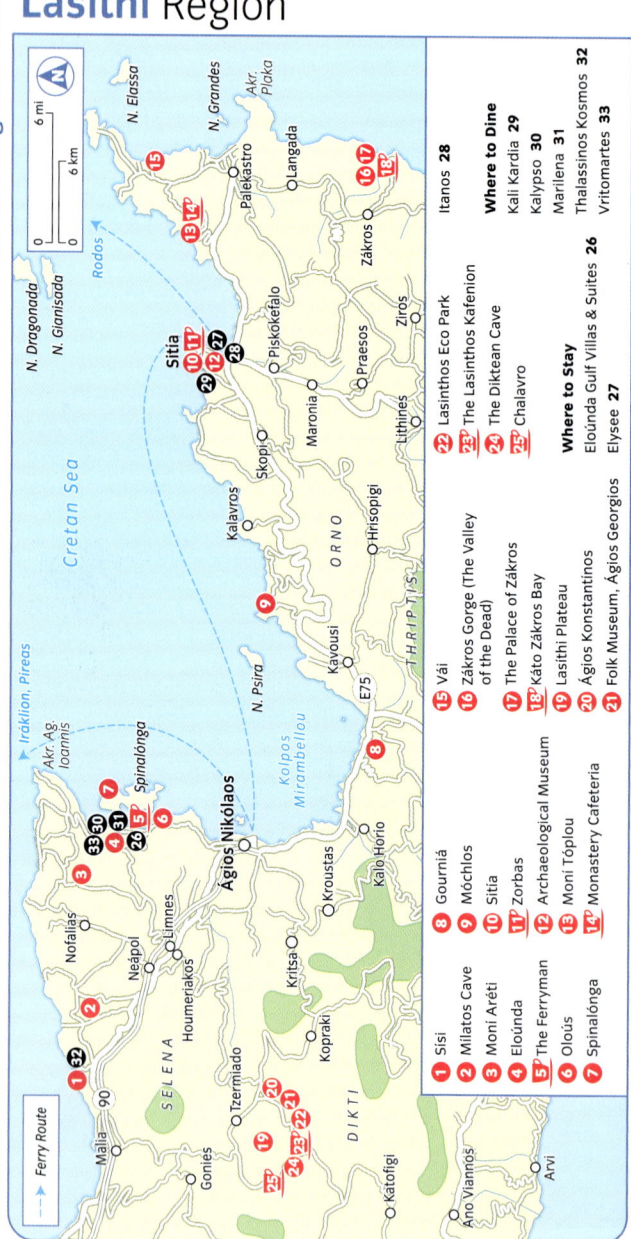

1. Sisí
2. Milatos Cave
3. Moní Aréti
4. Eloúnda
5. The Ferryman
6. Oloús
7. Spinalónga
8. Gourniá
9. Móchlos
10. Sitía
11. Zorbas
12. Archaeological Museum
13. Moní Tóplou
14. Monastery Cafeteria
15. Váï
16. Zákros Gorge (The Valley of the Dead)
17. The Palace of Zákros
18. Káto Zákros Bay
19. Lasíthi Plateau
20. Ágios Konstantínos
21. Folk Museum, Ágios Georgios
22. Lasinthos Eco Park
23. The Lasinthos Kafenion
24. The Diktean Cave
25. Chalavro

Where to Stay
Eloúnda Gulf Villas & Suites 26
Elysee 27
Itanos 28

Where to Dine
Kali Kardia 29
Kalypso 30
Marilena 31
Thalassinos Kosmos 32
Vritomartes 33

Lasithi has a character all of its own. It may lack the commanding ranges of the rest of Crete, but it is still very mountainous, especially around the huge Gulf of Mirabéllo, one of the island's most beautiful bays. The north-eastern end of the bay is largely rural. In this area, too, is the popular seaside town of Eloúnda and the eerie, ex-leper colony island of Spinalónga. Half way around the bay stands the provincial capital Ágios Nikólaos, once almost ruined by mass tourism, but now a uniquely striking, seaside-town-on-a-lake. Crete's 'far east' boasts a picturesque regional capital (Sitía), important Minoan sites, delightful fishing villages, and Crete's famous beach, Vái. The agricultural Lasíthi Plateau, high in the region's western mountains, pulls in large numbers of tourist coaches, drawn by its characteristic wind pumps, local crafts, and Crete's best-known cave. START: **All tours begin in Ágios Nikólaos.**

Tour 1: North of Ágios Nikólaos (Round trip 76km)
Take the National Road towards Iráklion. After 25km turn right towards Sisi. 31km.

1 ★ Sisi. A charming seaside village, Sísi (sometimes Sissi) with a harbour surrounded by trees, a handful of fishing boats, a forest of date-palms, and a good selection of cafés, restaurants, tavérnas, and pizzerias, makes an ideal stopping place for coffee or a full meal (see below). If you want to stretch your legs, a broad dirt path strikes east from the main square, along a low, rocky shore.

From the main road turn left towards Milatos. Near the village, follow signs for 'Milatos Cave' which leads you eventually to a right turn along a rocky dirt road. Don't worry—it's only 200 metres. When you get to the end, there's no sign but turn left. The cave is well marked on the right 2km up the mountain. Park on the road. 6km.

2 ★ kids Mílatos Cave. The roughly paved path to the cave climbs up the hillside. It's an easy ten-minute walk, rustic fencing keeps you safe, and there are extensive views back towards the sea.

Milatos caves.

One of the numerous Turkish atrocity sites which have long fed Cretan nationalism, the Milatos Cave was the scene of a famous massacre. The cave is, in fact, a network of chambers that penetrates far back into the mountain. There's a chapel built into it, about 20m from the entrance. *See p 41,* **10**. ⏱ *30 min. Free admission.*

Continue up the mountain, then down past olive groves and vineyards through Latsida and Neápoli. Turn left just before the ruined windmills at Nikithiano, following signs to Fourni. The

The busy harbour at Eloúnda.

road weaves up to Kastélli (look out for a good folk museum in the village, and ruined windmills climbing the conical hill beyond). Just beyond Fourni, with its large modern church, on the Eloúnda road, turn left and climb steeply to the monastery of Moní Aréti. 24km.

3 ★ Moní Aréti. With its tiny church, its little courtyard overlooked by stepped balconies, rustic benches and pots of flowers, archways and trees, Moní Aréti is the archetypal Greek monastery. It lies high in the hills, surrounded by its own honeycomb of dry-stone walls and flocks of sheep and goats. Wandering around in the cool upland air, with the sounds of goat and sheep bells all around you, the sense of peace and tranquillity is palpable. *15 min. Free admission.*

Go back down the mountain and turn left to Eloúnda. At an unsignposted fork in the road, bear right. Stop just beyond a row of ruined windmills on the left. One has been partially restored—climb up to the terrace. The view of Eloúnda and the Gulf of Mirabéllo beyond is out of this world. Then drive down through Pano Pines and Pano Eloúnda to Eloúnda. 16km.

4 ★★ Eloúnda. Curved around its busy harbour set in a range of low hills, Eloúnda is, despite its popularity as a holiday resort, extremely diverting. Its large paved central square opens directly onto the waterfront, along which boats bob and people stroll. To the left of the harbour is a clean and well-organised municipal beach with a large children's playground. *See p 103,* **13**.

5 The Ferryman. Eat or drink at this large tavérna, where, greybeards may remember, a 1970s British TV series called Who Pays the Ferryman was filmed. *$$.*

6 Oloús. Whilst you're in Eloúnda, make a diversion to the ancient remains of Roman Oloús. A few hundred yards beyond the harbour, on the road to Ágios Nikólaos, take a left off the main street (signposted *Hotel by Sea,* or, if you're driving into Eloúnda from Ágios Nikólaos, *Sunk City*) and cross the causeway. To the right, low walls sticking out of the lagoon show where Venetian salt pans once stood. At the end of the causeway there's a bridge across a canal built by the French, several windmills, and all around, the unexcavated remains of the Roman city of Oloús.

Return to Elounda, and catch a ferry from the port to Spinalónga.

❼ ★★ kids Spinalónga. A tiny island on the northern approach to Elounda, Spinalónga was heavily fortified by the Venetians in the late 16th century. So powerful was the fortress that, when the rest of Crete was conquered by the Turks, the island defied the invaders for a further 50 years, capitulating eventually in 1715. In the same way, Spinalónga provided a haven for Turks during the successive Cretan rebellions which led to independence and then unification with Greece in the early 20th century. In 1904 a leper colony was established on the island, and there must be some suspicion that this was a clever, if cynical, means of flushing out the Turks who still lived there. The colony wasn't closed until 1957—long after a cure for leprosy had been discovered! *Boat trips 10€ 9.30am–4.30pm. Admission 2€. Open 8am–7pm.*

Return to Ágios Nikólaos along the coast road. 12km.

Tour 2: The Far East (Round trip 252km)

Head south along the National Road towards Sitia. In about 20km, turn right along a dirt road to the ruins of Minoan Gourniá, just off the main road.

❽ ★★ Gourniá. One of the most under-visited and easily-comprehended Minoan sites in Crete, Gourniá is manageable in size, clear in layout, and has a wealth of context boards with admirably lucid explanations of what you're looking at. It's easy to get to, never crowded, and cheap to enter. The remains of a Minoan town, the ruins give a good idea of what ordinary life must have been like in Crete 3500 years ago. *See p 31,* ⑪. ⏲ *30 min. Admission 2€. Open 8.30am–3pm Tues–Sun.*

Continue along the main Sitia road, through Kavousi, Lastros and Sfaka. After the Panorama Tavern (terrific views!), turn left and drive down a switchback road through huge quarries to the coastal village of Móchlos. 23km.

❾ ★ Móchlos. The tiny fishing village of Móchlos is notable mainly for the little island that sits like a turtle just off the harbour. You can clearly see the ruins of a Minoan

The canal and some remains of the Roman city of Oloús.

Spinalónga fortress.

settlement, and there are also other Roman and Byzantine ruins, including the remains of fish tanks. Despite its diminutive size, Móchlos has a number of water-side tavérnas—if you want to cross to the island, simply ask, and negotiate a price. *See p 31,* ⓬.

Continue east after Móchlos, back to the main coast road, and drive the pleasantly bendy 20km to Sitia. When you get to the town, make for the port. After the last roundabout, just before the sea, the (free) car park is on the right. 35km.

❿ **Sitía.** The least touristy of Crete's north coast settlements, Sitia has all the advantages and disadvantages of a normal working Greek town. Though a bit down-at-heel, with back streets disfigured by overhead cables and parked motorbikes, walk out onto the quayside and you immediately appreciate why it is popular with Cretans themselves. Buildings climb picturesquely up from the sharp curve of a clean and modern quay to which working fishing boats are moored. The outline of a small Venetian fortress decorates the skyline, and men dangle fishing lines into the water from the dock. *See p 23,* ❼.

The little island off the coast of the fishing village of Móchlos.

⓫ **Zorbas.** On the corner where the quayside changes direction, Zorbas is usually packed with older men playing tavli (backgammon) and drinking coffee. Just right for drinks, snacks, or main meals. *No phone. $.*

Return to the car park, pass it, turn left and left again.

⓬ ★ **Archaeological Museum.** Although the bulk of Crete's Minoan sites are in Iráklion province, the 'Far East' has several important ones, including the one on the island at Móchlos (see above), the Palace of Zákros (see below) and a cemetery near Agía Fotia. Consequently, Sitía's Archaeological Museum, which covers the whole of the eastern end of the island, has a wealth of finds—tablets in Linear A script, vases, statues, agricultural tools, and some unique kitchen equipment. ⏲ *15 min. Admission 2€. Open Tues–Sun 8.30am–3pm.*

After Sitia follow signs to Palaiokastro, Vái and Zákros. After about 10km, turn left off the main road, and drive across 3km of bleak terrain to the monastery of Moní Tóplou. 15km.

🔴**13** ★ **Moní Tóplou.** Moní Tóplou has two opposing things going for it—the great beauty and peace of its flower-bedecked courtyards and balconies, and its defiantly bloodstained history of resistance to occupation. Tóplou was destroyed by pirates in 1498, captured by the Turks during the 1821 rebellion (12 monks were hanged from the main gate), and became a centre for the Cretan resistance during the World War II Nazi occupation. There's a small museum and a shady café. ⏲ *30 min. Admission 3€. Open 9am–1pm and 2–6pm.*

14 **Monastery Cafeteria.** Heavily patronised by Cretans (a good sign), stop for a drink or try their delicious diropittes (cheese pasties). *No phone. $.*

Continue to Vái. 9km.

🔴**15** ★ kids **Vái.** Vái is one of Crete's most famous sandy beaches, largely because of the huge groves of palm trees, once thought to have been introduced by Roman or Arab invaders, but now believed to be indigenous date palms (Europe's only ones) which have survived on Crete for thousands of years. Vái can be delightful, but is unbearably crowded at the height of the season. *See p 24,* 🔴**9**.

From Vái, head south to Káto Zákros. Just before the village, look out for a sign on the left 'Footpath Zákros Gorge—Cheese

The modern quayside at Sitia.

Dairy—Zákros Springs'. Park the car and take the path. 30km.

⑯ ★★★ Zákros Gorge (The Valley of the Dead).

The path soon peters out, but fear not. Go through a wooden door in a fence then climb steeply into the canyon beyond. It is really beautiful. Look out for flowers in spring, and caves high on the cliffs, used by the Minoans as tombs. The path is along the left-hand side of the canyon (there are red way-markers to help), and comes out eventually on a cement road. Turn left along it, and you'll get to the Palace of Zákros in about 10 minutes. The whole walk takes about 45 minutes down; an hour back (or get a bus or taxi from Káto Zákros). *See p 106,* ③.

⑰ ★ The Palace of Zákros.

Though worth visiting in its own right (it's a peaceful fishing village with a shingle beach and several fish restaurants), Káto Zákros is best known for the remains of the Minoan palace that sits just behind it. It wasn't excavated until 1962 (by Greek archaeologist Nikólaos Platon), and so has benefitted from all the modern mid-20th century techniques. A further bonus was that it hadn't been looted, therefore yielding a rich haul of everyday objects, which are now in the Iráklion and Sitía Archaeological Museums. *See p 30,* ⑨. ⏱ *1 hr. Admission 3 €. Jul–Oct 8am–5pm, Nov–Jun 8am–3pm.*

⑱ Káto Zákros Bay.

End the trip with a swim off the pebble beach and a cold drink or meal here. ☎ *28430 26887. $.*

Return the way you came to Ágios Nikólaos, or, for an exhilarating drive across mountainous inland Crete, turn left 3km north of Zákros for Karidi up a series of hairpin bends. A 15km drive across good mountain roads through Sitanos, Chadras, and Armeni brings you to the main Sitía–Ierapetra road. Turn left to Ierapetra, then follow signs for Ágios Nikólaos. 116km.

Tour 3: The Lasíthi Plateau (Round trip 115km)

Take the National Road towards Iráklion, and turn off after about 12km, following signs for Neápoli, then for 'Lasíthi Plateau'. After Mésa Lasíthi, you'll see the Lasíthi Plateau.

The path from the Dikteán Cave coming down onto the Lasíthi Plateau.

⑲ ★★★ Lasíthi Plateau. A flat patchwork of fields appoximately 9 km by 6 km, the Lasíthi Plateau lies in the Dikti Mountains—at over 800m above sea level, it's one of the highest permanently inhabited areas in the Mediterranean. The rich soil of the Lasíthi Plateau, washed down over eons from the surrounding mountains, has supported a human population since the New Stone Age—the only interruption was during the 14th and early 15th centuries, when the Venetians cleared it because of successive rebellions against their rule. The influence of the occupiers wasn't all bad, though—when Cretans were allowed back onto the plateau in the 15th century, the Venetians organised the building of a massive drainage system which channelled melt-water from the mountains and ground-water from wells through the farmland to a sink-hole on the western edge. Water from bore holes nowadays is pumped up by diesel or electric motors, but thousands of the old windmills survive. *See p 107,* ⑩.

Woman working on a loom in the village of Ágios Konstantinos.

Drive down to the first of the Lasíthi villages, and start the clockwise circumnavigation of the plateau on what is in effect a 'ring' road. 46km.

⑳ Ágios Konstantínos. This is the first village you come to, notable mainly for the numerous shops on its main street selling woven cloth and embroidery.

Continue to Ágios Georgios. 2km.

㉑ Folk Museum, Ágios Georgios. The folk museum in Ágios Georgios is almost as interesting for its architecture as for its contents. Housed in a whitewashed stone farmhouse with trees and flowers in the courtyard, and rough stone floors and ancient beams inside, the museum contains a variety of well-displayed pieces of domestic equipment. Next door a more modern mansion contains a diverting (if poorly presented) collection of photographs to do with Cretan writer Nikos Kazantzákis. *⏱ 15 min. Admission 3€. 10am–4pm Apr–Oct.*

The Lasinthos Eco Park is 1km outside Ágios Georgios, on the road to Psichro.

㉒ ★★ kids Lasinthos Eco Park. An attempt to recreate a Cretan village, the Lasinthos Eco Park is new enough not to appear in most guidebooks. Built around a square, it consists of a number of workshops where you see traditional crafts being practised—pottery, wood carving, weaving, ceramics, wax working. There's a café and several souvenir shops. Behind the park you can see all the main types of animal common in Crete—ducks, geese, chickens, horses, ponies, cows, dogs, wild boars, alpine goats, and the national animal, the kri-kri. Just outside the park is a large tavérna and also apartments to rent. *See p 64,* ⑱. *⏱ 1 hr. Ágios Georgios. ☎ 28440 89100. www.lasinthos.gr. Admission 4€. Open all year (for apartments, see 'Where to stay' below).*

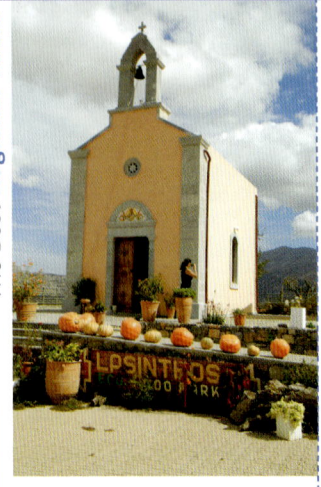

The village church at Lasinthos Eco Park.

23 **The Lasinthos Kafenion.** The Lasinthos Kafenion is good for cold drinks and nibbles. If you want anything more substantial, walk up the hill to The Lasinthos Restaurant, a large tavérna overlooking the park. ☎ 28440 89100. $.

Continue to the village of Psichro, and follow signs for the Diktean Cave. 4km.

24 ★★ kids **The Diktean Cave.** The Diktean Cave is one of several claimed as the birthplace of Zeus, and you can see its point—deep, dark, with visceral limestone shining on the walls and haze surrounding the entrance, it's like some huge natural womb. It's a 25-minute climb to the entrance (with two alternative routes—a paved switchback path (easy), or the one used by the donkeys straight up the mountainside (stiff). Donkeyrides cost 15€ one way, 20€ return. Once up at the cave and through the admission gate, it's a long climb down concrete steps to the bottom, then back up again on a loop. *See p 64,* **19**. ⏱ *2 hr. Admission 4€ (parking 2€). Open daily 8am–7pm.*

25 **Chalavro.** Refuel at this café/tavérna at the bottom of the paved path from the cave, or one of the ones that line the car park. *No phone. $.*

Continue round the loop to Lasithi's main town Tzermiado, then back to Neápoli and Ágios Nikólaos.

Where to Stay

★★★ Eloúnda Gulf Villas & Suites ELOUNDA   Luxury beyond the dreams of avarice. Built into the hillside above Eloúnda, the main hotel has suites, a restaurant, and a communal pool, whilst each villa has every luxury—including private terrace with infinity pool. Some also have their own gym and sauna. And if you order food from room service, expect creamy linen and a full place setting! Access roads are steep, though a golf buggy can be whistled up at the drop of a hat. Not cheap of course—many celebrities stay here, including the Queen of Jordan. Enough said! *Eloúnda.* ☎ *28102 27132. www.eloundavillas.com. 28 rooms. Suites 250€–900€, villas 600€–4750€ villas w/breakfast. AE, MC, V. Apr–Oct.*

Elysee SITIA   The Elysee is ideally located on the beach a five-minute walk from the centre of town. All rooms have balconies and air conditioning, and there's free WiFi within the hotel. A good basic business hotel, with rooms that are a little too small to encourage much sitting about. *14, Kalamanli St.* 📞 *28430 22312. www.elysee-hotel.gr. 26 rooms. Doubles 45€–80€. MC, V.*

kids **Itanos** SITIA Right on Sitía's main square, the Itanos couldn't be more central. It offers comfortable accommodation (A/C, TV, minibar in all rooms), a cafeteria and à la carte restaurant, and a roof garden with views across the town. A good choice for families—there are endless permutations of accommodation, with rooms with from two to four beds, many with connecting doors. *Platía Iroon Polytechniou.* 📞 *28430 22900. www.itanoshotel.com. 69 rooms. Doubles 59€–68€. AE, MC, V.*

★★ **Lasinthos Eco Park** PSICHRO Accommodation is on the hillside above the Eco Park, just outside Psichro. There's a choice of studios and maisonettes, all with kitchens, Internet access, balconies, and traditional Cretan furnishings. There is access to all animals and activities in the Eco Park, and the opportunity to muck in and help. *Ágios Georgios.* 📞 *28440 89100. www.lasinthos.gr. 13 rooms. Doubles 75€–90€; two-room apartments 100€–110€.*

Where to Dine

★ **Kali Kardia** SITIA *CRETAN* On the street that runs parallel to the waterfront, the Kali Kardia (*Good Heart*) is a typical Cretan tavérna/ouzeri. Run by a charming older couple, it attracts considerable local patronage, and the food's excellent—the next best thing to eating Cretan food privately prepared by an excellent traditional cook. *22 Fountalidou, Sitía.* 📞 *0843 22249. Entrées 4.50€–8€. Open 12.30–3.30pm, 6.30pm–late.*

★★ **Kalypso** ELOUNDA *MEDITERRANEAN* A relative newcomer in Eloúnda, the Kalypso, on the harbour side next to the church, aims for a cool, sophisticated ambience. A piano tinkles away each evening,

Infinity pool at the Eloúnda Gulf Villas.

Feast of traditional Cretan cuisine at Kali Kardia.

and the menu offers a broader range of meals than just Cretan or Greek. It's popular with the younger set and can get a bit noisy as the night progresses. *Port of Eloúnda.* ☎ *28410 31367. Entrées 5€–40€. MC, V. Open midday–11pm (midnight in Aug). Apr–Oct.*

★★ **Marilena** ELOUNDA *GREEK* Large and buzzing and for over thirty years one of Eloúnda's leading restaurants, the Marilena is famous for its mezzedes, fish and lobster, and for its Greek and Cretan nights (currently on Mondays). *Eloúnda.* ☎ *28410 41322. www.marilena restaurant.gr. Entrées 8.50€–20€. MC, V. Open midday–4pm, 7–11pm. 1st Apr–31st Oct. Reservations recommended.*

Thalassinos Kosmos SISI *FISH* A beautiful restaurant that sits on top of the hill above Sisi's pretty harbour. Good range of fish and other food, fast friendly service, terrific views. *Sisi.* ☎ *28410 71089. Entrées 6€–18€. Open midday–late. Apr–Oct.*

★★ **Vritomartes** ELOUNDA *CRETAN/GREEK* Perfectly positioned in the centre of the harbour, you might fear that the Vritomartes will be too touristy. Certainly its menu makes concessions to non-Greek taste (chips and rice with everything), yet the quality of the food is superb, from delicious *souvlakia* to out-of-this-world bread and dips, to the freshest of fish. And if you're not eating the fish, you can feed them—they swarm around the quay as diners throw bits of bread. *Eloúnda Harbour.* ☎ *28410 41325. www.vritomartesrestaurant.gr. Entrées 6.50€–25€ (more for lobster and some fish). AE, MC, V. Open 10am–11pm. Apr–Oct.* ●

Thalassinos Kosmos restaurant on Sisi's attractive harbour.

The
Savvy Traveller

Before You Go

Government Tourist Offices
In the US: Olympic Tower, 645 Fifth Ave, Suite 903, New York, NY 10022 (212 421 5777); www.greektourism.com. In the UK: Greek National Tourism Organisation, 4 Conduit St, London, W1S 2DJ (020 7495 9300); www.visitgreece.gr. In Australia: Hellenic tourism organization, 51–57 Pitt St, Sydney, NSW 2000. P.O.Box R203 Royal Exchange NSW 2000, Australia (00612 92411663/4/5-92521441); email: hto@tpg.com.au.

Visa Information
European Union, US, and Australian citizens need only a valid passport to travel to Greece—no visa is required. You may stay for up to 90 days—for longer visits you need a residence permit from the appropriate office. For further information, contact the Consulate General of Greece (0207 3135600).

The Best Time to Go
The Cretan holiday season lasts from the beginning of April to the end of October. Spring (Apr–May) and Autumn (Sept–Oct) are the best times to visit Crete—most attractions, hotels, and restaurants are open, yet it's not too hot, crowded, or expensive. July and August are, if at all possible, best avoided, with large crowds, summer heat, and the most expensive tariffs. High winds and rough seas can happen at any time.

Public Holidays in Greece
New Year's Day: 1st January
Epiphany (Baptism of Christ): 6th January
Clean Monday: Varies (41 days before Easter)
Easter: Varies
Independence Day: 25th March
May Day: 1st May
Pentecost Monday: Varies (7th Sunday after Easter)
Assumption of the Virgin: 15th August
Ochi Day: 28th October
Christmas Eve: 24th December
Christmas Day: 25th December
St Stephen's Day: 26th December

During any of these public holidays it's worth finding out in advance how they may affect your holiday. Government offices, banks, post offices, and many museums, restaurants, and tavérnas are closed, so if you are set on visiting any attractions, check beforehand that they are open and that you can get to them. The dates of some public holidays vary because they are linked to the date of Easter. An Easter holiday in Crete can be extremely enjoyable (see below)—there's a lot of eating, drinking, and dancing, the weather is mild, the spring flowers are out, and the birds are singing. But again, you could be faced with overcrowding and top prices as Greeks from abroad flood home for the celebrations. Greek and UK/USA Easters are sometimes on different dates:

Year	Date	Same as UK & Ireland?
2009	19th April	No
2010	4th April	Yes
2011	24th April	Yes
2012	15th April	No
2013	5th May	No
2014	20th April	Yes
2015	12th April	No
2016	1st May	No
2017	16th April	Yes

Previous page: Rethymnon harbour.

Useful Websites

www.greekisland.co.uk/wcrete/creteinfo.htm
www.explorecrete.com
You might try to get hold of the Cretan holiday magazine *Frappe* as well (**www.frappe-magazine.com**).
www.whitepages.gr and **www.xo.gr** are two excellent telephone directories offered by the Greek communications company OTE. The first is a normal directory; the second is the Yellow Pages. Both are searchable in a variety of ways, and you can opt for the Latin alphabet. The only problem is knowing how they've transposed from the Greek alphabet—put in 'Rethymnon' and you'll get nothing because they spell it 'Rethymno'. But once you've got used to trying different alternatives, they are both very useful sites.

Other Festivals & Special Events

JANUARY. New Year's Day. 1st January is a celebration of St Basil, who, somewhat like Father Christmas, gives out gifts. Tradition dictates that eating *Vassilopita*, a special basil cake, is a must.

FEBRUARY. Apokreas and Clean Monday. Apokreas is the period of eating, dancing, and celebration that leads up to the beginning of Lent. It is carnival time—people dress up and have to guess each other's identities. The final weekend of Apokreas is the most popular for dances, masked balls, and children's parties, culminating in carnival parades on the final Sunday. Apokreas ends on the public holiday that is Clean Monday, the beginning of Lent. Once Lent begins, so does the fasting, and no meat, eggs, oil, or dairy products may be eaten. The dates of Apokreas and Clean Monday vary as they depend on when Easter falls. Clean Monday traditionally sees families going to the countryside for Lent-friendly picnics or tavérna meals and kite flying.
Réthymnon Carnival. Art, culture, dancing, theatre, traditional Greek customs, games, and activities are all part of this Cretan carnival. There is a grand parade, treasure hunts, a graffiti festival, and fancy dress balls, and on Shrove Thursday there is a huge open-air party.

MARCH. Greek Independence Day and the Feast of the Annunciation (25th). This dual celebration of Greek independence and the day that the Archangel Gabriel told Mary that she was pregnant is a busy day that sees military parades and religious celebrations throughout Greece.

APRIL. Easter. Orthodox Easter is the main Christian holiday in Greece—far more important than Christmas. Good Friday sees processions in memory of the burial of Christ. They often go on all day and are watched and followed by big crowds. It's a very solemn day of mourning with church bells ringing slowly. Easter Saturday is a day of preparation for the following day. Just before midnight everyone, including children, goes to church for the miracle of the resurrection. It is announced that Christ has risen and candles are lit from the church's eternal flame and others are lit from those until everyone is carrying a lit candle. People then make their way home with their candles—hundreds of candles heading away from the church and along the streets is truly a sight to see. Easter Sunday celebrates the resurrection of Christ and marks the end of Lent. Lamb is roasted over hot coals on a spit and red-dyed eggs are eaten. It's a day for families and feasts and dancing. **Feast of St George (23rd).** This is the feast day of the patron saint of shepherds. It is an important rural celebration and involves dancing and a feast.

MAY. **May Day.** May Day is another family day for picnicking and traditionally, families go to the country to pick flowers and make wreaths. As elsewhere, it is also a day of left-wing celebration of the working class.

JUNE. **Summer Solstice (24th).** Also the feast of St John the Baptist. Lots of bonfires and celebrations. **Naval Week (late June).** Celebrations and fireworks in honour of the navy (particularly at Soúda Bay near Chaniá).

JULY. **Réthymnon Wine Festival (second half of July).** Held in the Municipal Gardens. You can sample a wide range of local wines and listen to traditional Cretan folklore music. **Renaissance festival of Réthymnon (July–August).** A rich arts festival, including theatre, dance, music, and visual arts. Past performances have included theatre by Cretan playwrights as well as Shakespeare and Molière. Musicians from around the world perform. For further information visit www.rfr.gr. **Iráklion Festival (July–August).** Wide range of cultural events at venues all over the city.

AUGUST. **Feast of the Assumption of the Virgin.** 15th August marks the day when Mary ascended into heaven. It is a huge holiday in Greece, in fact it's the third biggest religious holiday after Easter and Christmas. People return to their home towns and villages, so even remote areas are busy with family-orientated activities. The entire country is closed for people to celebrate, and church services and festivals, family gatherings and feasts make this a wonderful time to be in Greece. Travel can be difficult due to limited services and the fact that the entire population of Greece is moving around and has booked most modes of transport well in advance. **Paleochóra Music Festival.** Song contests and music are performed on an open-air stage in the village. It's worth heading there if you're in the area as there's a lovely party atmosphere. **Sitia Sultana Festival.** A week-long celebration of the local crop in mid-August. Not all the grapes have been turned into sultanas, so there's plenty of wine! **Ágios Titos's Day (25th).** Celebration all over the island of the patron saint of Crete. Big parade in Iráklion.

SEPTEMBER. **Feast of the Exaltation of the Cross (Ypsosis tou Timiou Stavrou) (14th).** This is an autumnal feast which marks the last of the outdoor summer festivals and feasts.

OCTOBER. **Ochi Day.** 28th October is a public holiday across Greece that commemorates the reply given by the Greeks, specifically General Ioannis Metaxa, in response to Mussolini's demand for surrender during World War II. Ochi (which means no in Greek) Day is a celebration involving military parades, folk music, and dancing. **Elos Chestnut Festival.** This tiny village celebrates the chestnut with local entertainment. Usually around 15th October, but it does change, so check locally before making a special trip.

AVERAGE TEMPERATURE & SUNSHINE IN CRETE

		JAN	FEB	MAR	APR	MAY	JUNE
TEMP (MIN)	(°C)	3C	5C	6C	8C	10C	11C
	(°F)	37.4F	41F	42.8F	46.4F	50F	51.8F
TEMP (MAX)	(°C)	16C	16C	17C	20C	23C	27C
	(°F)	60.8F	60.8F	62.6F	68F	73.4F	80.6F

		JULY	AUG	SEPT	OCT	NOV	DEC
TEMP (MIN)	(°C)	13C	12C	10C	7C	6C	4C
	(°F)	55.4F	53.6F	50F	44.6F	42.8F	39.2F
TEMP (MAX)	(°C)	29C	29C	27C	24C	21C	18C
	(°F)	84.2F	84.2F	80.6F	75.2F	69.8F	64.4F

NOVEMBER. **Arkádi (7th–9th).** Celebration of the explosion at the Arkádi Monastery. **St Minos Parade.** Iráklion honours its patron saint with a parade along Kalokerínou Street. St Minos saved the Christians from being slaughtered by the Turks in the 19th century.

DECEMBER. **Christmas.** Christmas Day and Boxing Day are public holidays in Greece. Traditionally, Christmas in Greece is not as big a celebration as Easter, but Western customs are infiltrating and turkeys and Christmas trees are quite common. As with many places all over the world, Christmas is a time for families, singing, and feasting. **New Year's Eve.** People sing, drink, and eat.

The Weather
Crete enjoys a Mediterranean climate, with hot summers and cooler, wetter winters. It is the farthest south of the Greek islands, and is therefore the hottest, with the longest summer season. Yet it has strong seasonal winds (see box on p 94), which can make it seem much cooler than it is, with a corresponding increase in the danger of getting serious sunburn or sunstroke. The combination of strong winds and great heat in the summer can also lead to forest fires.

Mobile Phones
Before you travel, let your mobile phone provider know that you are going abroad and check that there are no blocks on your phone that would prevent you from using it. Find out from your phone network which Greek network they recommend, as when you first switch your phone on in Crete you may be given a choice of networks. Your own provider will know if any of these networks will be cheaper for you. Another way of using your mobile phone abroad is to buy a local SIM card to slot into your phone. You can buy these from a mobile phone shop, electronics shop, and even from some kiosks for about 15€.

International Dialling Code
The international dialling code for the whole of Greece is 0030. Dial it, then add the ten-figure number.

Getting There

By Plane
From the UK and Ireland: The vast majority of people visiting Crete from the UK and Ireland do so by plane—it has never been so easy, or so inexpensive, to fly.

The principal providers of scheduled flights from the UK are:
British Airways: www.britishairways.com ☎ 0870 850 9 850
Olympic Airways: www.olympicairlines.com ☎ 0870 6060 460
Flights are from Heathrow, Gatwick, or Manchester.

The websites of the main no-frills airlines with routes to Crete are as follows:
Airtours: www.airtours.co.uk
Flythomascook: www.flythomascook.com
Thomsonfly: www.thomsonfly.com

Each of these provides numerous routes from a large cross-section of the UK's regional airports. There are also numerous charter flights, often as part of a flight + accommodation package. The prime destinations for package holidays in Crete are the area around Chaniá and Réthymnon, the stretch between Iráklion and Hersónisos/Mália, and the shores of the Gulf of Mirabéllo around Ágios Nikólaos and Eloúnda. Crete has two international airports which can give you access to the island—Kazantzákis Airport, just to the east of Iráklion, is convenient for eastern and central Crete, and Daskalogiannis Airport, on the Akrotíri peninsula just outside Chaniá is useful for the centre and west. Flight times from the UK are 3½ hours from London, 4 hours from Manchester.

From the USA and Australia: Visitors from North America or the Southern Hemisphere are best advised to fly to one of the major European hub airports—London, Paris, Rome, or Amsterdam—then fly from there to Crete. Olympic Airways has agreements with a number of airlines (American Airlines, for example, or America West Airlines) to allow through booking.

By Boat
As with most Greek islands, it's not feasible to get to Crete from the UK by sea. However, it is possible to visit it by boat—either on a cruise, or by ferry from Athens or from other islands. Take a look at www.pocruises.com or www.viamare.com.

Getting Around

On Foot & By Taxi
You can explore each of the Cretan towns covered in this book on foot—even in the capital Iráklion, everywhere you're likely to want to see is within walking distance, and the centres of Chaniá and Réthymnon are very compact. If you do want to range a little farther afield, grab a cab (Radio Taxis ☎ 28210 98700). If you do so, it's wise to negotiate a fare before you get in.

By Bus
Crete's bus system is excellent—it's well-organised, efficient, and cheap. Most fares fall into the 3€–6.50€ range (for example, Chaniáto Kastélli is 3.90€, Chaniá to Réthymnon is 6€, Réthymnon to Iráklion 6.50€). If you intend to use the buses a lot,

do visit KTEL's excellent website and run off the routes and timetables you need (www.bus-service-crete-ktel.com).

By Car

In Crete, a rented car is by far the best way of seeing the island. Car rental provision is widespread and easy to arrange. The roads are far better than you might expect, especially as many routes have been upgraded and resurfaced, courtesy of EU grants. The National Road that runs along the north coast of the island is fast and well-engineered, but apart from the odd section, is not dual carriageway. This can make turning across the traffic flow a little hairy, though a central lane is usually provided. Signposting is clear, and in most places is in both Greek and Latin lettering. Main roads from north to south are also in excellent condition. Secondary roads are sometimes subject to rashes of potholes, though they too can be surprisingly good. [Insider tip]: when facing what is marked on the map as a dirt track, check with locals—in many places they have been resurfaced since the maps were drawn. If determined to use a dirt track, check your insurance: many rental companies don't cover use on unsurfaced roads.

There are high numbers of road traffic accidents in Greece—the death rate on Greek roads is three times higher than, for example, in Britain. Extra care should therefore be taken whether driving or walking.

By Moped, Motorbike or QuadBike

Hiring motorcycles, mopeds, scooters, or quad bikes really isn't a good idea, especially if you're not very experienced—the rate of serious and fatal accidents involving tourists on these forms of transport is frightening. If you do hire a moped, scooter, or motorcycle you should be aware that Greek law requires you to wear a helmet (or a helmet and goggles if you are on a quad bike). Failure to wear a helmet is also likely to invalidate any travel insurance. A full driving licence is needed to drive a moped and it needs to cover category A1, light motorcycle, not category P which is valid in the UK for driving a moped up to 50cc.

By Boat

Most coastal towns offer boat excursions, and this can be a pleasant way of seeing more of the area. They are invariably advertised at the quayside. On the south coast, indeed, they or the coastal ferry are the only way of getting to many of the prettiest beaches and villages if you don't want to walk.

By Tourist Road Train

Many of the main towns and holiday areas on Crete offer tourist road trains which are a quick and easy way of getting an overview of the area.

Fast **Facts**

AIRPORT see 'Getting there by plane'.

AMERICAN EXPRESS Adamis Travel Bureau, 23 25th Augusto St, Iráklion (☎ 28103 46202)

ATMS There are cash machines throughout western Crete.

BANKING HOURS Banking hours for customers are generally 8.00am until 2.00pm, but check this with

The Savvy Traveller

your closest bank when you first get to Crete. It is worth taking the contact details of your card provider's global assistance in case your credit card gets lost or stolen. Below are the details of some of the main card providers. **American Express credit card** ☎ +044 (0) 1273 696 933. **American Express Traveller's Cheques** ☎ +044 (0) 1273 571 600. **Visa credit card** ☎ 00 800 11 638 0304. **Mastercard** ☎ 00 800 11 887 0303. If you need money in an emergency and banks are closed, it is worth knowing that you can have money transferred to you through Western Union (www.westernunion.co.uk). This can be done through an agent, over the phone.

BUSES KTEL information numbers are: **Chaniá** ☎ 28210 93306; **Réthymnon** ☎ 28310 22212; **Iráklion** ☎ 28102 45020.

BUSINESS HOURS Opening hours of businesses in Crete, as in the rest of Greece, can be somewhat complicated and you should bear in mind that many shops and businesses are closed for the afternoon siesta between 2 and 5.30pm. Supermarkets tend to be open from 8am–8pm, or 9pm during high season; they close at 6pm on Saturdays and are closed on Sundays and holidays. Shops open from 9am–2pm Monday–Saturday, then on Tuesdays, Thursdays, and Fridays they open again from 6–9pm. This may vary depending on the season and area. As with supermarkets, shops are closed on Sundays and holidays. Offices keep to the same hours as shops, but are not open on Saturdays. Gas stations are open throughout the day Monday–Saturday, they are very rarely open past 10pm, and Sundays and holidays are very much a matter of luck, so you may have to travel around a little in order to find an open one. Main Post Offices are open from 8am–8pm Monday–Friday and 8am–2pm on Saturdays. Other Post Offices tend to be open from 8am–2pm Monday–Friday. Kiosks keep their own hours and an open one can usually be found without any problems. The opening hours of tourist shops vary hugely, and they are often open later at night than normal shops, especially in the tourist season. Most car mechanics work from 9am–4pm Monday–Friday and some on Saturday mornings, so you shouldn't have a problem finding a garage.

CREDIT CARDS All larger establishments (hotels, restaurants, shops) accept the main credit cards, but a lot of smaller ones don't. And even when they have the technology to accept them, you may find a reluctance to do so. In service stations, for example, there are usually pump attendants, and they far prefer taking cash—they always seem to have enough money on them to give change—to returning to the office to process a credit card.

CUSTOMS When travelling into Crete from the UK or Ireland, visitors over the age of 18 may bring in 800 cigarettes or 200 cigars or 400 cigarillos or 1kg of loose tobacco, 10 litres of spirits or 90 litres of wine and 110 litres of beer. The import of plants in soil is strictly prohibited. While most sports and camping equipment have no restrictions, it should be noted that only one windsurf board per person may be imported duty free and a note of it will be made in your passport to ensure that the board is exported at the end of your stay. When travelling from Crete to the UK and Ireland there is no need to pay tax or duty on items that were bought on the island, as long as local tax was paid on purchase. This applies to purchases for personal use only and customs are likely to question you about goods that exceed the following limits: 3200 cigarettes, 400 cigarillos, 200 cigars, 3kg of loose tobacco, 110 litres of beer, 90 litres of wine, 10 litres of spirits, 20 litres of fortified wine. When travelling within the European Union you are permitted to pay tax-free prices on the following products: fragrances, cosmetics, skincare products, photographic goods, electrical goods, fashion and accessories, gifts and souvenirs. The export of antiquities out of Greece is strictly prohibited. Any genuine antiquity, particularly religious objects including icons, needs special permission to leave the country and you must provide receipts and a full explanation of how it was acquired. In addition to this, an export certificate must be provided for any object that dates from before 1830. This export certificate should be provided by the person, dealer, or shopkeeper who was responsible for the sale.

ELECTRICITY 220 volts AC. UK appliances should work, US ones will need a transformer. Sockets are of the two-pin, standard European design, so three-pin plugs will need an adaptor.

EMBASSIES & CONSULATES **UK:** British Vice Consulate, 16 Papa-Alexandrou St, 712 02 Iráklion ☎ 28102 24012. Open to the public Mon–Fri 8am–1pm. **US:** The American Citizen Services section of the US Embassy is located at the Kokkali St entrance near Dinokratous and Evzonon Streets in Athens. American Citizen Services: 8:30am–5:00pm. For emergencies on the last Wednesday of each month, call ☎ 21072 12951. For after-hour emergencies call ☎ 21072 94301 or ☎ (0030) 210-729-4444.

☎ 21072 02419/2415/ 2420/2408. **Australia:** The Australian Embassy, Level 6, Thon Building, Cnr. Kifisias and Alexandras Ave, Ambelokipi, Athens 115 23 (Postal Address: PO Box 14070 Ambelokipi, Athens 11510) ☎ 210 87 04000.

EMERGENCY ASSISTANCE Emergency (general) ☎ 112, Police ☎ 100, Ambulance ☎ 166, Fire Department ☎ 199, Tourist Police ☎ 171.

GAY & LESBIAN TRAVELLERS Homosexuality is legal over the age of 17, and in the major holiday resorts little prejudice is likely to be encountered, though overt gay behaviour in public is often frowned upon. There is no major gay scene in Crete as there is, for example, in Mykonos.

HEALTH No vaccinations are needed for travelling to Greece, but it's worth checking that inoculations are up-to-date. It also may be worth considering a vaccination for tick-borne encephalitis (TBE) if you are camping, rambling, or travelling to forested areas. A big health risk in the summer is the sun. Drink plenty of water, wear a high sun protection factor sun cream, cover up where possible, and wear a hat and sunglasses. It is highly recommended that you stay out of the sun during the hottest part of the day—you can be burned even through a parasol, as I know to my cost. Be extra careful when it comes to young children and babies.

HOSPITALS & HEALTH CENTRES Hospitals and medical centres in Crete are of varying standards and services may be limited in more remote areas—the ambulance service in particular can be rudimentary. It may be worthwhile finding out more information about what medical facilities are close to where you will be staying before you travel. Many of the big resort hotels have doctors on call, and smaller ones will certainly offer advice.

INSURANCE Travellers from the UK need to apply for a European Health Insurance Card (EHIC). This has replaced the old E111 and it entitles UK residents to free or reduced cost healthcare. The card is valid for 5 years and allows you, as a card holder, the same treatment as a resident of Greece if you become ill or have an accident during your trip. Each person travelling needs their own card and it's free. You can apply at www.dh.gov.uk/travellers, on ☎ 0845 606 2030 or you can pick up a form at the Post Office. Guidelines state that a postal application should take up to 21 days and telephone and online applications will take up to 7 days. The EHIC card isn't a substitute for travel and health insurance, and purchasing comprehensive insurance is recommended. Be sure to check carefully for exclusions and that you are covered for any activities that you are planning. It may be worth checking home insurance policies or credit card perks to find out if you are already covered for some things, such as contents away from home, and you may find it is more cost effective to extend one or more of these policies rather than buy a new policy. If you are not covered, then good quality comprehensive cover can be found at a reasonable price online. As it is quite a competitive market it is worth shopping around.

INTERNET ACCESS Big hotels usually offer Internet access, either in-room or in a dedicated 'Internet corner' on the premises. Internet cafés and bars are common in most towns visited by tourists, often with just two or three machines. Internet cafés come and go—try Vranas Studio Café ☎ 28210 58618, just behind the cathedral (Chaniá); Galero ☎ 28310 21324; near the Rimini Fountain (Réthymnon), the Konsova Internet Café on Dikeossinas (Iráklion), or the Café du Lac on the lake, above the Café du Lac restaurant (Agios Nikolaos) ☎ 28410 22414. But there are lots of others.

MONEY The euro has been the official form of currency in Greece since 2002 when the drachma was replaced. There are 7 denominations of notes: 500€, 200€, 100€, 50€, 20€, 10€, and 5€. Coins come in denominations of 2€, 1€, and 50, 20, 10, 5, 2, and 1 cents. You may hear the cents being referred to as *lepta*, which was to the drachma what the cent is to the euro. Although euros differ slightly in appearance from country to country, they are legal tender in all of the countries that use the euro. In smaller shops and restaurants there can sometimes be a problem using large denomination euro notes, as they cannot change them or don't always like to accept them, so ensure you carry smaller denomination notes with you. Most banks and travel agents and the Post Office offer foreign currency and traveller's cheques. The most convenient and safe way to obtain cash while on holiday is to get it from a cash machine (ATM), just as you do at home—either with your normal bank card, or with your credit card. Look out for the very useful ATM locators on providers' websites before you go (www.visa.co.uk and www.mastercard.co.uk). You just enter as much information about your intended location as you can provide, and it gives you addresses, telephone numbers, and a map of the closest ATMs. If in any doubt about using your card in Greece, contact the provider. It should be noted that smaller towns often have only one bank with an ATM, which may not accept your card so, again, it is worth checking first or having more than one type of card with you. Up-to-date currency exchange rates are displayed in the windows of banks in Greece, so you should be able to get some idea of how much you are withdrawing. Credit card companies charge a fee for currency exchange, though it's rarely high enough to outweigh the convenience. Depending on how the charges work, it may prove more cost effective to withdraw cash in larger sums and use it for transactions, rather than using the card direct. Check with your card provider before you go to work out the best method of payment for you. Another thing to note is that some banks and the Post Office offer a pre-paid credit card. As the name suggests, you put a set amount of money on the card before you go and you can only spend that amount, which could be useful for those on a strict budget. The card offered by the Post Office is a Visa card that costs a one-off charge of £10 per card (you can have up to three) and you can put as much money as you need on the card. You can top the card up by phone and if the card is lost or stolen, the card will be replaced, as will any outstanding balance that was left on the card. Visit www.postoffice.com to find out more.

Tip

When you arrive in Crete, you'll need a 1€ coin at the airport to secure a trolley, and there are often long queues at airport cash points. So it's worth buying at least some euros before you go.

PARKING Apart from the centre of main towns (where parking is strictly controlled) Cretans seem to park where they like, and there are few restrictions. (For the main towns see p 98.)

PHARMACIES Pharmacies keep the same hours as shops on Monday to Friday, and are closed at weekends. As with UK pharmacies, if you need an open one outside of normal hours, there will be a notice giving the nearest open pharmacy in the window.

POLICE If you need the police, your best bet is to contact the tourist police in the first instance—they are specially trained, and are more likely to speak English than their mainstream colleagues. Dial ☎ 171 or Chaniá ☎ 28210 25931, Réthymnon ☎ 28310 28156, Iráklion ☎ 28102 83190.

POST OFFICE **Chaniá:** Tzanakaki 3 (near Municipal Market) Mon–Fri 8am–8pm, Sat 8am–midday. Réthymnon: 37 Moatsu (east of the Public Gardens) Mon–Fri 8am–8pm, Sat 8am–midday. Iráklion: Plateia Daskaloyiannis (due south of the Archaeological Museum) Mon–Fri 7.30am–8pm, daily.

SAFETY Crime rates in Greece are relatively low, but tourism does attract pickpockets and thieves, especially in areas where there are crowds of people. So stay as vigilant as you would at home, and keep valuables in the hotel safe. Sexual assaults are rare, but they do occur: older teenage daughters should be warned against drinking too much, going off alone with strangers, and leaving drinks unattended.

SENIOR TRAVELLERS Reductions are available to over-60s in all state-run attractions, and some archaeological sites and museums are free. It's also worth asking on buses, ferries, and even flights—there may be discounts. Have your passport available to prove your age.

The Savvy Traveller

SHOPPING Details of shopping are to be found throughout this guide. For opening hours, see 'Business Hours' above.

SMOKING Smoking in all public places is to be banned in Greece from 1st January, 2010. How the Greeks—Europe's heaviest smokers—respond remains to be seen!

TELEPHONES Payphones in Greece tend to be card phones and phones that accept coins are not common. Cards can be bought at shops and kiosks and come in varying denominations from 3€ upwards.

TIME Crete is 7 hours ahead of Eastern Standard Time in the US and two hours ahead of the UK's GMT. Eastern Daylight Time in Australia is 11 hours ahead of GMT.

TIPPING In formal restaurants a tip of about 10% of the bill is customary, but elsewhere (cafés, tavérnas) it is usual simply to leave any odd coins that come back with your change. For small drinks bills, round up to the nearest euro. Leave 1€–2€ per night for chambermaids, and round up to the nearest five or ten euros for taxis (up to about 10% of the fare).

TOURIST INFORMATION OFFICES
The principal offices are: Iráklion: 1 Xanthoudidou ☎ 28102 28225, Mon–Fri 8am–2.30pm. Chaniá: National Tourist Office: 1866 Square ☎ 28210 92943, Mon–Fri 9am–2.30pm; Municipal Tourist Office: Kidonias 29 ☎ 28210 36155, Mon–Fri 9am–2.30pm. Réthymnon: Venizelou ☎ 28310 29148, Mon–Fri 8am–2.30pm. Ágios Nikólaos: 21 Akti I Koundourou St ☎ 28410 22357.

TRAVELLERS WITH DISABILITIES For those in wheelchairs, Crete, with its steep hills, stepped pavements, narrow alleys, and difficult access to buildings can be a nightmare. Furthermore, pavements in towns and cities are often uneven and obstructed by cars and motorbikes. Efforts are being made, however, to make holiday areas at least more wheelchair-friendly, and modern hotels usually have lifts and ramps. There doesn't seem to be any central source of information on Crete for those with disabilities, and where websites give advice it tends to be general (see www.holidays2crete.com, for example), or simply lists of accommodation suitable for those with disabilities (eg www.greekhotel.com). Many airlines, tour operators, and hotels now provide information about suitability for those with disabilities, so the best bet is to contact them direct.

VAT VAT rates in Crete vary from 4.5% to 19%, depending on the item.

WATER Tap water in Crete is usually safe, though in remoter areas it would be as well to ask. Chilled bottled water is available everywhere at prices which are, to prevent profiteering, fixed by law.

Crete: A Brief History

A knowledge of Crete's history adds immeasurably to the pleasures of visiting the island. Below are the edited highlights. But remember, Cretan history is chock-full of the unknown and the disputed, so this account is grossly over-simplified. The alternative would have been lots of 'it is believed that …' and 'expert opinion now seems to feel that …'. On holiday, you don't need it. Life's too short.

The Earliest Settlers

7000–3000 BC The earliest Cretans came across the Eastern Mediterranean from the north, east, and south. They lived in caves, had rudimentary tools, pottery and cloth, and grew crops and raised livestock.

The Minoans

Europe's first, and Crete's greatest, civilisation, Minoan Crete went through three phases—the early development of agriculture, crafts, and trade; the building of the first palaces; and, most famously of all, the great period of new palace building.

3000–1900 BC (PRE-PALATIAL)

Towns and villages spread across the island, and sophisticated arts and crafts developed—metalworkers, stone-cutters, potters, jewellers, and weavers produced hitherto unmatched clothes, stone, bone, and wooden tools, pottery, weapons, and jewellery. The olive and the grape were introduced, and Crete started to trade with her neighbours. And remember—this was still the Stone Age!

1900–1700 BC (FIRST PALACES)

Great palaces were built at Knossós, Mália, Festós and Zákros, their wealth and lack of defences suggesting a peaceful and prosperous society. Pottery, jewellery, and craft work were now highly sophisticated and beautifully decorated, and the presence of Cretan bronze-work and pottery all over the eastern Mediterranean bears witness to its powerful navy and burgeoning maritime and mercantile economy. Around 1700 BC the palaces were destroyed, probably by an earthquake, possibly followed by an opportunist early Mycenaean invasion from the mainland. But the civilisation carried on.

1700–1450 BC (NEW PALACES)

All the palaces to whose remains visitors nowadays flock date largely from the rebuilding of the great palaces that followed the 1700 BC earthquake. Though in the same places (Knossós, Mália, Festós and Zákros), they were even more magnificent, huge complexes of multi-storey buildings, elegant rooms, sweeping staircases, and colourful frescoes, with sophisticated plumbing, extensive workshops, and venues for elaborate religious ritual. The standards of architecture and of artistic achievement are staggering, especially when you take into account that this was 1500 years before Christ! Add the widespread use of the (as yet undeciphered) Linear A script, the other houses and towns dotted across the Cretan landscape, and the wide distribution of Cretan artefacts across the whole Mediterranean area, and you have Europe's first great civilisation, over a thousand years before the golden age of Classical Greece. Its end came catastrophically in 1450 BC when the palaces were totally destroyed, possibly by the after-effects— tidal wave, fires, clouds of ash— of the volcanic explosion of Santorini. This time Minoan civilisation didn't recover, and was overwhelmed, either by rebellion by its own lower orders, or by further Mycenaean invasion from the mainland, or both.

Mycenaean Crete

1450–1100 BC What happened next is confused, with little decisive evidence. The Mycenaeans took control of much of the island, with Crete becoming an

Crete: **A Brief History**

adjunct of Mycenaean Greece. Minoan culture, however, seems to have continued in a modified form.

Dorian & Classical Crete

1100–67 BC From about 1100 BC the Dorians dominated Crete, either by invasion or through settlement. New cities were established (Lató, for example, just outside Ágios Nikólaos), and a harsh, stratified society developed. The fascinating Law Code, which is the principal evidence for this period, was found inscribed on a wall in Górtys—though dating from 450 BC, it was a codification of laws which had already been in existence for centuries. As Greece entered its Golden Age from around 500 BC onwards, Crete was revered for its past glories, but had little practical involvement in the great classical Hellenic world.

Roman Crete

67 BC–395 AD Following attacks and raids from about 200 BC onwards by the increasingly confident Romans, the island was eventually conquered in 67 BC. Crete became, like Britain, a part of the Roman Empire which dominated Europe for the next 400 years. Górtys became the capital, there was much building of roads, aqueducts, bridges, and towns, and, in the wake of St Paul's visit to the island in 47 AD, Crete became Christian, with Ágios Titus as its first bishop.

Byzantine Crete

395–1206 AD Following the splitting of the Roman Empire into a Western and Eastern sector, ruled from Rome and Constantinople respectively, Crete became part of the Eastern, or Byzantine, Empire. Despite a lengthy interval of Arab rule (824–961 AD), during which Crete became largely a base for attacks on the rest of Greece and on passing shipping, this was a period of relative peace and prosperity, with many churches being built—for example Ágios Titos at Górtys—and icons and frescoes painted. Although this was a period of growing threat from the Muslim East, it was actually Christian politicking that led to the end of Byzantine rule. The Fourth Crusade, in 1204, intended as a campaign to drive the Muslims out of the Holy Land, turned instead on the Christian capital of Byzantium—Constantinople—and sacked it. Crete was ceded to the Venetian Empire.

Venetian Crete

1206–1648 AD It took the Venetians 4 years of heavy fighting to secure Crete from the Genoese, who had taken control of the island pre-emptively in 1206. Crete was an invaluable addition to the Venetian maritime empire. Its ports gave access to the whole of the Eastern Mediterranean, its land supplied food for its sailors and timber for its ships. So Venetian rule was quickly imposed—land was divided between feudal lords, who squeezed the conquered population until the pips squeaked. Catholicism replaced Orthodox Christianity as the official religion—another cause of bitter resentment among the Cretans. Rebellions were frequent during the first century of occupation, and were put down with ruthless ferocity by the occupying power. In 1453, however, the fall of Constantinople led to an influx of highly educated refugees, leading to a great burst of cultural and artistic endeavour. At the same time, pirate raids on Cretan towns were gathering strength, and, especially after 1573 when Cyprus fell, fear of the growing Turkish threat led to a burst of military activity as town walls were strengthened, fortresses built, and harbours and shipyards improved. To no avail. The Turkish conquest of Crete was largely completed by 1648, though pockets of resistance held out until 1715.

Ottoman Crete

1648–1898 AD It is the Turkish occupation of Crete that lives most strongly in the memories of Cretans, even today. The Ottoman Empire was interested not in developing the island, but in making money out of it. Investment in infrastructure was minimal (hence the shortage of major buildings, apart from mosques from this period), taxation was sky-high, corruption was rife. And although the Ottoman Empire allowed the return of the Orthodox church, taxation and the law favoured Muslims to such an extent that many Christians, at least nominally, converted. Rebellions were inevitable. The first major one occurred in 1770, led by Daskaloyannis who, when trying to negotiate terms, was seized and skinned alive in Chaniá's main square. Such brutality became par for the course during subsequent waves of rebellion, provoking a similarly ferocious response from the Cretans. Throughout this period the Turks easily held the major towns and the agricultural lowlands, but dared not venture into highlands invariably controlled by Cretan rebels. In particular, Sfakia, in the south-west, was never securely under Turkish rule.

The Fight for Independence & Union with Greece

1898–1913 From 1821, when a full-scale War of Independence started in the rest of Greece, rebellion in Crete became even more febrile, and from 1832, when the independent Greek state was established, most Cretans had only one aim—*enosis*, or union with Greece. Rebellion followed rebellion—in 1841, in 1858, in 1866, in 1889, and 1896. Support for the Cretans was widespread throughout Europe, but western governments, suspicious of each other and afraid that a collapse of the Ottoman Empire would lead to a dangerous power vacuum, stayed out of it. But in 1898, when the British vice-consul in Iráklion was killed, the British and their allies were forced to act. The Turks were expelled from Crete, and a national government was set up, still nominally under Ottoman rule. The drive towards *enosis* was now, though, unstoppable, and in 1913 Crete became part of Greece.

World War II

1939–1945 Most Cretan soldiers were mobilised at the beginning of World War II to fight in Northern Greece, first against the Italians, then against the Germans. When Greeks and Allies were driven off the mainland by the Germans, they fled to Crete, which was intended to be an impregnable bastion against the Nazi hordes, but which turned out to be, as a result of lack of preparation, poor communication, and incompetence on the part of the Allies, an unmitigated disaster. The Battle of Crete started on 20th May, 1941 when German paratroops invaded from the air and, though suffering horrific losses, managed to establish a

The Greek Language

Greek isn't an easy language to learn. For a start, there's the alphabet. You either have to learn it, or deal with its imperfect transliteration into the more familiar Roman script. Then there are the difficulties caused by pronunciation, and by the rapid-fire delivery of Greeks speaking their own language. Add regional dialects and accents (both are very noticeable in Crete), and you begin to see the problem. It is, though, really worth making an effort to learn at least a few words: Greeks are proud of their country and their language, and they'll be delighted with any effort that you make to learn a bit about either.

bridgehead at Máleme airfield west of Chaniá. Despite heroic bravery on the part of individual Allied soldiers and, in particular, the ordinary men, women, and children of Crete, Allied forces were unceremoniously chased across the island to the south coast, from where the majority were lifted off to Egypt. This began the second phase of the war in Crete, involving the German occupation and the Cretan resistance. The resistance was initially concerned with helping Allied soldiers who'd been left behind get off the island, then increasingly with harrying the occupying forces and supplying the Allies with information about defences and troop movements. They were helped in this by expertise, equipment, and supplies organised by Allied intelligence officers landed along the south coast. The fighting was brutal, with murderous German reprisals against the civilian population.

Post-War Crete

1945–PRESENT Since World War II, Crete's history has been very much that of Greece as a whole, though the island avoided the worst excesses of the Civil War that ripped the mainland apart—Crete has a liberal, republican tradition, so the vicious in-fighting between left and right never took hold. Always suspicious of mainland control (oddly, when you recall how hard they fought for unification!), Crete has benefitted from EU membership (particularly agricultural policy and road building), and from a huge increase in tourism, though it is now perhaps regretting the unbridled nature of 1960s and 1970s development, and is trying to broaden its appeal and extend its tourist season.

Useful Words & Phrases

Tip

When you're asking for or about something and have to rely on single words or short phrases, it's an excellent idea to use sas parakaló (if you please) to introduce or conclude almost anything you say.

ENGLISH	GREEK	PRONOUNCIATION
Hello/goodbye	Γειά σου Γειά σαζ	Ya-soo (singular, informal); Ya-sas (plural, singular polite)
Good morning	Καλημέρα	Ka-li-me-ra
Good afternoon/ evening	Καλησπέρα	Ka-li-spe-ra
Goodnight (night)	Καληνύχτα	Ka-li-nich-ta (nik-ta)
Yes	Ναι	Nai
No	Οχι	O-hi
Please/ you're welcome	Παρακαλω	Pa-ra-ka-lo
Thank you (very much)	Ευχαριστω (πολή)	Ef-ha-ri-stow (po-lee)
How are you?	Τι κάνετε?	Ti ka-ne-te?
Fine, thank you	Μιά χαρά, ευχαριστω	Mya ha-ra, ef-ha-ri-stow
Excuse me	Συγνωμη	Sig-no-mi
Sorry	Σόρι	So-ry
Give me . . .	Μου δωστε . . .	Mou dhos-te . . .
Do you speak English?	Μιλάτε αγγλικά?	Mi-la-te Angli-ka?
I understand	Καταλαβαίνω	Ka-ta-la-ve-no
I don't understand	Δεν καταλαβαίνω	Dhen ka-ta-la-ve-no
I know (it)	Το ξέρο	To gze-ro
Where is . . .	Που είναι . . .	Pou ee-ne . . .
the station	Ο σταθμόζ	o stath-mos
a post office	Το ταχιδρομίο	to ta-chi-dhro-mee-o
a bank	Η τράπεζα	ee tra-pe-za
a hotel	Το ξενοδοχείω	to xe-no-dho-hee-o
a restaurant	Το εστιατόριο	to estia-tow-ree-o
a pharmacy/chemist	Το φαρμακείο	to farma-kee-o
the toilet	Η τουαλέτα	ee tooa-le-ta
a hospital	Το νοσοκομείο	to no-so-ko-mee-o
Left	Αριστερά	A-ri-ste-ra
Right	Δεξιά	Dhex-ya
Straight	Ευθύα	Ef-thee-a
Tickets	Εισιτήρια	Ee-see-tee-ria
How much does it cost?	Πόσο κάνει?	Po-so ka-ni?
A one-way ticket	Ενα απλό εισιτήριο	E-na ap-lo is-i-ti-rio
A round-trip ticket	Ενα εισιτήριο με επιστροφη	E-na is-i-ti-rio me e-pi-stro-fi
Is there a discount for . . .	Ηπάρχει έκπτωσι γιά . . .	Ee-par-hi ek-pto-si yia . . .
family	Οικογένεια	ee-ko-gen-ya
children	Παιδιά	pe-dhia
students	Φοιτητέζ	fee-tee-tes
seniors	συνταξιούχοζ	syn-da-xi-ou-hos

ENGLISH	GREEK	PRONOUNCIATION
What time is it?	Τη ωρα είναι?	Ti o-ra ee-ne?
When?	Πότε?	Po-teh?
When does (it) leave?	Πότε φεύγει?	Po-teh fev-gi?
This	Αυτό	Af-tow
Here	Εδω	Eh-dho
There	Εκεί	Eh-key

Numbers

One (1)	Ενα	E-na
Two (2)	Δύο	Dhee-o
Three (3)	Τρία	Tree-a
Four (4)	Τέσσερα	Te-se-ra
Five (5)	Πέντε	Pen-de
Six (6)	Έξι	E-xi
Seven (7)	Επτά	Ep-ta
Eight (8)	Οκτό	Ok-to
Nine (9)	Εννιά	En-ya
Ten (10)	Δέκα	Dhe-ka
Eleven (11)	Έντεκα	En-dhe-ka
Twelve (12)	Δωδεκα	Tho-dhe-ka
Thirteen (13)	Δεκατρία	Dhe-ka-tree-a
Fourteen (14)	Δεκατέσσερα	Dhe-ka-te-se-da
Fifteen (15)	Δεκαπέντε	Dhe-ka-pen-de
Sixteen (16)	Δεκα-έξι	Dhe-ka-eh-xi
Seventeen (17)	Δεκα-επτά	Dhe-ka ep-ta
Eighteen (18)	Δεκα-οχτω	Dhe-ka ok-to
Nineteen (19)	Δεκα-εννιά	Dhe-ka en-ya
Twenty (20)	Εικοσι	Ee-ko-see
Thirty (30)	Τριάντα	Tri-an-da
Forty (40)	Σαράντα	Sa-ran-da
Fifty (50)	Πενήντα	Pe-nin-da
One hundred (100)	Εκατό	Eh-ka-to

Menu Terms

Food	Φαγητό	Fa-gee-to
Water	Νερό	Neh-ro
Coffee	Καφέ	Ca-feh
Tea	Τσάι	Tsa-ee
A kilo/half-kilo	Ενα κιλό/Μισό κιλό	Ena kee-lo/mi-so kee-lo
of red/white wine	κόκκινο/άσπρο κρασί	kok-kino/as-pro kra-see
The bill please	Το λογαριασμό παρακαλω	To lo-ga-ri-az-mo pa-ra-ka-lo

Roll the 'r's so they sound like a soft d. Dh sounds like the.

Index

A

Accommodations
  Ágios Nikólaos, 95–96
  Chaniá, 71–73, 124
  Iráklion, 88, 143–144
  Lasíthi Plateau, 154–155
  Réthymnon, 79–80, 134
Acquaplus Water Park, 63, 142, 143
Aegean bar (Ágios Nikólaos), 97
Aerakis (music shop, Iráklion), 86
Afráta, 118
Ágia Galíni, 19, 113, 130
Agia Paraskevi (Argiróupolis), 128
Agía Pelágia, 102, 113, 132
Agia Rouméli, 105, 113
Agía Triáda, 18, 29, 141
Ágios Konstantínos, 153
Ágios Nikólaos, 22, 90–98, 103, 107, 113
Ágios Títos, 14, 160
Ágios Títos church (Iráklion), 14, 85–86
Ágios Títos's Day, 160
Agritourism, 10
Agrotiko (Réthymnon), 76
Águis Konstantínos, 51
Airports, 162
Akrotiri Peninsula, 121–123
Alaoum, 61–62
Ali, Mehmet, 41
Ali, Uluch, 33
Allied War Cemetery, 45, 122
Almirída, 101, 114, 123
Almyros beach (Ágios Nikólaos), 93
Amári Valley, 107, 129, 139
Ammos beach (Ágios Nikólaos), 93
Amnesia disco (Hersónisos), 138
Amusement parks, 5, 61–62, 117. *See also* Water parks
Andistatis market (Réthymnon), 76
Animal parks and zoos, 109
  Aquaworld (Hersónisos), 62, 142
  Ark (Georgioúpolis), 54, 60, 109, 123
  Lasinthos Eco Park (Ágios Georgios), 57, 64, 109, 153
  Stone Garden, 53, 59–60, 122
Anópoli, 38–39
Ano Zákros (Upper Zákros), 106
Apodóulou, 130
Apokreas festival, 159
Apostolos, Kourtis, 71
Aquariums
  Aquaworld (Hersónisos), 62, 142
  Cretaquarium (Gournes), 14, 64, 109, 143
Aquarius Pub and Sports Bar (Ágios Nikólaos), 97
Aquaworld (Hersónisos), 62, 142
Aradena Gorge (Loutró), 107
Archaeological Museum (Ágios Nikólaos), 94, 95
Archaeological Museum (Archánes), 139
Archaeological Museum (Chaniá), 69
Archaeological Museum (Iráklion), 5, 14, 17, 27, 29, 83, 141, 152
Archaeological Museum (Réthymnon), 76, 78
Archaeological Museum (Sitía), 30, 150–152
Archánes, 139
Argiróupolis, 3, 128
Ariadne, 15
Ark (Georgioúpolis), 54, 60, 109, 123
Arkádi festival, 161
Arkádi Monastery, 3, 4, 40–41, 128–129
Arsenáli, 67, 70, 87
Art museums, 48–51
  El Greco Museum (Fodele), 50, 132
  Folk-Art Museum (Ágios Nikólaos), 91, 92
  Folk Museum (Ágios Georgios), 153
  Historical and Folk Art Museum (Réthymnon), 77–78
  Museum of Religious Arts (Iráklion), 17, 49
Askifou Plateau, 45, 46, 119
Atelier Ceramica (Ágios Nikólaos), 93
ATMs, 163, 166–167
Averof (shoe shop, Iráklion), 86
Avidou, 108
Avli Raw Materials (Réthymnon), 76

B

Bali, 4, 102, 132
Banking hours, 163–164
Barbarossa, Aruj, 33
Bars. *See* Nightlife
Battle of Crete Museum (Iráklion), 14, 17
Beaches, 100–103
  Afráta, 118
  Ágia Galíni, 19, 131
  Agía Pelágia, 132
  Ágios Nikólaos, 93
  Bali, 132
  Chaniá region, 101–102, 120
  Elafonísi, 3, 118
  Eloúnda, 148
  Georgioúpolis, 60, 127
  Hersónisos, 14, 21, 62–63, 142
  Iráklion region, 102–103, 142
  Lasíthi region, 103
  Mátala, 18–19, 141
  Paleochóra, 118
  Plakiás, 131–132
  Réthymnon region, 75, 102, 131, 132
  Stavrós, 121
  Váï, 24, 151
Bembo Fountain (Iráklion), 84
Bicycling, 61, 110–111
Boat houses, 67, 70, 87
Boating, 162, 163
  in Ágia Galíni, 19
  in Almirída, 123
  in Bali, 132
  with children, 19, 60–62, 120, 142
  in Eloúnda, 22
  ferries, 3, 9–10, 19, 60, 71, 113, 120
  in Hersónisos, 142
  on Lake Kournás, 127
  in Plakiás, 131–132
Bottomless Lake (Ágios Nikólaos), 92
Boyd, Harriet, 31
Buses, 162–164
Business hours, 9, 164
Byzantine Empire, 67, 170
Byzantio (icon workshop, Ágios Nikólaos), 93

C

Cameo Club (Hersónisos), 138
Car rentals, 9
Caves
  Diktean Cave (Psichro), 64, 154
  on Lasíthi Plateau, 6

Index

Caves (cont.)
  in Mátala, 5, 18–19, 103, 141
  Milatos Cave, 21, 41, 147
Cell phones, 161
Chaniá Cathedral, 69–70
Chaniá region, 116–125
  accommodations, 71–73, 124
  Akrotiri and Drapano Peninsulas tour, 121–123
  beaches, 101–102, 120
  city of Chaniá, 19, 37–38, 59–62, 66–73, 113
  dining, 72, 125
  nightlife, 72
  shopping, 70
  south coast tour, 119–121
  west coast tour, 116–119
Children, activities for, 58–64
  amusement parks, 5, 61–62, 117
  animal parks, 53, 54, 57, 59–60, 62, 64, 109, 122, 123, 142, 153
  aquariums, 5, 14, 62, 64, 142, 143
  beaches, 3, 14, 18–19, 21, 24, 60, 62–63, 101–103, 118, 120, 131, 132, 141, 142, 151
  boating, 19, 60–62, 120, 142
  caves, 18–19, 21, 41, 64, 103, 141, 147, 154
  clubs, 59, 72
  glass blowing factories, 60, 123
  golfing, 5, 61–62
  historical sites, 5, 13, 14, 17, 22, 27–28, 34, 35, 54, 55, 62, 87, 128, 133, 137–138, 142, 149
  horse riding, 61, 62, 108
  Internet cafés, 59
  museums, 3, 19, 33, 44–45, 50, 56, 59, 64, 67–68, 71, 87, 109, 132
  music-related, 51, 59, 72, 139
  playgrounds, 57, 60, 61
  shopping, 57, 60–61
  tourist road trains, 60, 62, 75–76, 142
  Voúves Olive Tree, 53, 117
  walking and trekking, 19, 61, 106, 107, 120, 130
  water parks, 5, 61, 63, 142
Children's World (Georgioúpolis), 60
Christmas, 161
Church of the Three Martyrs, 69
Clean Monday festival, 159
Climate, 158, 161
Consulates, 165
Cooking, 110
Credit cards, 10, 163, 164, 167
Cretan Village (Arolíthos), 54, 55, 133
Cretan winds, 110
Cretaquarium (Gournes), 14, 64, 109, 143
Crete
  family life in, 4
  favourite moments in, 2–6
  history of, 168–172
  strategies for seeing, 8–10
Crete Golf Club, 63, 107, 108, 142–143
Currency, 10, 166–167
Customs, 164–165

D

Daedalus, 15
Daliani minaret, 37
Dalianis, Hatzimichaelis, 39
Daly, Ross, 51, 139
Damaskenos, Michael, 49
Daskaloyannis, 38–39
Dedalou (Iráklion), 86
Deligiannakis, Nikos, 39
Destijl nightclub (Agia Marina), 72
"Dew Men," 39–40
Diadromés (Armeni), 61
Dialing code, 161
Diktean Cave (Psichro), 64, 154
Dikti Mountain, 153
Dimakopoulous, Ioannis, 40
Dimitrakaki market (Réthymnon), 76
Dining
  Ágios Nikólaos, 96–98
  Argiróupolis, 3
  Chaniá, 72, 125
  Iráklion, 89, 144–145
  Lasíthi Plateau, 155–156
  Réthymnon, 80–81, 135
Disabilities, travellers with, 168
Discos, 138
Diving, 113
Dorian Law Code, 140, 170
Drapano Peninsula, 121–123
Drinking water, 168
Driving, 9, 46, 163
Drossoulites, 39–40

E

Easter, 159
East Mediterranean (specialty foods, Ágios Nikólaos), 93
Elafonísi, 3, 101, 118
Electricity, 165
Eleftherios Venizélos Square (Chaniá), 69
El Greco Museum (Fodele), 50, 132
El Greco Park (Iráklion), 14, 86
Ellinadiko bar (Ágios Nikólaos), 97
Elos Chestnut Festival, 160
Eloúnda, 22, 35, 91, 103, 148
Embassies, 165
Emergency assistance, 165
Enosis, 171
Erotokrítos (Vitsentzos Kornaros), 84
Erotokrítos and Aretoúsa (statue), 84
Etz-Hayyim Synagogue (Chaniá), 68–89
Evans, Arthur, 13, 17, 27–29, 137
Éxo Moulianá, 57

F

Falásarna, 101
Feast of St George, 160
Feast of St John the Baptist, 160
Feast of the Annunciation, 159
Feast of the Assumption of the Virgin, 160
Feast of the Exaltation of the Cross, 160
Fere Silver and Gold (Réthymnon), 76
Ferries, 3, 9–10, 19, 60, 71, 113, 120

Festivals, 159–161
Festós, 18, 140–141
Firka, 67
Folk-Art Museum (Ágios Nikólaos), 91, 92
Folk Museum (Ágios Georgios), 153
Fortezza at Réthymnon, 33, 78–79
Frangokástello, 39–40, 102
Full-day tours, 12–24
 three-day, 12–15
 seven-day, 16–19
 fourteen-day, 20–24
Fun Park Pantou, 61–62

G
Galatás, 44
Gas stations, 10
Gay and lesbian travellers, 165
Georgioúpolis, 60, 101, 108, 127
German War Cemetery (Máleme), 117
Glass blowing factories, 60, 123
Glatás Village, 44
Golden Fun Park (Chaniá), 61–62, 117
Golfing, 5
 Crete Golf Club, 63, 107, 108, 142–143
 Golf Land, 61–62
Goniá Monastery, 117
Gorge of Zaros, 107
Górtys, 18, 140, 141
Gournía, 22–23, 31, 149
Grand Stairway (Festós), 140
Greece, 170, 171
Greek Independence Day, 159
Greek language, 172–174
Greek mythology, 15
Gulf of Mirabéllo, 21–22

H
Halbherr, Federico, 28–29
Harbour at Chaniá, 33
Harbour Square (Chaniá), 69
Hay, Robert, 130
Health issues, 165–166
Hersónisos, 5, 21, 62–63, 108, 113, 142
Hersónisos stables, 108
Hill 107 battlefield, 43–44
Hippocrates, 54, 123
Hippopotamos club (Chaniá), 59, 72
Historical and Folk Art Museum (Réthymnon), 77–78
Historical Museum (Iráklion), 14, 17, 49, 86
Hogarth, David, 30
Holidays, 158
Homo Sapiens Museum, 56, 64
Hóra Sfakíon, 19, 46, 105, 113, 120, 131
Horse riding, 61, 62, 108–109
Hospitals, 165–166
Hunt, Bob, 107

I
Icarus, 15
Ierapetra, 114
Ímbros Gorge, 19, 106, 120
Independence Day, 159
Inland Crete, 24
Insurance, 166
International dialing code, 161
Internet access, 59, 166
Ippikos stables (Karteros), 109
Iráklion Festival, 160
Iráklion region, 136–145
 accommodations, 88, 143–144
 beaches, 102–103, 142
 city of Iráklion, 14, 17, 34, 41, 62–64, 82–89, 113
 dining, 89, 144–145
 east of Iráklion, 142–143
 Knossós area, 136–139
 nightlife, 138
 road to Mátala, 140–142
 shopping, 86
Iron Gates, 105

J
Jeep safaris, 111
John the Teacher, 38

K
Kalamáki go-kart track, 61
Kalivaki beach (Georgioúpolis), 60, 127
Kalives, 122
Kalokerinou (Iráklion), 86
Kandanoleon Massacre, 35
Kándanos, 119
Kara Pasha mosque (Réthymnon), 40
Karteros, 108
Káto Zákros (Lower Zákros), 24, 103, 106–107, 152
Kazantzákis, Nikos, 5, 13, 17, 34, 49, 83, 85, 86, 153
Kazantzákis Museum (Mirtiá), 5, 13, 17, 50, 138
Kippenberger, Howard, 44
Kitroplatia (Ágios Nikólaos), 93, 94, 103
Klik Scandinavian Bar (Chaniá), 72
Knossós region, 136–139. *See also* Palace of Knossós
Kokkinó Horió (Georgioúpolis), 60, 123
Komboloi, 54
Komitades, 106
Kornaros, Vitsentzos, 84
Kotsifou Gorge (Plakiás), 107
Koules (Iráklion), 34, 87
Kourtaliotiko Gorge (Plakiás), 107, 131
Krási, 56
Kreipe, Karl Heinrich, 45, 129, 138, 139
Kreipe Monument, 129, 138, 139
Kritsá (Ágios Nikólaos), 22, 51, 91, 93, 95

L
Labyrinth, 15
Labyrinth Musical Workshop (Houdétsi), 51, 139
Lake Kournás (Georgioúpolis), 60, 127
Lake Voulisméni (Ágios Nikólaos), 92
Lampros Karandreas (musical instrument maker), 51
Langouvardos, Agathangelos, 131
Lapa Avocado Beauty Products (Argiroúpolis), 128
Lasinthos Eco Park (Ágios Georgios), 57, 64, 109, 153
Lasíthi region, 146–156
 accommodations, 154–155
 beaches, 103
 dining, 155–156
 far east, 149–152
 Lasíthi Plateau, 5–6, 21, 107, 152–155
 north of Ágios Nikólaos, 147–149
Lató (Ágios Nikólaos), 22, 95
Lighthouse (Chaniá), 71
Limnoupolis Water Park (Varipetro), 61
Loggerhead turtles, 114
Loggias, 14, 76, 85

Lotus bar (Ágios Nikólaos), 97
Loutró, 3, 15, 19, 60, 107, 120
Lychnostatis Museum (Hersónisos), 14, 55, 62, 142
Lynch, Peter, 114
Lyra, 51, 139

M

Máleme airfield, 43, 117
Mália, 94
Mambo dance club (Ágios Nikólaos), 97
Margarites (Réthymnon), 51
Marinakis, Gabriel, 40
Maritime Museum of Crete Permanent Exhibition (Chaniá), 71
Markets, 70, 75, 76, 86
Mátala, 5, 18–19, 103, 141
May Day festival, 160
Melanouri stables (Pitsidia), 109
Melindóni Cave, 41
Mesa Moulianá, 57
Messara Plain, 140
Milatos Cave, 21, 41, 147
Minoa (ship), 71
Minoan Crete, 26–31, 169
Minoan Palace (Festós), 140
Minoan Palace (Mália), 14
Minoa Winery (Peza), 139
Minos, King, 15
Minotaur, 15
Mirthios, 114
Mobile phones, 161
Móchlos, 23, 31, 94, 149–151
Mochós, 6, 55–56
Monasteries
    Arkádi Monastery, 3, 4, 40–41, 128–129
    Goniá Monastery, 117
    Monastery of Agía Triáda, 122
    Préveli Monastery, 47, 130, 131
Moní Aréti, 21, 148
Moní Tóplou, 23, 151
Moni Zangarolo (Monastery of Agía Triáda), 122
Mopeds, 163
Morosini, Francesco, 85
Morosini Fountain (Iráklion), 14, 85
Mortiz bar (Ágios Nikólaos), 97
Mosque of the Janissaries (Chaniá), 37, 69
Motorbikes, 163
Mountain biking, 61, 110–111

Mount Psiloritis, 107
Mourtzanos 1907 (Réthymnon), 76
Moutsounas (Zénia), 57
Municipal Beach Club (Ágios Nikólaos), 93
Municipal Market (Chaniá), 70
Museums
    Archaeological Museum (Ágios Nikólaos), 94, 95
    Archaeological Museum (Archánes), 139
    Archaeological Museum (Chaniá), 69
    Archaeological Museum (Iráklion), 5, 14, 17, 27, 29, 83
    Archaeological Museum (Réthymnon), 78
    Archaeological Museum (Sitía), 30, 150–151
    Battle of Crete Museum (Iráklion), 14, 17
    El Greco Museum (Fodele), 50, 132
    Folk-Art Museum (Ágios Nikólaos), 91, 92
    Folk Museum (Ágios Georgios), 153
    Historical and Folk Art Museum (Réthymnon), 77–78
    Historical Museum (Iráklion), 14, 17, 49, 86
    Homo Sapiens Museum, 56, 64
    Kazantzákis Museum (Mirtiá), 5, 13, 17, 50, 138
    Lychnostatis Museum (Hersónisos), 14, 55, 62, 142
    Maritime Museum of Crete Permanent Exhibition (Chaniá), 71
    Museum of Religious Arts (Iráklion), 17, 49
    Museum of the Battle of Crete and National Resistance 1941-1945 (Iráklion), 83–84
    National Museum (Iráklion), 5
    Natural History Museum of Crete (Iráklion), 87, 109
    Naval Museum (Chaniá), 3, 19, 33, 44–45, 59, 67–68
    War Museum 1941-1946 (Askífou), 119

Musical instruments, 51, 76
Music venues
    rock, 59, 72
    traditional, 51, 139
Mycenaean Crete, 169–170
Mylos Club (Plantaniás), 72
Mythology, 15

N

National Museum (Iráklion), 5
Natural History Museum of Crete (Iráklion), 87, 109
Naval Museum (Chaniá), 3, 19, 33, 44–45, 59, 67–68
Naval Week festival, 160
Negalo Neorio (Chaniá), 70
Nerandzes Mosque (Réthymnon), 40, 77
New Year's Day, 159
New Year's Eve, 161
New York disco (Hersónisos), 138
Nightlife
    in Ágios Nikólaos, 97
    in Chaniá, 72
    in Iráklion region, 138
    in Réthymnon, 80–81
Nikos Papalexakis (Réthymnon), 51, 76
Nily, Mustapha, 69
Notos (Chaniá), 59

O

Ochi Day, 160
Octavius, Augustus, 128
Oddball Crete tour, 52–57
Odos 1866 (Iráklion), 86
Odysseia Stables (Avidou), 108
Old City (Chaniá), 68
Old Town (Chaniá), 37–38
Old Town (Réthymnon), 40
Oloús (Eloúnda), 22, 94, 103, 148–149
Omalos, 105
Omirou (Ágios Nikólaos), 92
Ottoman Crete tour, 36–41
Ottoman Empire, 39, 171
Outdoor activities, 100–114
    best beaches, 100–103
    on land, 104–111
    at sea, 112–114

P

Palace of Festós, 28–29
Palace of Knossós, 5, 13, 17, 27–28, 137–138
Palace of Mália, 29, 142
Palace of Zákros, 24, 30, 107, 151, 152

Paleochóra, 101–102, 113, 118
Paleochóra Music Festival, 160
Pallavicini, Sforza, 33
Palm Beach (Ágia Galíni), 19, 102, 131
Palme, Olof, 55–56
Panagia Kera (Ágios Nikólaos), 94, 95
Paradise Beach (Balí), 102
Paragliding, 111
Parking, 98, 167
Pasiphae, 15
Paximadia Islands, 19, 130
Petrol stations, 10
Phaistos Disc, 18, 29
Pharmacies, 167
Pitsidia, 108
Plakiás, 107, 113, 114, 131–132
Platia Eleftherias, 17
Platia minaret, 37
Platia Nikiforou Fokas (Iráklion), 14, 84, 138
Platia Venizelou (Iráklion), 14, 17, 84, 138
Platon, Nikólaos, 24, 30, 151
Playgrounds, 57, 60, 61
Police, 167
Porta Guora (Réthymnon), 77
Poseidon, 15
Post offices, 167
Préveli Monastery, 47, 130, 131
Psaraki, Kalitsa, 130
Psiloritis Mountains, 107, 129, 141
Public Gardens (Chaniá), 37
Public Gardens (Réthymnon), 77, 81
Pubs. *See* Nightlife

Q
QuadBikes, 163

R
Rafting, 111
Regional tours, 116–156
  in Chaniá region, 116–125
  in Iráklion region, 136–145
  in Réthymnon region, 126–135
Religious sites, 111
  Agía Paraskevi (Argiróupolis), 128
  Ágios Titos (Iráklion), 14, 85–86
  Arkádi Monastery, 3, 4, 40–41, 128–129
  Chaniá Cathedral, 69–70
  Church of the Three Martyrs, 69
  Etz-Hayyim Synagogue (Chaniá), 68–69
  Goniá Monastery, 117
  Kara Pasha mosque (Réthymnon), 40
  Monastery of Agia Triáda, 122
  Moní Aréti, 21, 148
  Mosque of the Janissaries (Chaniá), 37, 69
  Nerandzes Mosque (Réthymnon), 40, 77
  Panagia Kera (Ágios Nikólaos), 94
  Préveli Monastery, 47, 130, 131
Renaissance festival of Réthymnon, 160
Réthymnon Carnival, 159
Réthymnon region, 126–135
  accommodations, 79–80, 134
  Arkáki Monastery, Amári Valley and South Coast, 128–132
  beaches, 75, 102, 131, 132
  city of Réthymnon, 19, 40, 74–81, 102, 113, 114
  dining, 80–81, 135
  east of Réthymnon, 132–133
  nightlife, 80–81
  shopping, 75, 76
  west of Réthymnon, 127–128
Réthymnon Wine Festival, 77, 160
Rimondi Fountain (Réthymnon), 78
Rock music, 59, 72
Rodopou Peninsula, 107, 118
Roman Empire, 170

S
Safety, 167
Sailing, 113, 114
St Minos Parade, 161
Samariá Gorge Walk, 19, 105, 120
San Marco Basilica (Iráklion), 85
Sanmicheli, Michele, 34
Senior travellers, 167
Shopping, 168
  Ágios Konstantinos, 153
  Chaniá, 70
  Iráklion, 86
  Réthymnon, 75, 76
Sisi, 21, 147
Sitía, 23, 150
Sitía Sultana Festival, 160
Skridlof (Chaniá), 70
Smoking, 168
Sorrento nightclub (Ágios Nikólaos), 97
Soúda Bay, 45, 122
Sougia, 113
Special events, 159–161
Special-interest tours, 26–64
  art museums, 48–51
  child-friendly, 58–64
  Minoan Crete, 26–31
  oddball Crete, 52–57
  Ottoman Crete, 36–41
  Venetian Crete, 32–35
  World War II, 42–47
Spíli, 107, 130
Spinalónga, 5, 22, 35, 149
Splantzia, 38
Star Beach (Hersónisos), 14, 62–63, 142
Stavrós, 121
Stergiou (Iráklion), 86
Stone Garden (Kalives), 53, 59–60, 122
Summer Solstice, 160

T
Talos Express (Georgioúpolis), 127
Taxes, 168
Taxis, 10, 162
Telephones, 161, 168
Theotokópoulos, Doménikos (El Greco), 49, 50, 83, 86, 132
Theseus, 15
Thrapsanó, 51
Thrónos, 107, 129
Time zone, 168
Tipping, 168
Tomb of Kazantzákis (Iráklion), 49–50, 85
Tombruk, 103
Tourist offices, 91, 158, 168
Tourist road trains, 9, 163
  in Ágios Nikólaos, 91
  in Balí, 132
  in Hersónisos, 142
Tourist road trains *(cont.)*
  in Réthymnon, 75–76
  Talos Express (Georgioúpolis), 60, 127
Tour packages, 108
Traditional music, 51, 139

Index

Trains. *See* Tourist road trains
Trekking. *See* Walking and trekking
Turkish relics, 37–38, 40

U
Unicorn Trails (Avidou), 108
Urban tours, 66–98
　Águis Nikólaos, 90–98
　Chaniá, 66–73
　Iráklion, 82–89
　Réthymnon, 74–81

V
Vacation packages, 108
Vái, 24, 103, 151
Valley of the Dead. *See* Zákros Gorge
Value-added tax, 168
Vámos, 10, 123
Vámos S.A. (company), 123
Venetian Crete, 32–35, 170–171
Venetian Empire, 34
Venetian Fortress (Chaniá), 67
Venetian Fortress (Iráklion), 87
Venetian Harbour (Iráklion), 87
Venetian Harbour (Réthymnon), 77
Venetian Massacre, 35
Venizélos, Eleftherios, 38, 67, 121
Venizélos, Sophocles, 38, 121
Vicky M (jewelry shop, Ágios Nikólaos), 93
Vineyards, 17, 139
Visas, 158
Vlachos, Ioannis, 38
Votomos Lake (Zaros), 141
Voûves Olive Tree, 53, 117
Vrísses, 119

W
Walking and trekking, 104–107, 162
　Askifou Plateau, 119
　Diadromés (Armeni), 61
　Ímbros Gorge, 19, 106, 120
　in Plakiás, 131–132
　Samariá Gorge Walk, 19, 105
　in Spíli, 130
　Zákros Gorge, 24, 106–107, 152
War Museum 1941-1946 (Askífou), 119
Water, drinking, 168
Water City (Anapolis), 63
Water parks, 5
　Acquaplus Water Park, 63, 142, 143
　Limnoupolis Water Park (Varipetro), 61
　Water City (Anapolis), 63
Water sports, 109, 113–114, 132
Weather, 158, 161
Websites, useful, 159
　bicycling, 111
　boating and watersports, 108, 113–114
　horseriding, 108–109
　Jeep safaris, 111
　walking and trekking tours, 108
West coast tour (Chaniá), 116–119
White Mountains, 105, 123
Wildlife, 109
　Ark (Georgioúpolis), 54, 60, 109, 123
　Lake Kournás (Georgioúpolis), 127
　Lasinthos Eco Park (Ágios Georgios), 57, 64, 109, 153
Wildlife and Conservation Volunteering (Peter Lynch), 114
Wind turbines, 94
Wineries, 4–5, 139
Wine Roads area, 17, 139
Wine Roads of Heraklion Prefecture booklets, 139
World War II, 42–47, 120, 171, 172
Worry beads, 54

X
XS Icons (Iráklion), 86

Y
Yoga Plus (Ágios Pavlos), 109, 110

Z
Zákros Gorge, 24, 94, 106–107, 152
Zaros, 107, 141
Zenia and Dolce (Réthymnon), 76
Zoos. *See* Animal parks and zoos
Zoraidas stables (Georgioúpolis), 108
Zorba the Greek (film), 121, 123

Photo **Credits**

Front Matter Credits: i: © Agita Leimane / Shutterstock; © Karel Gallas / Shutterstock; © Robert Harding Travel / Photolibrary

All images: © Jos Simon

Notes

day by day™

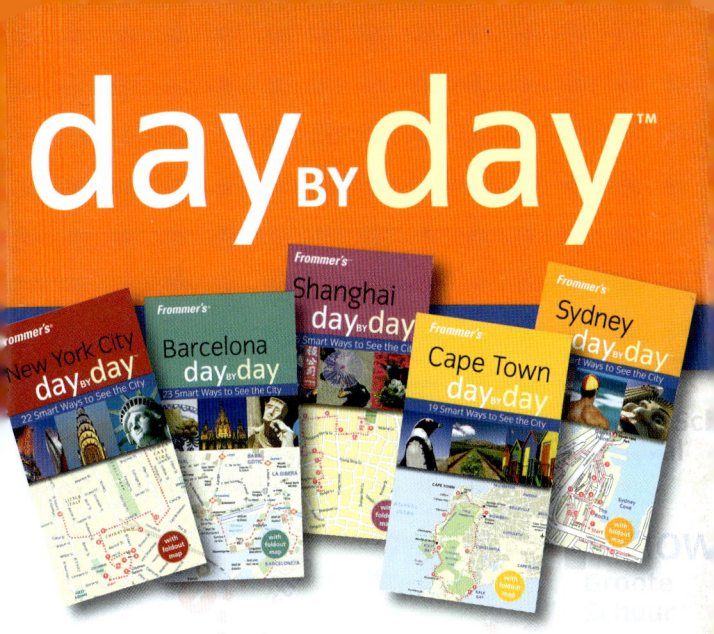

Get the best of a city or region in 1, 2 or 3 days

Day by Day Destinations include:

Europe
Amsterdam
Athens
Barcelona
Berlin
Brussels & Bruges
Budapest
Cornwall
Dublin
Edinburgh & Glasgow
Florence & Tuscany
Lake District
Lisbon
London
Madrid
Malta & Gozo
Moscow
Paris
St Petersburg
Prague
Provence & the Riviera
Rome
Seville
Stockholm
Valencia
Venice
Vienna

Canada and The Americas
Boston
Cancun & the Yucatan
Chicago
Honolulu & Oahu
Los Angeles
Las Vegas
Maui
Montreal
Napa & Sonoma
New York City
San Diego
San Francisco
Seattle
Washington

Rest of the World
Bangkok
Beijing
Hong Kong
Melbourne
Shanghai
Sydney
Toronto

Frommer's®

Available wherever books are sold

Explore over 3,500 destinations.

TOKYO — 7766 miles
LONDON — 3818 miles
TORONTO — 4682 miles
SYDNEY — 5087 miles
NEW YORK — 4947 miles
LOS ANGELES — 2556 miles
HONG KONG — 5638 miles

Frommers.com makes it easy.

Find a destination. ✓ Book a trip. ✓ Get hot travel deals.
Buy a guidebook. ✓ Enter to win vacations. ✓ Listen to podcasts.
Check out the latest travel news. ✓ Share trip photos and memories.
And much more.

Frommers.com